Asian Women in Corporate America:

Emerging Research and Opportunities

Sambhavi Lakshminarayanan
Medgar Evers College, City University of New York, USA

A volume in the Advances in Human Resources Management and Organizational Development (AHRMOD) Book Series

IGI Global
PUBLISHER of TIMELY KNOWLEDGE

Published in the United States of America by
IGI Global
Business Science Reference (an imprint of IGI Global)
701 E. Chocolate Avenue
Hershey PA, USA 17033
Tel: 717-533-8845
Fax: 717-533-8661
E-mail: cust@igi-global.com
Web site: http://www.igi-global.com

Library of Congress Cataloging-in-Publication Data

Names: Lakshminarayanan, Sambhavi, 1962- author.
Title: Asian women in corporate America : emerging research and opportunities / by Sambhavi Lakshminarayanan.
Description: Hershey : Business Science Reference, 2021. | Includes bibliographical references and index. | Summary: "This book discusses the experiences of Asian women in American (business) workplaces and anticipates future developments regarding their organizational careers"-- Provided by publisher.
Identifiers: LCCN 2020042213 (print) | LCCN 2020042214 (ebook) | ISBN 9781799843849 (hardcover) | ISBN 9781799868248 (paperback) | ISBN 9781799843856 (ebook)
Subjects: LCSH: Corporate governance--United States. | Asian American women employees--United States. | Minority women executives--United States.
Classification: LCC HD2741 .L315 2021 (print) | LCC HD2741 (ebook) | DDC 331.4089/95073--dc23
LC record available at https://lccn.loc.gov/2020042213
LC ebook record available at https://lccn.loc.gov/2020042214

This book is published in the IGI Global book series Advances in Human Resources Management and Organizational Development (AHRMOD) (ISSN: 2327-3372; eISSN: 2327-3380)

British Cataloguing in Publication Data
A Cataloguing in Publication record for this book is available from the British Library.

Advances in Human Resources Management and Organizational Development (AHRMOD) Book Series

ISSN:2327-3372
EISSN:2327-3380

Editor-in-Chief: Patricia Ordóñez de Pablos, Universidad de Oviedo, Spain

MISSION

A solid foundation is essential to the development and success of any organization and can be accomplished through the effective and careful management of an organization's human capital. Research in human resources management and organizational development is necessary in providing business leaders with the tools and methodologies which will assist in the development and maintenance of their organizational structure.

The **Advances in Human Resources Management and Organizational Development (AHRMOD) Book Series** aims to publish the latest research on all aspects of human resources as well as the latest methodologies, tools, and theories regarding organizational development and sustainability. The **AHRMOD Book Series** intends to provide business professionals, managers, researchers, and students with the necessary resources to effectively develop and implement organizational strategies.

COVERAGE

- Outsourcing HR
- Worker Behavior and Engagement
- Employee Evaluation
- Coaching and Mentoring
- Employment and Labor Laws
- Talent Identification and Management
- Human Relations Movement
- Corporate Governance
- Personnel Retention
- Succession Planning

IGI Global is currently accepting manuscripts for publication within this series. To submit a proposal for a volume in this series, please contact our Acquisition Editors at Acquisitions@igi-global.com or visit: http://www.igi-global.com/publish/.

The Advances in Human Resources Management and Organizational Development (AHRMOD) Book Series (ISSN 2327-3372) is published by IGI Global, 701 E. Chocolate Avenue, Hershey, PA 17033-1240, USA, www.igi-global.com. This series is composed of titles available for purchase individually; each title is edited to be contextually exclusive from any other title within the series. For pricing and ordering information please visit http://www.igi-global.com/book-series/advances-human-resources-management-organizational/73670. Postmaster: Send all address changes to above address.

Titles in this Series

For a list of additional titles in this series, please visit:
http://www.igi-global.com/book-series/advances-human-resources-management-organizational/73670

Transforming Human Resource Functions With Automation
Anchal Pathak (Bule Hora University, Ethiopia) and Shikha Rana (IMS Unison University, India)
Business Science Reference • © 2021 • 192pp • H/C (ISBN: 9781799841807) • US $195.00

Examining the Career Development Practices and Experiences of Immigrants
Jared Keengwe (University of North Dakota, USA) and Kenneth Kungu (Clayton State University, USA)
Business Science Reference • © 2021 • 362pp • H/C (ISBN: 9781799858119) • US $215.00

Future of Work, Work-Family Satisfaction, and Employee Well-Being in the Fourth Industrial Revolution
Ethel Ndidiamaka Abe (University of KwaZulu-Natal, South Africa)
Business Science Reference • © 2021 • 382pp • H/C (ISBN: 9781799833475) • US $215.00

Handbook of Research on Cyberbullying and Online Harassment in the Workplace
Leslie Ramos Salazar (West Texas A&M University, USA)
Business Science Reference • © 2021 • 717pp • H/C (ISBN: 9781799849124) • US $265.00

Integration and Application of Business Graduate and Business Leader Competency-Models
Donta S. Harper (University of Washington, USA)
Business Science Reference • © 2021 • 275pp • H/C (ISBN: 9781799865377) • US $195.00

Human Resource Management Practices for Promoting Sustainability
Sulaiman Olusegun Atiku (Naimbia University of Science and Technology, Namibia) and Tinuke Fapohunda (Lagos State University, Nigeria)
Business Science Reference • © 2021 • 326pp • H/C (ISBN: 9781799845225) • US $195.00

For an entire list of titles in this series, please visit:
http://www.igi-global.com/book-series/advances-human-resources-management-organizational/73670

IGI Global
PUBLISHER of TIMELY KNOWLEDGE

701 East Chocolate Avenue, Hershey, PA 17033, USA
Tel: 717-533-8845 x100 • Fax: 717-533-8661
E-Mail: cust@igi-global.com • www.igi-global.com

Table of Contents

Preface

Asian women have been making their mark in America for many years. Recently we have seen the rise of high-profile Asian women in varied areas of American society and life such as government, entertainment, education, and business. These women are not exceptions; Asian women's participation in different spheres of activity in the U.S. has been steadily increasing.

There is every reason to expect that in the future there will be more Asian women among senators and representatives, judges and lawyers, movie stars and producers, doctors and nurses, teachers and principals, professors and presidents. However, their entrance in corporate America and their increasing numbers in corporate workplaces are more recent, driven largely by societal, cultural, and immigration-related legislative changes. Of special interest to this book are Asian women's futures in organizational workspaces and C-suites of businesses large and small. (As a matter of clarification, the term "Asian women" in this book refers to women with ancestry in the countries of Asia; this group includes immigrants as well as women born in the U.S.)

This book was motivated by conversations with Asian women working in businesses in the U.S. Their experiences of working in different corporations, large and small, showcase their achievements but also provide stark pictures of their struggles. Often with little family or community support, they faced great hardships in attempting to meet the often competing demands of work and family. Some Asian women found family to be a source of exceptional support, such as parents who provided childcare and encouraged their pursuit of a demanding career. Others had a contrasting experience of not only having to work and help provide for the family but also taking care of their children and elderly parents (or in-laws). Many immigrant women managed a complex life balancing family (and often parents') demands in the U.S. and in Asia. Some felt a commitment to bring children over to Asia for visits with grandparents, which meant a commitment of time and money. Not having the option to take time off from work for such family reasons led some women to routinely quit their jobs to make these trips. The willingness to persist and a clarity of purpose propelled most of these women, and they relied on their experiences in crafting career strategies.

While many Asian women in corporate environments had followed a general playbook of getting education and skill-training for their jobs, they often had a lack of awareness and knowledge of the necessity of participating in organizational life in other ways. Additionally, Asian women appeared not entirely knowledgeable about how their identities and roles as women, Asians, and Asian women impacted their navigation of the organizational workplace.

There has been extensive and exceptional research done in the area of women (in general) and organizational work. At the same time, there is a paucity of published work on Asian women in corporate workplaces. Women are not a monolith; what is relevant and useful for one group might not be so for another. Thus, many aspects of general research on women might not apply directly to Asian women, and there is a need to modify those findings. Indeed, without details on Asian women's careers and experiences, the picture of women in American organizations is incomplete.

The aim of this book is thus threefold: to provide information about Asian women and American work environments; to highlight areas where there is need for more research and a deeper understanding of the situations of Asian women in corporate America; and to function as a primer on work in business organizations for Asian women at entry and middle levels. Knowledge of the complexity and breadth of women's experiences, outlooks, and effective strategies across all groups will be invaluable for businesses, organizations, and society at large.

SOCIETAL CHANGES AFFECTING WOMEN IN THE U.S. AND ASIA

American society—like all societies—is constantly changing, with steady shifts punctuated by periods of intense change. Each wave of transformative changes has impacted a wide swath of American life in a deep and lasting manner, and eventually these developments had global impacts as well. The 1960s, for instance, was a period of seismic societal and legislative changes.

Of particular interest to this book is the evolution of the status and role of women in American society, which has profoundly changed over the last few decades as women began seeking to earn a livelihood by pursuing education and working for pay. This was a drastic shift from earlier social norms that dictated women's role as (unpaid) homemakers. As women envisioned a different social role for themselves, they began entering the labor market in increasing numbers and affected prevalent attitudes about women's work. It is now the societal norm in the U.S. for women to work outside the home (even if such employment is sporadic rather than continual). This major change has been the result of steady persistence at the individual and employee levels as well as demands by certain high-profile women for impactful social and legal changes (such as parity in pay).

On the other side of the world, cultures in Asian countries underwent major changes of their own. These changes gained momentum after the 1950s (historical explanations for this are available through many sources). Specifically, the status, lifestyle, and role of women in these cultures started changing as women in many countries began to pursue education in increasing numbers. With every generation the level of education rose. Thus, for a middle-class woman reaching adulthood in the 1970s and 1980s, it was likely that her great-grandmother had had no formal schooling, while her grandmother went through elementary schooling and her mother was probably a high school—or even a college—graduate. For such women, obtaining a college education was not only possible, it was expected.

This shift in norms related to women's education aligned with a general societal view that education was a reliable pathway to socio-economic progress. Increasing socio-economic development in Asian countries gave rise to many professional careers that require specialized education, such as doctors, engineers, lawyers, and accountants, to name a few. Professional careers like these were considered not only prestigious but also secure and well-compensated. Thus, there was a general willingness to pursue higher education as a means to a financially stable future. Asian cultures underwent another wave of change with the advent of technology, which opened up opportunities in new kinds of jobs. Even as these technological advances created new jobs and altered current ones, societal views on what could be considered "good" jobs also changed. Technology-related jobs were considered desirable, both because they were seen as good career choices and because they were well-compensated. Over time all these changes made it easier for women to be educated (and employed) in Asian countries.

Meanwhile, in the U.S., major changes in immigration policy in the 1960s and 1990s had a major impact on patterns of Asian immigration. As a result immigration increased in numbers, but the kinds of immigrants (related to their reasons for immigrating) changed as well. Qualified and educated Asian immigrants, many of whom had been educated in Asian countries, immigrated in search of employment in the U.S. There was also a corresponding increase in the number of students from Asia seeking higher education (graduate and doctoral programs) in the U.S. These groups, consisting of employment-seekers and students, included women, although not in the same numbers as men. Some women also came to the U.S. as spouses of members of these two groups. They were likely to be educated, and some were even trained professionals. In other words, there was a significant increase in the number of Asian women who were ready to enter the American workforce. While other kinds of immigration continued (for example, family members of those who had already arrived), these three groups had arguably the biggest impact in terms of entry into corporations.

ASIAN WOMEN AND CORPORATE WORKPLACES

In many ways, corporate workplaces have been a good fit for Asian women. Employment in the U.S. is overwhelmingly located in the private sector; data from the Bureau of Labor Statistics show 78% of the labor force is in the private sector, with only 15% in the public sector and about 7% in nonprofits (U.S. Bureau of Labor Statistics). In the private sector, the workforce is split almost fifty-fifty between small businesses and large ones. Thus, it is not surprising that many Asian women have sought employment in the corporate world. These workplaces can be fairly structured and even regulated environments (in certain areas), and in many workplaces the work and role requirements are clear. The private sector might offer quicker entry into the workforce (although these jobs could have an equally swift exit) compared to public-sector jobs and better compensation compared to nonprofits. Departments and specialized work are a good fit for Asian women with education, professional qualifications, and training in related fields.

Thus, businesses both large and small continue to be attractive workplace options for Asian women. Larger corporations can offer more stability, possibilities for specialized work, and better compensation than smaller firms. Their organizational environments are likely to be more structured and to operate under clearer guidelines. On the other hand, smaller firms can be more flexible, less impersonal, and offer more opportunities to develop complex and diverse work skills. However, as the recent coronavirus pandemic has shown, smaller businesses are far more vulnerable to economic and social upheavals. Thus, both large and small corporate environments can be equally challenging for women, albeit in different ways. Ultimately, the skills necessary for negotiating business workplaces are more similar than distinct across organizations of different sizes or even located in different industries.

Corporate workplaces are not immune to social, legal, and cultural transformations in the U.S. Indeed, changes in these workplaces have made it easier for Asian women to enter and develop their careers. Women's increased participation in the U.S. labor force has meant more women working in corporations. Over the years, their experiences have shined light on gender-related disparities and discrimination, including in compensation and career progress; sometimes women have even sued their employers for this reason. At the same time, the media and researchers have also kept the focus on these issues. This multi-pronged effort has influenced broad changes in organizations. One indicator of their impact is the presence of women in positions of organizational power, such as the number of women in Fortune 500 board positions and across executive levels (Deloitte, 2018). The women who were among the early entrants to corporate workplaces, and their allies inside and outside corporations, did not have an easy time. However, their persistence and refusal to accept status-quo situations have influenced organizational change and their efforts eased the path for later generations of women, including Asian women.

Another significant change has been the increasing diversity of the workforce, reflecting larger demographic and cultural changes in U.S. society. Diversity has been defined in various ways in workplaces, including ethnic diversity, diversity in sexual orientation, and ability, to name a few. Once again, corporations have had to respond to pressure from employees, the media, and society in general to adapt. Early responses were primarily aimed at educating and increasing employees' awareness of specific minority groups within the organization, commonly through diversity training (sometimes referred to as "sensitivity" training). Over the years corporations have moved through cycles of diversity-related initiatives as they attempted to match workplace environments with employee needs. These changes too eased the way for Asian women. However, even as they benefit from these past attempts, they can look to be active participants in shaping the workplaces of the future.

It should be expected that Asian women's workplace experiences are similar in some ways and (perhaps wildly) different in others, due to cultural differences stemming from the country of origin, family influences, occupational variations, and personality characteristics. One expected difference, which has been established across many different immigrant groups, is the generational effect. This can be viewed in terms of immigration-related generations, with adult immigrants being Generation 1, their children born in the U.S. being

Generation 2, and so on. It can also be understood in terms of immigrants' presence in workplaces. Asian women who were the first entrants to the labor market, especially in corporate workplaces, can be considered as Generation 1. Because a significant number of women entered the country after changes in immigration law, these women would have been entering the labor market in the 1980s and 1990s. Thus, Asian women entering corporate workforces at present (for instance, the daughters of immigrants) can be considered as Generation 2. The labeling is not as important as understanding the implications of these circumstances. Generation 1, either immigrants to a new society or those entering a new workplace environment, typically have a determination to learn and adapt. These early entrants can influence, if not shape, how later entrants from their group are perceived. They can also pass along their understanding of the environment and effective ways to negotiate it. Even though corporate and social environments have changed greatly, the experiences of these first- and second-generation Asian women will be relevant and invaluable guides to the future.

Most often, Asian women (like other employees) enter corporate organizations in search of a paying job. Some might view the job as an economic necessity or as a means to improve the family's standard of living. Some (more likely second-generation women rather than immigrants) might seek to fulfill more personal career ambitions or aspirations. In any case, almost everyone can expect to encounter setbacks and failure in every job. Overcoming setbacks and building on successes requires inner strength and strong motivation. More than that, navigating the workplace and managing one's work requires specific knowledge and skills.

To this end, Asian women need to have a strong sense of self, and they need to understand how workplaces function. Developing a sense of self includes understanding and reconciling various identities that are part of living in a complex society. Understanding workplaces requires learning about how they function and planning one's responses to circumstances that arise at work. For example, this might include recognizing which parts of one's work are valued (and which are not), assessing the vulnerability of one's position to organizational changes, understanding communication patterns and protocols in the workplace, intuiting power distribution in the organization, and grasping the general workplace culture.

An important precursor to career management is clarity regarding one's motivation to work. Viewing a job as a transactional relationship (in which the employee produces work output in exchange for money) is unlikely to lead to long tenure or upward progress in an organization. Not everyone can be in a leadership position, nor does everyone aspire to obtain such positions. At the same time, a sustained career at any level, not just an upwardly mobile one, requires long-term thinking and goal orientation. In less turbulent times, some organizational jobs might have been stable despite a low degree of involvement by the employee. However, at present (and likely in the future) that is not the case. Employees not only have to deliver on the job but develop relationships and be prepared to move to other jobs or other organizations as needed. In dynamic environments, every employee in every position must be nimble, alert, and prepared.

Asian women who might have viewed their careers as secondary (to their spouse's) or as a backup might face the harsh reality that every career is likely to be tenuous. The backup might need a backup. However, since most careers are housed in organizations, any skills women have in navigating workplaces will be of use over their careers. Even if they transition from working for corporations to running their own businesses, the lessons learned about managing work and relationships will not be in vain. They might, in fact, turn out to be a distinct advantage.

A BRIEF DESCRIPTION OF CHAPTERS IN THE BOOK

Knowledge of the structures and dynamics of organizational workplaces is fundamental to understanding work and careers in corporate settings. To that end, each chapter in this book addresses a unique topic and can be perused individually. The book provides a comprehensive view of organizational workplaces and careers and includes specific issues relevant to Asian women while also framing these issues in a more general context. In this quest, the book is interdisciplinary in its approach and spans several disciplines. It draws materials from research in management, women's studies, sociology, psychology, and business.

Chapter 1 provides an introduction to the two main themes of this book: Asian women and corporate workplaces in the U.S. It presents an overview of the Asian women under consideration, specifically with regard to the impact that changes in U.S. immigration laws and Asian social situations have had on them. This chapter also lays the foundation for understanding the professional environment relevant to this book, namely organizational workplaces.

Chapters 2, 3, and 4 relate to organizational structures and functioning. Chapter 2 discusses basic concepts such as authority, performance evaluation, and decision-making in organizations. Power within organizations is an important issue for Asian women but it is often neglected in career strategizing. Chapters 3 and 4 focus on the interpersonal aspects of organizational work. A diverse workforce is a reality in most workplaces but it is also one that continues to pose challenges. While organizations have responded to diversity-related employee issues and concerns in a variety of ways, the effect of their actions on the careers of Asian women is not clear. Chapter 4 discusses networks and mentors in the workplace. The importance of mentors and networks for career success has been well studied, yet there is a lack of information on how Asian women fare in this regard. Similarly, this chapter addresses another well-researched topic—organizational leadership—in which little is known about Asian women in terms of their leadership approaches and styles.

Chapters 5 and 6 turn towards the individual, specifically the Asian woman. While the previous chapters viewed members of this group primarily from an employee perspective, these chapters focus on them as individuals who happen to work in an organizational workplace. The work experiences of Asian women are shaped, to a large extent, by how they are perceived and how they perceive themselves in work environments. Asian women have had to manage perceptions that include stereotypes as well as role expectations both within the workplace and within their families and communities. Chapter 5 addresses stereotypes in more detail, as well as Asian acculturation processes and the ways in which Asian women attempt to negotiate multiple cultures. Chapter 6 discusses the various identities relevant to Asian women, including racial/ethnic, gender, professional, and organizational.

Careers are the focus of Chapter 7, which presents models and theories that have been proposed for understanding organizational careers. This includes more recent models that delineate the differences between the careers of women and men, as well as present-day careers that are likely to span multiple organizations. Of special importance for Asian women is the concept of at-will employment, a special feature of U.S. corporations that immigrants might not be familiar with.

Chapter 8 provides a summary of the preceding chapters. It identifies the challenges that Asian women are likely to face in corporate workplaces in the future and proposes strategies they could use to navigate these workplaces. The chapter concludes with opportunities for future research by identifying understudied topics that Asian women will find to be relevant and important in their careers.

AUDIENCES FOR THIS BOOK

This book was motivated by the need to discuss the experiences of Asian women in American (business) workplaces and to anticipate future developments regarding their organizational careers.

The limited amount of research on Asian women in workplaces meant that discussions had to be framed in the broader context of all women, general organizational environments and careers, and broad sociological behaviors. This book identifies areas and topics for further discussion and research to fill gaps in our knowledge about Asian women's careers. This would be useful to researchers in the field who seek to add to a comprehensive view of women in workplaces.

College courses on women in business and management should ideally include sections addressing different groups of women. This book can serve as a text for such courses. Students will get an overarching view of topics related to women and organizational workplaces, with special emphasis on Asian women. For students who are about to enter the workforce, this book will also be useful as a practical guide.

An intent of this book is to translate and make available the findings of academic research to (Asian and all other) women in corporate settings. Understanding how organizations work and how other groups have handled similar challenges can only strengthen Asian women's resolve and help them develop practical strategies. Women, regardless of whether they identify as Asian or not, can use the material in the book to understand the complexities of organizational workplaces, develop an understanding of what to expect in the future, and formulate career strategies.

Finally, anybody who has Asian women co-workers or serves in some way as a sounding-board for them on career matters, will find this book of help in forming a nuanced understanding of their experiences in organizational workplaces.

REFERENCES

Deloitte. (2018). *Missing pieces report: The 2018 board diversity census of women and minorities on Fortune 500 boards*. https://www2.deloitte.com/us/en/pages/center-for-board-effectiveness/articles/missing-pieces-report-industry-view.html

U.S. Bureau of Labor Statistics. (n.d.). *Current employment statistics*. https://www.bls.gov/ces/

Acknowledgment

I began this book project with little more than determination and passion, and without any prior ideas on what ought or ought not to be included in it.

The project would not have been completed without the generosity of many people who made time to share their experiences and thoughts. They provided guidance and invaluable encouragement.

Students in my class on women in business at Medgar Evers College (City University of New York) triggered the initial idea of writing this book. Their brilliant, and sometimes unexpected, comments showed how much society has changed and how far women have come. These students were ready to explore, and wanted to understand, the experiences of different groups of women in greater depth and complexity.

Many women shared information about their professional journeys, knowledge gained, and life strategies. These individuals represented corporations, academia, health care, even venture capitalists. Their insights into issues of importance clarified the decision on topics to be included in the book.

A special group, the raison d'etre for this book, consisted of younger/junior Asian women. They worked in a variety of organizations: small and big corporations, for-profits and nonprofits. They vetted the book's contents and gave consistent support to my endeavor. I wrote this book for them.

Finally, I would like to thank my family. They patiently heard about corporations, women, and Asian women (in rotation), over many months. Sometimes their comments were useful.

My children were great sounding boards and provided deep insights. My daughter's views and opinions were sharp, relevant, and meaningful. Her clarity regarding her career goals and ambitions convinced me a book such as this needed to be written. My son, although not an Asian woman, contributed significantly to the chapter on careers. My understanding of new career forms deepened and became more detailed by his sharing thought processes on how he made career decisions.

Chapter 1
Asian Women in America:
An Overview

ABSTRACT

The presence of Asians in the U.S. has a lengthy history, although not a very well documented one. This book is concerned with the presence of Asian women in American corporations, which spans a shorter period. The beginnings of a significant increase in the numbers of Asian women in American workplaces can be traced to the 1960s. Since then, Asian women have entered all spheres of American life, including but not limited to businesses, government, education, healthcare, and nonprofits. The experiences of Asian women in American workplaces overlap with that of women in general as well as that of Asian men. Yet, certain aspects of Asian women's experiences are unique to them. This chapter provides a brief historical overview of Asian women's entry into American workspaces and their professional experiences. It also discusses the contexts in which to view Asian women in American corporate environments.

INTRODUCTION

Asia is more a "geographic term than a homogenous continent" and encompasses a great diversity of geographies, peoples, and cultures (Encyclopedia Britannica).

In the U.S., people with Asian ancestry can choose to identify as "Asian/Pacific Islander." This is an officially categorized group that was created for

DOI: 10.4018/978-1-7998-4384-9.ch001

data gathering purposes. Such ethnic categorization is a way to group people on a broad basis of culture and race (Phinney, 1996, p. 919). Categorization can serve practical purposes if the assumption that people within a category have similar experiences is accepted. If that is so, it would be possible to design effective approaches to aid group members in navigating the challenges they face, which are assumed to be similar as well. However, the process of determining categories has been criticized as being imprecise and arbitrary, and it changes over time (Phinney, 1996). Despite these criticisms, the current API categorization in place for the last many years seems to have been accepted, to an extent.

Researchers have used "Asian" and "Asian American" quite widely, apparently for the sake of simplicity, even as these terms represent complexities (Hyun, 2005). "Asians" include various ethnicities, cultures, and nationalities (Read & Cohen, 2007; Zhou & Gatewood, 2000). Similarly, "Asian American" is a concept that "subsumes, under one heading, various cultures, social histories, and experiences of immigration" (Srinivasan, 2001, p. 155). Researchers acknowledge this diversity but have mostly chosen to focus instead on the commonalities that inform experiences of group members.

"Asian American" typically includes both U.S.- and foreign-born individuals (Gee et al., 2015). The Asian American population is estimated to be around "21.8 million, approximately 7% of the U.S. population" (Nielson Reports, 2018, p. 8) and is projected to grow over time. An interesting prediction is that, by the year 2050, approximately 10% of Americans will have Asian ancestry (Kim & Hong, 2004, p. 15). Asian Americans have made their presence felt in all parts of American society and its economy. They have been especially active participants in the professional and business sectors. Dhingra (2012), writing about Indian-American motel owners, linked Asian Americans to the business world by contending that Asian immigration "has been, and continues to be, a product of US needs in global capitalism" (Dhingra, 2007, p. 17).

An interesting and intriguing subsection of the Asian American population is women working in business sectors. Some of them, such as Andrea Jung of Avon and Indra Nooyi of PepsiCo, have been high-profile success stories. Andrea Jung was named CEO of Avon in 1999 and Indra Nooyi became the CEO of PepsiCo in 2006. Since that time, Asian American women have been making steady inroads into the business world. However, despite their hard work, professional presence, and progress, Asian women remain a largely under-researched group in corporate America (Arifeen & Gatrell, 2019). There is a real lack of detailed knowledge about their professional lives, the challenges they face, and how they manage their careers.

It is possible to focus on work experiences in corporate settings across industries and geographies in the U.S. mainly because of similarities in work environments among large business organizations. For instance, hiring processes are subject to similar legal constraints across business domains. These similarities make it possible to discuss broad approaches to individual careers and organizational practices. The career strategies and work experiences presence of Asian women entrepreneurs and small businessowners is distinctly different from those of employees in large organizational settings.

There is extensive research available on women in the workplace, with a specific focus on women's career pathways. Although that body of research does not address Asian women specifically, it is used as reference to bring up important points with which to inform, compare, and contrast them with other groups of women. Further, as minority group members, Asian women's workplace experiences are significantly impacted by race and ethnicity. We will thus discuss related issues of racial stereotyping and ethnic identity, both broadly as well as in the context of Asian women.

Finally, this book presents a comprehensive view that pulls together all aspects of organizational functioning that are likely to be especially influential on Asian women's career experiences. These include general career management, mentors, networks, impression management and leadership.

The book concludes with strategic recommendations for Asian American women on managing their careers. Their success will be informed by organizational practices and (Asian) communities' efforts. Women have been nimble in adjusting to changing life and societal environments. So too should be these macro-entities in recognizing and responding to the presence and efforts of Asian women in American workplaces.

A Brief Look at U.S. Immigration Policy and Asian Immigration

Immigrants have different reasons for moving from one country to another. Regardless of their motivations, immigrants to the U.S. gain entry only by fitting into one of the various classes determined by the U.S. government. These classes include family reunification, family preference, immediate relatives, employment visas, and refugees. The U.S. can and does alter its immigration policy, such as in fixing the number of immigrants who are granted entry in each class and from each country.

According to Seller (1982, p. 137), immigration policy involves "value judgments about the motivations and potential contributions of particular individuals and groups, the probable ease of their adjustment to America and America's adjustment to them, and the political, social and economic consequences of admitting them—or the moral consequences of not admitting them." Balancing such complex considerations inevitably leads to policy changes over time. The U.S. had open migration until 1882, at which time exclusions of certain groups were put in place (Seller, 1982, p. 148). The first excluded group was Chinese immigrants; by 1924, the policy had changed to exclude almost all Asian and African immigrants.

A watershed moment in immigration policy was the Hart-Cellar Immigration Act of 1965. This act gave more equitable consideration to immigrants from all countries and shifted priority to relatives of those already in the U.S. and persons with special skills. Asian immigrants with good English language skills realized there was an opportunity for improving their economic conditions, relative to their countries of origin, by using their professional skills in the U.S. (Lobo & Salvo, 1998). Thus, many professionally qualified Asians began immigrating to the U.S. in the 1960s and 1970s. This resulted in concerns in the U.S. about American jobs going to immigrants, and conversely in Asian countries to preoccupations about brain-drain. The U.S. government responded to local concerns by placing certification requirements on immigrants in the employment category. Such labor certification needed to indicate that the immigrant's employment would not negatively impact the available American labor market (Seller, 1982, p. 156).

The Immigration Act of 1990 changed employment visa types to include "extraordinary ability or exceptional skills" (Lobo & Salvo, 1998). This modification further accelerated immigration from Asian countries, resulting in a seven-fold increase over three decades. Many Asians began immigrating in the employment class, rather than in the family category. Since employment-related immigration was contingent on successfully passing through screening for specific jobs, these immigrants had very high skill levels (Lobo & Salvo, 1998). Interestingly, many immigrants in the "family preference" and "immediate relatives" categories were professionally qualified as well (Lobo & Salvo, 1998). This focus on skills and education in Asian communities appears to have continued over time. About half of Asians in the U.S. ages 25 and older (in 2015) had a bachelor's degree or a graduate degree, a higher percentage than in other races and ethnicities (Budiman et al., 2019). Asians constitute around 5% of the total U.S. population but represent about 8.3% of undergraduate degree recipients (Smith, 2013).

One basis of variation in the Asian American population is the country of origin. About 85% of Asian Americans "belong to one of six origin groups—Chinese (23%), Indian (19%), Filipino (18%), Vietnamese (9%), Korean (9%), and Japanese (7%)" (Budiman et al., 2019). This population broadly consists of the native-born Generation 1, who came to the U.S. as adult immigrants primarily for employment or family reasons; Generation 1.25, who came as adults with basic schooling in their countries of origin, with the goal of obtaining higher-level education and training in the U.S.; and Generation 1.5, who came as children. The generational distribution of Asian Americans has been determined by U.S. immigration policy. Zhou (2004) noted that an overwhelming percentage (60%) of this group's members are foreign-born, with those from the second generation being the next largest group (28%), with relatively few third-and-higher-generations (12%). Among immigrants, Generation 1.25, many of whose members came as students, currently constitutes the largest group; this group also has a high average gross income (Kim & Zhao, 2014, p. 644).

The socio-economic achievements of some Asian Americans have led to the popular "model minority" stereotype. Coinage of this well-known term is attributed to articles in the *New York Times Magazine* and *The US News and World Report* in the mid-1960s. This stereotype has portrayed Asian Americans as hard-working, adhering to rules, persistent in pursuing educational and professional goals, and not seeking help from others in these pursuits. The academic and professional success of some second-generation Asian Americans, from all family backgrounds, has reinforced this perception (Zhou, 2004). However, as with stereotypes, the model minority description does not apply to all Asian Americans and has even worked against their interests on occasion.

Asian American Women

The pattern of female Asian immigration also changed as a result of the 1965 and 1990 legislations. In the past, women had entered the U.S. primarily as spouses or family members, but as societies in Asia underwent cultural changes and U.S. policy also changed, there was an increase in women immigrating directly as either students or workers. However, since their predominant mode for migration had not been as skilled labor, Asian women had been "relatively invisible in labor market narratives" (Killian & Manohar, 2016, p. 139). In general, the career experiences of ethnic minority women have not been well documented (Kamenou & Fearfull, 2006, p. 157). Asian women, as relatively recent immigrants into the U.S., have received even less attention. Little has been researched or documented about their varied experiences in the corporate world.

Many Asian women immigrants found that once in America, they had to work to earn an income (Yamanaka & McClelland, 1994). Although they were more likely to work in the U.S. than in their countries of origin, their participation rate has been lower than the overall rate for women (Omori, 2016). Culturally, their employment was contingent on gender and family roles and the availability of professional opportunities (Kang & Cohen, 2018). Asian women's employment patterns showed heterogeneity due to influencing factors like social class, family income levels, and cultural and other demographic features. A study in 2012 found that about a quarter of Asian American women were employed in the service sector (Smith, 2013). Some professions attracted specific groups, such as Filipino and Indian women immigrating as nurses.

Studies of immigrant Asian women have revealed some interesting employment patterns. Many researchers have noted the importance of family for Asian communities at large and for Asian women in particular. In the Asian context, the meaning of family went beyond that of spouse and children and often included parents on both sides and even siblings. In Asian countries, such extensions were a result of socio-economic forces and became culturally established practices. These practices carried over in some measure to Asian American communities. Women's employment had to be negotiated within this arrangement, and extended family could be either a strength or a constraint (Kang & Cohen, 2018). Sometimes older or female family members would support working women, but that was not the norm and it varied across different Asian groups. Kang and Cohen (2018) noted that the labor participation of married immigrant Asian women was likely to be higher when they lived with their parents (in-laws) in traditional arrangements. They noted that this was ironic considering that traditionally women did not work outside the home in many Asian countries of origin.

For many Asian women, entering the labor market was necessary in order to ensure the family's economic well-being (Grahame, 2003). Even though work and family typically have different purposes and even contrasting cultures (Clark, 2000), Asian women have found a way to reconcile the two by considering paid employment as a way to act as role-models to their children. These women experienced work not as separate or in competition with personal life, but as an extension of their family responsibilities. They viewed providing for the family through earning an income in similar terms as nurturing family members (Grahame, 2003). However, this negotiation was not done without paying a price. They necessarily had less time to address family needs and often settled for jobs that paid less than their qualifications merited (Yamanaka & McClelland, 1994). For some Asian women, particularly those with college educations, work was a means to fulfill career ambitions (Grahame, 2003).

Regardless of the kind of work they engaged in, many immigrant Asian women found it difficult to gain employment. Even after they gained employment, Asian women had to contend with double challenges. It was estimated that, for Asian women, ethnic and racial effects were several times more negatively impactful than gender effects (Gee et al., 2015). Immigrant women often realized that educational and occupational achievements in the country of origin were of little advantage in the U.S. (Omori, 2016). Human capital accumulated there did not transfer over. One experience common to the heterogeneous group of Asian women was that they typically needed to work harder, and sometimes for longer hours, than white women to achieve the same income levels (Yamanaka & McClelland, 1994, p. 108).

Along with Asian men, Asian women (were) fit into the "model minority" stereotype. Some data has supported that perception. A 2013 study found that they had the highest college graduation rate among different groups of women: 49.4% as compared to the next highest rate of 45.8% for white women (Smith, 2013). Asian women also had an added "model minority" aspect: a perception that they had stable families and gave considerable importance to being married (Fong, 1997, p. 2). Again, some data did support this perception: a survey reported that 69% of Asian women executives spoke of their spouses as "close confidants and partners in their career success" (Carlton & Tang, 2016, p. 80). However, while this trend was partially true, these stereotypical model minority images served to cover up inconvenient or non-confirmatory facts, such as inequity in gaining employment and blocks to career progression.

The time has come to emphasize that Asian American women are differentiated from both Asian American men and non-Asian women. They differ in their outlooks, cultures, and sensibilities. There are internal variations too, such as those along generational lines. Interestingly, immigrants often have strengths like "hardiness and dual frames of reference, that the current situation is better than past" (Varghese & Jenkins, 2009), whereas later generations have the advantage of knowing the society and culture. Second- and third-generation Asian American women are likely to have similarities with each other from having spent their formative years in the U.S. On the other hand, Generations 1, 1.25, and 1.5 might be more similar to each other based on the experience of having grown up in another country. Thus, the former group might be more aware of race-related disadvantages than the latter (Zhou, 2004, p. 35). The former might also struggle with issues of identity while the latter struggle with learning to survive economically and socially.

Women in American Workplaces

The topic of women in organizational settings has been extensively studied and there is plenty of information available on their situation in workplaces. Despite this attention and increasing numbers of women entering the workforce, they continue to be under-represented in higher organizational levels. There has not been a significant change in the percentages of women at managerial levels in corporate America (McKinsey Report, 2018). In 2015, less than 5% of CEO positions and 20% of board seats in the U.S. were occupied by women (Kossek et al., 2017, p. 228). There is considerable unevenness in managerial opportunities across countries, but significant challenges for women to take on senior roles are found everywhere (World Economic Forum, 2018).

The pipeline argument contends that the lack of women at the top is due to a lack of sufficient numbers of women in higher, middle, and even lower-level positions. A counter to this argument holds that women have been doing their share: they have been closing in on the educational gender gap by earning undergraduate degrees (World Economic Forum, 2018), remaining in the workforce despite having to fulfill family responsibilities, and learning to behave more assertively, as when asking for promotions and negotiating salaries (McKinsey Report, 2018). However, companies have failed to step up; they might state a commitment to gender diversity but do not translate that into concrete action.

Women have faced serious challenges as a result of gender stereotyping in the workplace. Gender stereotypes are deeply entrenched, and they can be descriptive as well as prescriptive (Heilman, 2001, pp. 657–658). Descriptive stereotypes of what women are like set expectations in specific ways. Prescriptive stereotypes of how women should behave affect the responses of their co-workers, subordinates, and superiors, especially in the context of performance evaluations. Combined, these expectations have worked as powerful forces against women's progress in the workplace.

These forces had affected criticism of women's workplace attitudes and behaviors. For instance, a common generalization held that women were relational and inclined to factor in other people's needs in decision making, whereas men were goal-oriented and decisive (Mainiero & Sullivan, 2005, p. 111). Communication styles were another issue; women were critiqued as not being direct and assertive enough. Researchers like Hakim (2006) went beyond these seemingly fixable behavioral issues to state that some women were simply not committed enough to a corporate career. Gender-based perceptions held men as more agentic and focused on action, and women as more communal and focused on relationships (Abele & Wojciszke, 2017, p. 752). However, more recent studies have shown such differences declining, as women have exhibited more agentic behavior in their motivations and styles (Kossek et al., 2017, p. 229). Thus, rather than innate qualities, it appears that these differences were socially and culturally constructed ideas.

There was reason to hope for change. Research findings informed women about existing organizational issues and challenges as well as ways to navigate them. Simultaneously, organizations were under pressure to react to these situations and to show that women's issues were addressed. Reasons advocating for organizational responses fell into the category of the business case or the ethical one. The business argument held that businesses were under-utilizing the talents and skills of women, and hence a resource was under-leveraged. The ethical case held that all employees ought to be treated fairly and in an equitable manner, and thus women should not be penalized for their gender. Either reasoning pointed to the need for change.

Despite these motivations for change, women's progress in the workplace has been unevenly distributed. Factors such as industry, geography, type of work, and level of work cause variation in women's success. For instance, women in academia appeared to face challenges in getting hired, but tenure and promotion processes appeared gender-neutral (Ceci at al., 2015). Another kind of variability is that of race and ethnicity. For instance, data from certain Silicon Valley technology companies showed that, among all groups, executive-level representation levels were lowest for Asian women, at 1:285, in comparison to 1:123 for white women (Gee et al., 2015).

Women's career pathways, even those of highly visible, successful women, differ from those of men. Recognizing the reality that most women have to fulfill family responsibilities even as they pursue corporate careers, researchers have described these career paths in various ways. For example, women might have to put together a combination of full-time and part-time jobs, whereas many men in organizational careers have linear paths (Mainiero & Sullivan,

2005, p. 110). According to Mainiero and Sullivan (2005, p. 111), a woman's path is similar to a kaleidoscope with changing patterns, as "she shifts focus to different aspects of her life." Echoing this non-linearity, Eagly and Carli (2007) likened a woman's career path to a labyrinth, which they noted was a complex journey towards a worthy goal. Models such as Alpha and Beta careers (Sullivan & Mainiero, 2007) attempt to descriptively capture the presence of discontinuities and the absence of long-term organizational tethers in women's careers. Other career models considered useful for understanding women's careers were the "protean" model (Hall, 2004), which refers to an individualized and self-directed path, and the "boundaryless" model, which describes a career that moves across different organizations over time (Cabrera, 2009). It is ironic that, given current organizational environments, the career models that used to be considered unconventional for women could very well become the norm for everyone.

Asian Women in Asian Workplaces

Given the strength of cultural influence on Asian women (especially immigrants), it is informative, if not instructive, to consider Asian women in Asian workplaces.

In general, the participation of women in the labor force in Asia has increased (Yukongdi & Benson, 2005, p. 139). Yet, underutilization of female talent has been widespread in many regions (Choa et al., 2015, p. 407). As can be expected, the situation of women in the labor force varies from country to country. In general, labor force participation has tended to be higher in East Asian countries than in South Asian ones (Tuminez, 2012, p. 31). In some countries, women had more economic opportunities as businessowners than as organizational employees. Women have had parity in educational opportunities in China and high literacy rates in Sri Lanka. Countries like India, Japan, and Korea still require women to fulfill traditional roles, whereas in Thailand more women work outside the home. Malaysia, in particular, has a good representation of women in senior positions (Choa et al., 2015).

The common thread among working women in Asian countries has been the degree of domestic work women are expected to take on. This refers to work done in the home, including taking care of (extended) family, which contrasts with paid work done outside the home. It appears that women in many countries in Asia are expected to handle most, if not all, domestic responsibilities, even if they work outside the home. Women in Asia have tried to close the gender gap in education and in workplaces, but cultural and social norms have been slow to change (Tuminez, 2012, p. 13).

Asian women managers reported that even as their workplace conditions improved, their jobs continued to be treated as secondary to their husbands' and their "status and roles at home remain entrenched" (Tuminez, 2012, p. 51). Even aspirational career-oriented women had to factor in the centrality of family, especially parents (in-law), to their decision making, and accordingly adjust their commitment to long hours or to travelling for work (Community Business, 2011). Hence, there is a need for systemic effort on the part of societies, governments, and organizations (Choa et al., 2015, pp. 423–424) to enable improvement of the situation of working women in Asia.

Organizational Workplaces

Working for a business can take many forms, one of which is as the owner (or co-owner) of a business. That role carries certain rights, responsibilities, and rewards. A businessowner has far more influence over the decisions and actions of the business than an employee does. Similarly, the owner accrues profits (if any) to a greater extent than an employee would. At the same time, this role comes with commitment and risk. The owner is responsible for generating revenue and managing costs, and their decisions affect both the success and survival of the business. Additionally, the lives of many small businessowners are intertwined with their businesses, and often they are forced to give higher priority to responding to the demands of the business over other personal matters.

In organizations, the onus of decision making is spread over several individuals. Additionally, large organizations have a relatively greater level of stability due to how they are structured and how they function. In some areas of their functioning, they are also held to legal standards regarding their practices (such as in hiring and promotion) and decisions (such as product design and production). Due to their size and scope, large organizations also offer opportunities for specialists to succeed. This is in contrast to smaller organizations where employees might be required to pick up different kinds of work as needed and to function as generalists. All this implies that working for a large corporation has different implications in terms of career planning and strategy than either owning one's own business or working for a smaller business.

The focus of this book is on organizational careers, particularly within large organizations (for the reasons listed above). We will discuss organizations and workers from the perspective of employees, addressing topics that are likely to impact their career strategizing. A caveat, however, is that large organizations have been changing in drastic ways over the last few decades, so an organizational career of the future is likely to look very different from those in the past.

A special case to consider is that of jobs, or work, in the gig economy. The gig economy is exemplified by companies such as Uber and GrubHub. While these are large corporations that have elements of "traditional organizations," they differ significantly from large corporations of the past in many ways. A telling statistic is their number of employees. For instance, Walmart "employs 2.2 million associates around the world—1.5 million in the U.S. alone" (Walmart), whereas for Uber, the number of full-time employees is 28,600 (Yahoo). In other words, many gig workers are not employees. Organizational work in such businesses is mostly performed by individuals who are treated as contractors rather than employees.

Paths Forward for Asian Women

Asian women have been making their presence felt in corporate America. They have faced challenges but, at the same time, have utilized latent strengths.

The model minority stereotype that has been used as an overarching description for this group has been used by Asians as an asset (Dhingra, 2007, p. 151) while for others it is a restrictive and distorted perception. The relatively recent entry of relatively larger numbers Asian women into American society and corporate workplaces might imbue them with a degree of unfamiliarity. Again, this could work to their advantage or be a disadvantage.

Identity is considered a "root construct" (Ashforth et al., 2011, p. 1144) essential to attitudes and behaviors. Individuals often possess multiple identities (Little et al., 2015, p. 8), each of which becomes more or less salient depending on circumstances. Such individual identities form the basis for social and organizational interactions (Ashforth et al., 2011). Of particular interest to this book is ethnic identity, which includes heritage, holding cultural values, and following cultural practices (Phinney, 1996). Ethnicity is not a label but a complex construct that can vary across members of a group and across time in an individual (Phinney, 1996, p. 922). Interestingly, an individual might have a strong ethnic identity even if she prefers to have little cultural involvement with that ethnic group (Phinney, 1996, p. 922). It is difficult for individuals to shed their unique life histories (Holland, 1996, p. 404), and it may not be in their best interest to do so. Thus, Asian women have to contend with their ethnic heritage and whether (and how) to display that identity. One option is to consider their distinctive difference as an asset and to seek to leverage it (Carlton & Tang, 2016, p. 46). For instance, one Asian woman executive stated that, in her workplace, the "combination of assertiveness and humility makes her stand out" (Carlton & Tang, 2016, p. 80).

Cultural competence is defined as having a strong personal identity, knowing the beliefs and values of the culture, displaying sensitivity, communicating clearly, and maintaining active social relations within the culture group (LaFromboise et al., 1993, p. 396). Asian women are at an advantage in having the opportunity to negotiate different cultures and deepen their multidimensional cultural competence as well as sharpen their skills for understanding differences among people (Carlton & Tang, 2016, p. 43). In a diverse society, such as the U.S., "all members must learn how to effectively navigate their interactions with people from different cultural backgrounds" (Roberts, 2005, p. 685). Asian women will find that their cultural competency skills will be increasingly prized in organizational settings as the workforce grows ever more diverse.

Asian women's professional experiences are likely to vary across generational lines, as do the challenges they face and the tactics they use. Immigrant women who mostly grown up in Asian cultures where they were part of the majority might pay little heed to a minority status in their preoccupation to adjust and succeed in a new environment. Women who have grown up in the U.S., in contrast, might have a more acute sense of their status as a minority and struggle with issues of ethnic identity. Regardless of their internal sense of identity, all Asian women are likely to face challenges related to racial stereotyping.

Progressing in an organizational career means taking on leadership roles. Becoming a leader means more than occupying a position; it might necessitate "acquiring new skills and adapting one's style to the requirements of that role" (Ibarra et al., 2013, p. 62). Ambitious Asian women will need to develop an identity as a leader and assert themselves by taking actions towards a shared purpose (Ibarra et al., 2013, p. 62). This might require some of them to get out of their comfort zones but could yield rich rewards.

The past experiences (and successes) of Asian women in corporate settings occurred during a time of relative stability in U.S. organizations. In the more recent past, however, businesses have been facing increasingly complex environments and responding to these changes in a variety of ways. One response has been to engage in constant restructuring to fit changing strategic imperatives. As a result, long-term, stable organizational careers have been a casualty of such restructuring, as increasingly the responsibility for career development has fallen on individuals (Seibert & Kraimer, 2001, p. 1). At the same time, competition for talent has become more intense (Cabrera, 2009, p. 1). These shifts have also prompted businesses to broaden their employee pools, which results in greater diversity in the workplace. Correspondingly, the need for organizations to manage diversity well has grown, if they want to retain valued employees. Finally, these changes might result in performance appraisals that are less biased based on gender, race, and ethnicity than they were in the past.

Communities can play an active role in the advancement of women in the workforce in many ways, particularly by helping women develop professional networks and negotiate gender-related roles. Socialization patterns for Asian women, especially those with children, might already include regular interaction with community members. However, such social capital is rarely converted to professional and human capital. There must be organized ways for women to leverage these resources. Finally, Asian American women still adhere to traditional gender roles and expectations to a large extent within Asian communities. If they are to truly experience success in both their professional and personal lives, their communities and families will need to adjust their expectations.

REFERENCES

Abele, A. E., & Wojciszke, B. (2007). Agency and communion from the perspective of self versus others. *Journal of Personality and Social Psychology*, *93*(5), 751–763. doi:10.1037/0022-3514.93.5.751 PMID:17983298

Arifeen, S. R., & Gatrell, C. (2019). A blind spot in organization studies: Gender with ethnicity, nationality and religion. In A. Antoniou, C. Cooper, & C. Gatrell (Eds.), *Women, business and leadership: Gender and organisations* (pp. 435–454). Edward Elgar Publishing. doi:10.4337/9781786432711.00034

Ashforth, B. E., Rogers, K. M., & Corley, K. G. (2011, September-October). Identity in organizations: Exploring cross-level dynamics. *Organization Science*, *22*(5), 1144–1156. doi:10.1287/orsc.1100.0591

Budiman, A., Cilluffo, A., & Ruiz, N. G. (2019). *Key facts about Asian origin groups in the U.S.* Pew Research Center. https://www.pewresearch.org/fact-tank/

Business, C. (2011). *Community Business Gender Diversity Benchmark for Asia*. Board Agenda. Retrieved June 5, 2020, from https://www.boardagender.org/files/Community-Business-Gender-Diversity-Benchmark-for-Asia-2011.pdf

Cabrera, E. F. (2009). Protean organizations: Reshaping work and careers to retain female talent. *Career Development International, 14*(2), 186–201.

Carlton, P., & Tang, L. (2016). Eve of change: Women redefining corporate America. *The Everest Project Initiative*. Retrieved June 5, 2020, from https://static1.squarespace.com/static/53065799e4b0be631aa1d70c/t/56f401e3356fb06d548dbd41/1458831856875/2016-Eve-of-Change-Report_03.pdf

Ceci, S. J., Ginther, D. K., Kahn, S., & Williams, W. M. (2015, January-February). Women in science: The path to progress. *Scientific American Mind, 26*(1), 62–69. doi:10.1038cientificamericanmind0115-62

Choa, Y., McLean, G. N., Amornpipat, I., Chang, W., Hewapathirana, G. I., Horimoto, M., Lee, M. M., Li, J., Manikoth, N. N., Othman, J., & Hamzah, S. R. (2015). Asian women in top management: Eight country cases. *Human Resource Development International, 18*, 1–22. doi:10.1080/13678868.2015.1020717

Clark, S. C. (2000). Work/family border theory: A new theory of work/family balance. *Human Relations, 53*(6), 747–770. doi:10.1177/0018726700536001

Dhingra, P. (2007). *Managing multicultural lives: Asian American professionals and the challenge of multiple identities*. Stanford University Press.

Dhingra, P. (2012). *Life behind the lobby: Indian American motel owners and the American Dream*. Stanford University Press. doi:10.1515/9780804782029

Eagly, A. H., & Carli, L. L. (2007). Women and the labyrinth of leadership. *Harvard Business Review*. https://hbr.org/2007/09/women-and-the-labyrinth-of-leadership

Encyclopedia Britannica. (n.d.). Asia: Continent. In *Encyclopedia Britannica*. https://www.britannica.com/place/Asia

Fong, L. Y. S. (1997). Asian-American women: An understudied minority. *Journal of Sociology and Social Welfare*, *24*(1), 91–111.

Gee, B., Peck, D., & Wong, J. (2015). *Hiding in plain sight: Asian American leaders in Silicon Valley*. Ascend Report.

Grahame, K. M. (2003). "For the family": Asian immigrant women's triple day. *Journal of Sociology and Social Welfare*, *30*(1), 65–90.

Hakim, C. (2006, August). Women, careers, and work-life preferences. *British Journal of Guidance & Counselling*, *34*(3), 279–294. doi:10.1080/03069880600769118

Hall, D. T. (2004). The protean career: A quarter-century journey. *Journal of Vocational Behavior*, *65*(1), 1–13. doi:10.1016/j.jvb.2003.10.006

Heilman, M. E. (2001). Description and prescription: How gender stereotypes prevent women's ascent up the organizational ladder. *The Journal of Social Issues*, *57*(4), 657–674. doi:10.1111/0022-4537.00234

Holland, J. L. (1996). Exploring careers with a typology: What we have learned and some new directions. *The American Psychologist*, *51*(4), 397–406. doi:10.1037/0003-066X.51.4.397

Hyun, J. (2005). *Breaking the Bamboo Ceiling*. Harper-Collins.

Ibarra, H., Ely, R., & Kolb, D. (2013, September). Women rising: The unseen barriers. *Harvard Business Review*, 62–66.

Kamenou, N., & Fearfull, A. (2006). Ethnic minority women: A lost voice in HRM. *Human Resource Management Journal*, *16*(2), 154–172. doi:10.1111/j.1748-8583.2006.00010.x

Kang, J., & Cohen, P. N. (2018). Household extension and employment among Asian Immigrant: Women in the United States. *Journal of Family Issues*, *39*(1), 128–154. doi:10.1177/0192513X15606489

Killian, C., & Manohar, N. N. (2016). Highly skilled immigrant women's labor market access: A comparison of Indians in the United States and North Africans in France. *Social Currents*, *3*(2), 138–159. doi:10.1177/2329496515620644

Kim, B. S. K., & Hong, S. (2004). A psychometric revision of the Asian values scale using the Rasch model. *Measurement & Evaluation in Counseling & Development*, *37*(1), 15–27. doi:10.1080/07481756.2004.11909747

Kim, C., & Zhao, Y. (2014). Are Asian American women advantaged? Labor market performance of college educated female workers. *Social Forces*, *93*(2), 623–652. doi:10.1093fou076

Kossek, E. E., Su, R., & Wu, L. (2017, January). "Opting out" or "pushed out"? Integrating perspectives on women's career equality for gender inclusion and interventions. *Journal of Management*, *43*(1), 228–254. doi:10.1177/0149206316671582

LaFromboise, T., Coleman, H. L. K., & Gerton, J. (1993). Psychological impact of biculturalism: Evidence and theory. *Psychological Bulletin*, *114*(3), 395–412. doi:10.1037/0033-2909.114.3.395 PMID:8272463

Little, L. M., Major, V. S., Hinojosa, A. S., & Nelson, D. L. (2015). Professional image maintenance: How women navigate pregnancy in the workplace. *Academy of Management Journal*, *58*(1), 8–37. doi:10.5465/amj.2013.0599

Lobo, A. P., & Salvo, J. J. (1998). Changing U.S. immigration law and the occupational selectivity of Asian immigrants. *The International Migration Review*, *32*(3), 737–760. doi:10.1177/019791839803200307 PMID:12293999

Mainiero, L. A., & Sullivan, S. E. (2005). Kaleidoscope careers: An alternate explanation for the "opt-out" revolution. *The Academy of Management Executive*, *19*(1), 106–123. doi:10.5465/ame.2005.15841962

McKinsey, R. (2018). *Women in the Workplace*. https://www.mckinsey.com/featured-insights/gender-equality/women-in-the-workplace-2018

Omori, M. (2016). Educated and staying at home: Asian immigrant wives' labor participation in the U.S. *Journal of Comparative Family Studies*, *47*(4), 463–481. doi:10.3138/jcfs.47.4.463

Phinney, J. S. (1996). When we talk about American ethnic groups, what do we mean? *The American Psychologist*, *51*(9), 918–927. doi:10.1037/0003-066X.51.9.918

Read, J. G., & Cohen, P. N. (2007). One size fits all? Explaining U.S.-born and immigrant women's employment across 12 ethnic groups. *Social Forces*, *85*(4), 1713–1734. doi:10.1353of.2007.0077

Reports, N. (2018). *Asian Americans: Digital lives and growing influence*. https://www.nielsen.com/us/en/insights/report/2018/asian-americans-consumers/

Roberts, L. M. (2005). Changing faces: Professional image construction in diverse organizational settings. *Academy of Management Review*, *30*(4), 685–711. doi:10.5465/amr.2005.18378873

Seibert, S. E., & Kraimer, M. L. (2001). The five-factor model of personality and career success. *Journal of Vocational Behavior*, *58*(1), 1–21. doi:10.1006/jvbe.2000.1757

Seller, M. S. (1982). Historical perspectives on American immigration policy: Case studies and current implications. *Law and Contemporary Problems*, *45*(2), 137–162. doi:10.2307/1191406

Smith, M. (2013). *Fact sheet: The state of Asian American women in the United States*. Center for American Progress. https://www.americanprogress.org/issues/race/reports/2013/11/07/79182/fact-sheet-the-state-of-asian-american-women-in-the-united-states/

Srinivasan, S. (2001). "Being Indian," "being American": A balancing act or a creative blend? *Journal of Human Behavior in the Social Environment*, *3*(3/4), 135–158.

Sullivan, S. E., & Mainiero, L. A. (2007). The changing nature of gender roles, Alpha/Beta careers and work-life issues: Theory-driven implications for human resource management. *Career Development International*, *12*(3), 238–263. doi:10.1108/13620430710745881

Tuminez, A. S. (2012). *Rising to the top? A report on Women's Leadership in Asia*. Asia Society. http://sites.asiasociety.org/womenleaders/wp-content/uploads/2012/04/Rising-to-the-Top.pdf

Varghese, A., & Jenkins, S. R. (2009). Parental overprotection, cultural value conflict, and psychological adaptation among Asian Indian women in America. *Sex Roles*, *61*(3-4), 235–251. doi:10.100711199-009-9620-x

Walmart. (n.d.). Retrieved June 20, 2020, from https://corporate.walmart.com/newsroom/company-facts

World Economic Forum. (2018). *The Global gender gap report*. http://reports.weforum.org/global-gender-gap-report-2018/

Yahoo. (n.d.). Retrieved June 20, 2020, from https://finance.yahoo.com/quote/UBER/profile?p=UBER

Yamanaka, K., & McClelland, K. (1994). Earning the model-minority image: Diverse strategies of economic adaptation by Asian-American women. *Ethnic and Racial Studies*, *17*(1), 79–114. doi:10.1080/01419870.1994.9993814

Yukongdi, V., & Benson, J. (2005, June). Women in Asian management: Cracking the Glass Ceiling? *Asia Pacific Business Review*, *11*(2), 139–148. doi:10.1080/1360238042000291225

Zhou, M. (2004). Are Asian Americans becoming "white"? *Contexts*, *3*(1), 29–37. doi:10.1525/ctx.2004.3.1.29

Zhou, M., & Gatewood, J. V. (2000). Mapping the terrain: Asian American diversity and the challenges of the twenty-first century. *Asian American Policy Review*, *9*, 5–29.

Chapter 2
Structures and Functioning of Business Organizations

ABSTRACT

The experience of Asian women in corporate America is largely one of working in organizational workplaces. Thus, it is important for employees to understand the structures and functioning of organizations. This chapter discusses research and foundational concepts in organizational structures, specifically as they related to businesses. The profit motive that drives businesses affects how employees' careers unfold within them. Specifically, it affects metrics for performance evaluation. The various organizational positions an individual occupies shapes her career path. The placement of an employee's work position within the hierarchy has numerous implications. For instance, positions are attached to decision making responsibilities and influence. Power is a significant aspect of organizational functioning that is often overlooked by employees who rely primarily on technical performance to propel their careers forward. This chapter addresses these topics as well as performance evaluation, which is the final determinant of an employee's career progress.

INTRODUCTION

Businesses in the U.S. are set up and function as organizations. An organization can be defined in a general way as a group of people working together towards a common goal (Uhl-Bien et al., 2014).

DOI: 10.4018/978-1-7998-4384-9.ch002

In this chapter the focus is on "working together" and how that process is aided through the organization's explicit structure and planned functioning. Organizations consist of individuals who differ from each other in a myriad of ways. Despite these differences, they need to work together to achieve organizational goals and objectives. The scope of organizational work thus requires the division of collective work into individual parts and the combining of all such individual work to achieve outcomes.

Organizational structure is the framework within which individuals work together. The two basic components of this structure are the division of work and its coordination. The division of work is reflected in the structures of units, departments, roles, and jobs. Work is coordinated through the mechanisms of hierarchy, authority, and assigned responsibility. The functioning of organizations includes processes, procedures, policies, philosophies, and culture. It includes not only how work is accomplished but also the behavior of the individuals involved.

We begin this chapter with a brief description of a long-running debate on whether the core goals of businesses should be financial or social. Business goals and objectives drive executive decisions, which are translated into organizational actions. Business actions have a direct impact on employees and indirect effects on the entire society. In the recent past, the debate regarding a business's responsibilities towards the social and environmental impacts of its actions has been renewed. Interestingly, some businesses have taken a strategic stance in this debate. For instance, Sorkin (2018) reported that the investment firm Blackrock informed business leaders that their companies "need to do more than make profits—they need to contribute to society as well if they want to receive the support of Blackrock." If such changes in perspective about the essential mission of business were to become widespread, this could signal a corresponding change in expectations about acceptable performance for top-level executives. Over time, these expectations could percolate to lower levels.

Not every organizational employee can influence strategic decisions. However, for organizations to function successfully, every employee must understand the work they need to do and the role they need to play in the collective effort. Asian women, like almost everyone else, often enter organizations without a complete understanding of how they will be situated within them or the dynamics that will affect their experience. Beyond understanding organizational structure, certain aspects of functioning are likely to be of special importance to these women in their career planning and management. Specifically, these areas include different types of work, performance evaluation, decision making, and organizational power.

Profit Motive or Social Motive?

A key question that has been debated for some time, and which is likely to become more prominent in the future, relates to the essential motives for a business to exist and function. This dilemma can be phrased simply: Should a business function with a profit motive or with a social motive?

One theoretical framing of this issue presents it as the contrast between "ownership theory" and "stakeholder theory" (Lawrence & Webber, 2015, p. 6). Businesses convert inputs, which are resources of various kinds, into outputs, which are products of use and value to customers (Schermerhorn & Bachrach, 2015). Because customers pay for the goods and services they receive, an argument can be made that every business inherently fulfills social needs in the form of products that customers want or need and are willing to pay for. Thus, some researchers view businesses as exhibiting elements of both models and so can be considered as "goal-oriented social entities that have structured systems" (Bedian & Zamnuto, 1991, p. 9).

A business accrues profit when it can sell products to customers for more money than it costs to produce them. A profit motive implies that the business functions in a way that maximizes its profit (Carson, 1993). This model immediately benefits owners and stockholders. The profit motive is supported by ownership theory, which views businesses as the property of their owners and holds that the purpose of businesses is to maximize long-term stockholder value (Lawrence & Webber, 2015). It should be noted that stockholders are not only individuals but also large institutional investors and entities such as pension funds.

The profit motive has been criticized because it could be used to justify a business pursuing profit at all costs, even when it is detrimental to the interests and well-being of groups affected by the business (other than stockholders). Hence, there has been an urge for businesses to consider adopting a social motive to "serve a broader public purpose: to create value for society" (Lawrence & Webber, 2015, p. 6), and not just for stockholders. This perspective acknowledges that businesses need to be profitable for their survival and sustainability but stresses that they need to fulfill other obligations as well.

Broadly, a stakeholder is any individual or group that affects, or is affected by, the business's actions (Lawrence & Webber, 2015, p. 7). Stakeholder groups include employees, local communities, customers, and general society. According to the stakeholder theory, a business is an "entity through which numerous and diverse participants accomplish multiple, and not always congruent, purposes" (Donaldson & Preston, 1995, p. 71). This definition acknowledges the reality that not all stakeholder groups are the same, and they could well have conflicting interests. It might not be possible for a business to meet all the needs of all its stakeholders. Businesses often need to engage in stakeholder management (Donaldson & Preston, 1995) and prioritize different interests.

The ownership and stakeholder theories differ in how they view the relationships a business has with other entities. To illustrate the ownership theory, Donaldson and Preston (1995, fig. 1, p. 69) placed the business in the center of their "input-output model." In this model, inputs come from suppliers, investors, and employees to a business as one-way flows. Similarly, outputs move from the business to customers as one-way flows. Donaldson and Preston (1995, fig. 2, p. 69) contrasted this with the "stakeholder model" where again the business is in the center, but the input and output form two-way flows between the business and stakeholder groups.

Over the past few decades, businesses have made distinctive contributions to the social good, separate from profit motives, in the form of Corporate Social Responsibility initiatives, commonly referred to as "CSR." For some businesses, CSR is closely tied to the business's products and functions. For others, these activities are quite unrelated. Some organizations explicitly connect their mission and purpose to social responsibility, and others make contributions as they see fit. In more recent times, businesses have started to significantly increase their efforts to contribute positively and to proactively minimize the negative impact of their actions on society and the environment. The strongest possible way these changes can be instituted is in defining how organizational performance is evaluated (Bunge, 2020; Safdar, 2020; Sorkin, 2018; Stoll, 2020).

The goal of business decisions and functioning is to obtain results. These results, namely business performance, are most frequently measured through various financial data. Indeed, linking financial performance to executive compensation signals its importance. Revenue and profit are clear indicators of whether an organization has financial viability. Financial ratios such as ROI (return on investment) and ROA (return on assets) indicate different aspects of financial well-being. Stock performance is another common performance measure that is often tied to executive compensation. Although stock prices can and do vary due to a multitude of factors, significant changes in stock prices or long-term trends can be interpreted to reflect shareholder confidence in executive leadership.

Businesses that rely solely on financial information in appraising firm performance are placed in the profit motive category. This profit orientation could also influence executive decision makers' focus on short-term results (Keller, 2013). The explicit role of stock performance to CEO compensation has been criticized as leading executives to focus excessively on decisions that avoid near-term pain at the cost of building long-term assets (Bogle, 2008), hence the shift to a different metric for firm performance by companies such as Blackrock (Sorkin, 2018).

Position and Authority

A generic organizational chart is a visual depiction of an organization's formal structure (see Appendix 1). Organizational charts also illustrate how work is intended to be accomplished within the organization. These visualizations are a response to an organizational need for order and help support a range of organizational functions such as separation of duties, resource allocation, and performance management (Oxman & Smith, 2003, p. 78). All work positions and reporting relationships are shown on the chart, along with job titles and the name of the person occupying each position (Schermerhorn & Bachrach, 2015, p. 243). Each box represents a position and shows the flows of authority connected to that position through lines. Together these lines of authority form the chain of command, which links every position to a higher position in the organization, up to the CEO (Schermerhorn & Bachrach, 2015, p. 257).

According to classical organization theory, business organizations have goals regarding making and selling products. Production is achieved through the use of resources and "maximized through specialization and division of labor" (Dessler, 1986, p. 28). Organizational structures are required to make the best use of available resources (Shafritz et al., 2005, p. 30). For instance, work should not be duplicated, and there should be a good match between the tasks and the skills of the person completing those tasks.

Organizational structures reflect the reality that organizational work is the collection of efforts by several people (employees). It is the formalization of two fundamental aspects of collective work: division of labor and the coordination of work towards common goals. Division of labor is the "subdivision of work into separate jobs," which could be assigned to different people (McShane & Von Glinow, 2019, p. 279). Since organizational work is essentially repetitive, such subdivided work is often narrowly focused and this leads to specialization (McShane & Von Glinow, 2019, p. 280). With work division and specialization comes the need for coordination, which is especially important due to the time-imperative nature of most organizational work.

Organizational coordination includes processes that are designed to align and unify the efforts of different interrelated units towards common goals (Dessler, 1986, p. 148). Techniques used for coordination include organizational rules and procedures, standardization of work, direct supervision and use of authority, formal and information communications, committees and other cross-unit groups, and liaisons (Dessler, 1986, p. 152). Each of these approaches is effective in different ways in different situations. The use of authority and hierarchy is common in almost every situation and is integral to organizational functioning. An emphasis on rules and procedures works well in predictable environments where tasks do not change much over time (Dessler, 1986, p. 149). In more unpredictable environments, frequent feedback, rather than rules, might be more appropriate (Dessler, 1986, p. 150).

The key aspects of organizational structures that are relevant to employees can be summed up as: position, specialization, hierarchy, and authority. Although organizational charts reflect the basics of work division (horizontally, through work positions and specialization) and hierarchy (vertically, through hierarchy and lines of authority), they do not show other aspects of organizational functioning such as how work is done in each position, the distribution of power in the organization, and organizational culture (Uhl-Bien et al., 2014).

There has been plenty of research on how organizations (ought to) function. Max Weber's idea of a bureaucracy was an idealized form, an "epitome of rationality and efficiency" (Eisenstadt, 1958). Weber emphasized jobs as duties, with strict adherence to hierarchy, use of rules, impersonality in performing duties, technical qualifications, and protection of employees from arbitrary dismissal (Eisenstadt, 1958, pp. 103–104). Fayol, another important thinker in this area, believed his concept of management applied to every type of organization. Fayol's principles included division of work, authority, discipline, unity of direction, centralization, initiative, and esprit-de-corps (Shafritz et al., 2005, p. 31). Taylor's scientific management focused on efficiencies of production, particularly in planning and controlling operations (Shafritz et al., 2005, p. 32).

Weber's classic description was later extended to include formalization and centralization. Formalization is the use of clearly stated policies, rules, and procedures. It was thought that as organizations grow in size and complexity, formalization could be used for control and consistency (Sandhu & Kulik, 2019, p. 621). A criticism of formalization is that, while it provides for structure and stability, it can also stifle creativity and individual initiative. Centralization refers to the distribution of decision-making authority and the degree to which it is concentrated in higher levels of the organization (Sandhu & Kulik, 2019, p. 621). In a sense, centralization helped with specialization since it freed lower-level employees from larger concerns. Centralization did make for consistent decisions across the organization. However, in centralized organizations, lower-level employees did not participate in most decisions, often not even in those decisions that could impact them significantly.

Specialization was considered as a contributing element to organizational efficiency by Herbert A. Simon, along with the appropriate grouping of members (such as into departments and divisions) and the hierarchy of authority (Shafritz et al., 2005, p. 112). Every organizational position represents a job, and the employee occupying that position is responsible for doing that job. Typically, every job is a collection of tasks, a set of prescribed activities (Wrzesniewski & Dutton, 2001). Specialization occurs when an employee repetitively performs the same kind of task over time and becomes an expert in doing it. Specialization serves many purposes, both organizational and individual. The importance given to specialization in organizational theories reflects the benefits it provides. Typically, specialization leads to increases in efficiency and productivity, and even in quality. It can benefit the employee, too, in terms of expert power.

Departmentation is the structure that supports unit-level specialization. It is the process through which "organizational functions/activities are grouped logically and assigned to managers" (Dessler, 1986, p. 125). Departments can be functional or divisional (Dessler, 1986, p. 125). Functional areas include business, managerial, and technological. Departmental divisions can be organized along product lines, customers, or geographies. In practice, most organizations are hybrids, combining different forms of departmentation (Dessler, 1986, p. 135).

Roles are an aspect of organizational functioning. They relate to behaviors that people are expected to exhibit because they hold a certain position (McShane & Von Glinow, 2019). For instance, an individual in a leadership position is expected to perform that role through actions such as decision making, planning, communicating, and motivating. This implies that an employee will need to change behaviors to adjust to role expectations as her career moves through different positions in the organization.

In an organization, hierarchy and authority are interrelated means of coordination. Authority is the right to give orders and is built into the organizational structure via supervisory relationships. A manager has authority over his or her reports; this structure of authority defines the organization's hierarchy. Running through the organization, the hierarchy connects all dispersed units, from the highest level to the lowest. Sometimes authority is also found in non-supervisory situations, such as when certain tasks are delegated or in cross-functional teams.

Differences Between Positions

An organizational position refers to a job as well as a place in the overall hierarchy. Positions are differentiated by how and where they are located within the organizational structure, and they are characterized by the units they are located in. These units could be specific departments and divisions, and they are related to the specific work and specializations of the employees. The location of a position is important because it has implications for employees' job security and career advancement.

Positions in an organization can be broadly divided into line or staff positions. According to Dessler (1986, p. 142), line functions are "those that have direct responsibility for achieving the goals of the organization" while staff functions "assist and advise line managers in accomplishing those objectives." According to Schermerhorn and Bachrach (2015, p. 14), line managers are "responsible for work that makes a direct contribution to the organization's outputs." In other words, line jobs are directly connected with production and sales of the business's products, whereas staff jobs provide organizational support. Staff jobs can be generalized as personal, such as executive or departmental assistants, or specialist, including human resources and information technology (Dessler, 1986).

Line positions are generally understood to directly affect the success and sustainability of the organization, while staff positions do not (Schermerhorn & Bachrach, 2015, p. 259). Thus, staff positions might not be considered essential to the organization and staff employees thus tend to have low visibility (Kanter, 1980). Most often, CEOs come from line positions, especially those that have responsibility for major initiatives (Ibarra, 2019, p. 3). However, there are two caveats to these common conceptions. First, some staff positions can become mission central depending on environmental factors and organizational needs. For instance, HR might acquire strategic importance in situations where there is fierce competition for talent and retention of skilled and experienced employees is important for business success. Second, some individuals have risen through their organizations' hierarchies via staff positions and have even become CEOs. For instance, the legal counsel's job might become critical to a business that is facing an existential legal challenge, a situation in which business strategy might be guided by legalities (Warner, 2002).

When organizations (re)structure, whether for economic or strategic reasons, it is likely that positions considered important to core functioning will be retained and those not considered essential will be let go or will no longer be part of the organization. In the latter case, the organization might decide to outsource that function or not to perform it at all. For instance, many organizations contract out cleaning services, food services, and even HR services (Patel et al., 2019). Staff positions are not the only positions that might not be considered part of the core organization, and consequently disposable. The same can happen to some line positions. For instance, a business could decide to exit a product category or a geographic region. Employees in such positions face job insecurity. Ironically, some positions that offer security might not offer a prospect for growth.

Organizational position is an important factor that determines whether an employee progresses upward or not. Researchers have noted that women are often found in staff positions. This might be due to organizational reasons, namely that women are simply preferred in support positions rather than in those that have direct profit and loss (P&L) responsibility. Indeed, organizations have been called out for posting employment numbers that seem to indicate gender parity but in reality obscure the fact that women mostly hold staff or inconsequential line jobs. However, this disparity might also reflect a preference among some women for the more predictable work and hours of staff positions. Women might even shift from line to staff jobs and from roles in major projects to those providing specialized expertise or assistance (Ibarra, 2019, p. 3). Many line positions, especially in projects critical to the firm, pose risks: they require political skills in acquiring resources, managerial skills in getting the team to deliver, and self-promotional ability in claiming credit for results. These positions might also require longer and more unpredictable work hours or travel. Although men might also choose to step out of these roles, women often do so due to the nature of the familial responsibilities they shoulder.

Many organizational positions, especially those at higher levels where decisions can have a consequential impact on the business, have attached risks. Some researchers have contended that women have been intentionally placed in precariously risky positions, an occurrence they labeled the "Glass Cliff" (Ryan & Haslam, 2007). An example of this would be a woman being hired as the CEO of a struggling company. If the company failed, it would reinforce the gender stereotype that women are not competent leaders. If the company overcame the challenges, the woman would be replaced by a male CEO. Ryan and Haslam (2007) proposed this idea based on financial data in the U.K. However, other researchers have countered its generalizability, noting that data from U.S. companies did not support this contention (Adams et al., 2009). Yet other researchers have proposed that Asian business executives have had similar experiences of being placed in leadership positions where the chance of failure is extremely high (Gündemir et al., 2019). The debate on whether data indicated that women and Asians were put in risky leadership positions was primarily based on financial indicators. However, it could be argued that financial data might not capture the entirety of a position's risk, especially in management positions that are not at the highest levels or those with P&L responsibilities (Ryan & Haslam, 2009).

Performance Evaluation

Performance evaluation has been identified as one of the areas of organization functioning where prescriptive gender biases play a role in halting or impeding employee progress (Heilman, 2012), thereby creating the Glass Ceiling. Similarly, performance evaluations play a role in the Bamboo Ceiling and can limit the progress of Asians (Burris et al., 2013). Both women, based on their workplace experience, and researchers, from analyzing data (Schein, 1978), have noted that when evaluation criteria are clear, unambiguous, and implemented based on performance alone, there is little room for gender bias in career progress.

Evaluation is included in the broader area of performance management, along with employee development (Lussier & Hendon, 2013). Several methods are used for this purpose, such as ratings of different kinds (behaviorally anchored, graphic, and ranking), management by objective, and descriptive narratives including critical incidents (Lussier & Hendon, 2013, pp. 297–300). The question of who should assess an employee's performance is critical, but the answer depends on the situation (Lussier & Hendon, 2013, p. 305).

Self-appraisals are commonly a part of employee evaluation, but in the last few decades, evaluations by individuals other than the direct supervisor have also been factored in. The 360-degree evaluation is one such technique that has found wide use in larger corporations.

Due to the impact of evaluation on an employee's continuation and progress within the organization, performance evaluations have been an area of organizational, legal, and social concern. In general, performance evaluation measures must have both validity and reliability, and they should be tied into specific organizational missions and objectives. It must also be possible to equitably implement evaluation techniques. Finally, the evaluations must find widespread acceptance among employees (Lussier & Hendon, 2013, pp. 287–288), and they must hold up to scrutiny in case they are challenged legally.

Despite the implementation of boundaries and guidelines, it would be difficult in practice to have uniform appraisal criteria across all jobs, companies, and industries. Evaluations necessarily have built-in variation and flexibility since businesses differ from each other in so many ways. There is job variability within every organization as well as across industries, arising from each business's unique specialization and hierarchy. For instance, evaluating a salesperson's performance will necessarily be different from evaluating an accountant. Some criteria could be uniform across an organization (such as whether an employee is a "team player") but others must be job-specific. Additionally, the complexity and scope of decision-making based on individual judgment differs according to employees' positions within the organizational hierarchy. Work at lower levels is typically more well-defined and thus lends itself to clearly defined evaluation criteria as well. Jobs higher up in the hierarchy become less structured and more complex; evaluation criteria for such positions must reflect that complexity.

A common issue in performance evaluations is bias, which appears from the need for subjective appraisal (Prendergast & Topel, 1993). A bias is a general tendency in favor of or against something and is often developed a priori. In their study, Prendergast and Topel noted that different kinds of biases occur, some intentional and others unintentional, on the part of evaluators or through the evaluation system itself. Bias can occur due to stereotyping, which is the categorizing of a person into a group and attributing assumed group characteristics to the individual. Typically, stereotypes work against, rather than in favor of, the individual. The halo effect of bias is limited to the individual; the evaluator extends an already formed favorable or unfavorable judgment to all aspects of that person. Non-bias-related inaccuracies can also occur due to the evaluator's internal tendencies, such as evaluating everybody either too hard or too leniently or too similarly. Attribution is another problematic aspect of evaluation inaccuracies that arises when the evaluator is required, or chooses, to give reasons for employee performance or judge its impact (Lussier & Hendon, 2013, pp. 306–307).

Women and minorities in particular have been affected by attribution errors, especially in performance evaluations. This happens because stereotype-related expectations affect attributions regarding competence and ability (Abele & Wojciszke, 2007). Negative attribution errors typically take the form of an individual being held accountable for problems and failures when external factors, rather than the individual, were responsible for those issues. For instance, this could occur when the individual is provided fewer resources than their peers but is expected to deliver the same outcomes. Failure to deliver those results is then attributed to incompetence or lack of effort on the part of the individual. A positive attribution error, in contrast, occurs when an individual is credited with a positive outcome or success when other people or external circumstances were the major factor driving that outcome. The experience of their work being attributed to others, and of others taking credit for their achievements, has been a common one for women and minorities. This error's occurrence might be related, in part, to self-presentation. Individuals can choose to communicate self-attributions for achievements by enhancing internal factors such as ability and skills, or they can shift credit away from themselves in an effort to be modest (Wosinska et al., 1996). Asian women should be aware that modesty might not be effective in all situations.

Decision Making in Organizations

Decision making can be defined as "the process of choosing a course of action for dealing with a problem or an opportunity" (Uhl-Bien et al., 2014, p. 190). Not all decisions are equal and they differ importantly in terms of impact. Making decisions requires being comfortable in dealing with uncertainty and ambiguity. There is an inherent risk to any decision since most organizational choices need to be made without complete and reliable information. Sometimes it might not be clear that a problem or opportunity exists (Chandan & Lakshminarayanan, 2006, p. 184). However, failing to act on time is a decision as well, and it could be the wrong one.

Decisions must be made on a continual basis in organizations. Every job can include, and is subject to, inconsistencies and unpredictability. It can be argued that if a job is specified and standardized to the extent that there is little variability in the work, it might be well-suited for automation. Thus, employees at all levels and in every type of job have to be prepared to make decisions. Fayol's model for organizational functioning recommends that every job allow initiative on the part of the employee, which might mean proactively instituting changes or resolving problems. Either of these actions would require decisions, and Fayol recommended that the employee be given leeway to make those decisions.

Decentralization, delegation, and individual initiative are different forms of decision making in organizations. Delegation is a personalized and focused manner of providing employees with the scope to exercise initiative. The supervisor chooses to assign responsibility for the completion of specified work to a specific employee (Dessler, 1986, p. 169). The authority for completing the work, including obtaining resources needed to do so, is given to the employee by the supervisor. However, the ultimate responsibility for the outcome of that task, good or bad, remains with the supervisor (Dessler, 1986, p. 169). Thus, delegation requires a level of trust in the employee since the supervisor essentially gives over the right to make and execute certain decisions (Schermerhorn & Bachrach, 2015, p. 257) while being held accountable for the results.

Decentralization can be understood as a broader, unit-level delegation. More decision-making authority is given to lower-level managers, and top-level executives maintain control only over essential matters (Dessler, 1986, p. 169). Decentralization is a more formalized process than delegation and involves developing rules, processes, and procedures to be followed (Dessler, 1986, p. 169). Decentralization is also a powerful way to simultaneously develop a deep bench of effective managers in the organization and to free up time for top-level executives to focus on strategic issues. It may not work out well, however, if lower-level managers do not have the skills and competence to take on the work, or if there are not good coordinating mechanisms in the organization. Finding the right balance between lower-level managers practicing autonomy and higher-level executives exercising control is the crucial issue in decentralizing (Dessler, 1986, p. 171).

Although decisions are almost always made under conditions of uncertainties of various kinds, a planned approach might reduce the likelihood of poor decisions. One such approach is the rational decision-making process (Chandan & Lakshminarayanan, 2006, p. 193). This is a multi-step process of defining or recognizing a problem or opportunity; identifying and analyzing alternative courses of action; choosing a preferred course of action; implementing the preferred course of action; and evaluating results and altering as needed (Uhl-Bien et al., 2014). This model works well if one has all the required information. However, since that is often not the case, this model has been adapted to the "bounded rationality model." This is the process of accepting a decision that is satisfactory in certain important dimensions, even if it is not optimal in meeting all requirements (Chandan & Lakshminarayanan, 2006, p. 200). The bounded rationality model explains why different people might arrive at different decisions in the same situation, since each person might identify different criteria as (un)important.

A way to reduce risk that is inherently attached to decisions is to have them made by a group or team. Group decisions can be the choice of the majority, a minority, a group consensus, or (rarely) group unanimity (Uhl-Bien et al., 2014, p. 203). A caveat of this approach is that group decisions that are not unanimous can have powerful and important detractors in those whose opinions were overridden.

A special kind of decision making is that made during a period of organizational crisis. A crisis occurs either when there is an unexpected problem that needs a quick response or when a long-term issue reaches the point of doing extensive harm. Some might contend that the true test of an organizational leader depends on how they handle a crisis, because it might be easy to be a good leader when conditions are favorable and the business is doing well. In particular, there have been criticisms that organizations turn to members from under-represented groups to lead during times of crisis. This was discussed in an earlier section in the context of the "Glass Cliff" (Ryan & Haslam, 2007). Such decisions could set these employees up for failure since chances of failing are likely to be high due to uncertainties and limitations on resources.

The central aspect of decision making is the choice—both of who makes the decision and who is held responsible for it. The impact of decisions can be uncertain and can have extreme consequences, such as threats to brand image, problems with production and delivery, and regulatory failures (Uhl-Bien et al., 2014, p. 196). Being a leader includes the willingness to make momentous choices for courses of action.

Power in Organizations

An important aspect of managing an organizational career is understanding power. Organizational power varies in type, value, and potential for impact.

Every individual in an organization has power, some of which is inherent to a position or a job. Individuals can also create power for themselves through their initiatives and actions. The quantity of power in an organization is not necessarily limited. For instance, it could be expanded through acts of delegation. Strategic knowledge of power includes knowing the kinds of power that exist, the value placed in each type of power, and the kinds of power that different individuals in the organization have. In other words, it is important to have an understanding of the power distribution specific to that organization.

Power can be defined as the ability of an individual to "influence or control some aspect of another person or group" (Uhl-Bien et al., 2014, p. 260). In organizations, it is manifest as the ability to "marshal resources of all kinds, including human, material, and informational" to achieve outcomes (Chandan & Lakshminarayanan, 2006, p. 310). Thus, having power can mean that the individual is central to networks, has a high status in the organization, and can access or control resources within the organization (Ibarra, 1993).

Two major sources of organizational power are positional and personal (Uhl-Bien et al., 2014, p. 263). Personal power is related to an individual's expertise, seniority, education, and other personal characteristics. Positional power is formal and related to the organizational position. Two other kinds of power, connectivity and information, can arise from both positional and personal bases.

Positional (structural) power can be of three kinds: legitimate, reward, and coercive. Legitimate power is the direct authority derived from hierarchy, that is, the power that a manager has over his or her subordinates. This form of power provides the right to give directives and evaluate performance. A caveat, however, is that simply giving an order does not mean that the subordinate will carry it out. Indeed, there is often resistance to following orders when the manager is a woman. Reward and coercive powers refer to the ability to administer positive and negative outcomes, respectively. Direct managers have both reward and coercive power over their subordinates, but these types of powers occur in other contexts as well. For instance, if the organization uses 360-degree performance evaluations as a factor in promotions, any rater has both reward and coercive power over the individual being evaluated. Finally, in the supervisor-subordinate relationship, a subordinate has power over the supervisor as well: the supervisor is evaluated on how well he or she gets work done through subordinates. This gives power to subordinates, as their job performance can reflect on the supervisor's job performance. Subordinates often exhibit this power through tactics like job slow-down, call-outs, or performing poor quality work even if they are capable of a better performance.

Personal power flows from the individual's characteristics and is separate from positional power. There are two kinds of personal power: expert and referent. Expert power refers to special knowledge and skills that are valuable to the organization and that other employees do not have. The importance of expert power is related to its value to the specific organization, and it might not transfer across organizations. An individual has referent power, sometimes called charisma, when others voluntarily identify with him or her. Typically, others also want to develop attitudes and behaviors that are advocated for or exemplified by this individual. For someone with the requisite ability and interest, it is possible to acquire expert power through experience and learning. On the other hand, referent power is generalized and related to an individual's personality and is thus rather more difficult to develop.

Connectivity and information powers are interrelated and can influence each other. Connectivity refers to who an individual is connected to and in what manner. Individuals are connected to others through the organization's hierarchy, but there are other formal connections and networks related to the position and job. Most people have some kind of connection with their peers, even those from other departments or units. For example, they might need to work with employees in line and staff units other than their own, or they might work in groups such as project teams, task forces, or committees. Beyond these situations, individuals can also form connections with others in the organization on a personal basis. These connections are not required or necessitated for organizational purposes, although they could be used by the organization. Unions, employee groups, and affinity groups can be the basis for such connections.

Connections can serve both professional and personal purposes for individuals. Professionally, such relationships might be needed for an employee to perform assigned tasks, or they can affect work quality. On a personal level, relationships can serve to motivate, encourage, or advise. Mentoring, a special kind of organizational relationship, has been extensively analyzed along these two dimensions. Brass (1985, p. 327) noted that the development of formal and informal relationships was one of the most significant ways to acquire organizational power. Social capital can be understood to mean the power latent in connections and relationships.

Not all organizational connections or networks are the same. Researchers have studied individuals' networks based on the strength of relationships and variation among contacts. Each relationship was classified as a "weak tie" or a "strong tie" (Granovetter, 1983). Weak links were used more for information exchange and advising purposes. Strong links were used for more explicit advantages such as advocating, sponsoring, and getting resources. Another kind of network analysis sought to identify whether an individual was "central" to a network or not.

A major implication of belonging to networks is access to information. Information power is important in organizations and can flow from both positional and personal bases. Certain positions require individuals to have certain information. For instance, a regional manager would have information on which locations were slated for closure before other employees in the region. This type of information would be part of formal communication in the organization. Individuals can also obtain information informally, through their position or contacts in organizational networks. For instance, the executive assistant to the regional manager is likely to possess the information regarding closures, and this assistant might choose to share that news with another employee, as could the regional manager. Simple possession of information is not powerful; only its use makes it so.

Although power is invested in an organization's structure, in practice an employee might experience powerlessness. This feeling of a lack of autonomy and participation occurs when employees feel they "must comply with what someone else says" (Uhl-Bien et al., 2014, p. 260). In particular, women managers often experience special power failures from levels both above and below them (Kanter, 1980). Their superiors might hold them accountable for results yet give them neither the authority nor the resources needed to achieve the desired outcomes. This can lead to frustration and failure (Kanter, 1980). On the other hand, women managers' subordinates might not accept their authority or follow their directives.

The two central issues regarding power and career management are the possession of power and the use of power. As mentioned above, individuals possess the power that is invested in their positions and jobs. Beyond that, individuals can actively seek to acquire (more) organizational power, both positional and personal. For example, a department manager can seek to expand their position power by taking over parts of another department or bidding for a project. Accumulating power includes building credibility and expertise as well as gaining access or control over people, information, resources, processes, and policies (Ramaswami et al., 2010, p. 390). A successful attempt to accumulate power requires both motive and resources on the part of the individual (Burns, 1978, p. 12).

An individual's organizational power is determined by the extent of the institutional and personal resources he or she can access (Burns, 1978). In turn, this access is related to the individual's "power base," or others in the organization to whom an individual can turn for such resources. Maintaining a power base is related to both position and personal characteristics (Ibarra, 1993). Successful use of the base might be a determining factor in career progress. Mentors and sponsors, for instance, could be part of an employee's power base, as well as talented and loyal subordinates.

Arguably, the most important aspect of power is its usage. Power, or conversely the lack thereof, is a critical element in effective management (Kanter, 1980). To be effective, individuals must use power. To get desirable results, they must use the resources to which they have access, the information they possess, and the cooperation they can gain from others (Kanter, 1980). Hesitation or delay in the use of power can result in another individual taking it away. Some Asian women might have to overcome cultural and gender conditioning to become comfortable in the use of power. It might help to view power as a means to achieve desirable goals in an efficient and timely way rather than implying dominance and control (Kanter, 1980).

Notes in Conclusion

Every business has a purpose which can be inferred from the customer needs it seeks to fulfill through its products and the industry in which it is situated. Some businesses articulate their purpose through a mission statement, which can indicate their broad purpose as well as information such as values and beliefs. Businesses use these statements to signal that they have a social motive along with a profit motive. The mission and purpose, whether explicit or implicit, affect how the business organization makes decisions.

Business organizations typically have structured environments. Within that structure, every employee has an organizational position which is attached to a title, a job description, and a supervisor (boss). Each job, in turn, consists of tasks and responsibilities, and employees are evaluated based on how well they perform the job. In almost every job, some aspects are clearly defined and others are left unspecified. Thus, employees have to be comfortable with a certain amount of ambiguity about how the job is to be performed, and even understanding the full scope of the job. At the same time, this uncertainty provides an opportunity for creativity and innovation. Job evaluation, usually the responsibility of the supervisor, considers how well the employee performs all aspects of the job. Thus, doing a job well requires that the employee not only complete tasks as specified but show initiative in doing less well-defined work. When jobs are not well specified, there is room for variability in performance evaluation between peers, and there is also the possibility for supervisor biases to impact employee-related decisions.

Unspecified work might be communicated as responsibilities. For instance, a supervisory position implies the responsibility of getting subordinates to do their jobs. It is up to the supervisor to choose approaches that will lead to this desired outcome. The organizational structure provides the supervisor with authority to give work directives to subordinates and to evaluate subordinates' performance. Without these structures in place, it would be almost impossible for the supervisor to effectively fulfill that responsibility.

Almost every job involves decision making of some kind. Employees need to be comfortable in (taking the risk of) making decisions to do their jobs well and to progress in their careers. An employee's decisions can impact themselves or others; in the latter case, these decisions contribute to the employee's power. For instance, the organizational structure gives a supervisor power to select tasks for a subordinate. Thus, power is built into the structure through positions, organizational relationships, and work overlaps. For instance, a subordinate has power over the supervisor as well, since the supervisor will be evaluated based on how well they manage their subordinates. It is also possible for employees to acquire different kinds of power. For example, both expertise in an area of importance to the organization and influential connections represent power. Employees can use this power to enhance their work performance as well as to expand the scope of work attached to their position.

Not all jobs in an organization are the same. Specifically, they can differ based on specialization, which is typically reflected in departmental structure: positions related to the same type of work are grouped in a unit. A job that requires specialized skills often requires education or training, experience, and expertise in that area. Specialized skills, in contrast to general skills, have a narrower scope. Examples of specialized areas in most corporations are accounting and information technology. Jobs also differ based on the organizational level. Typically jobs at lower organizational levels have a greater emphasis on short-term planning and efficiency. Going up the hierarchy, jobs become more complex, with more emphasis on the long-term and factoring in more uncertainty. Even though the problems that need to be solved become harder at higher levels of the organization, these positions provide scope for independent and complex decision making (Shafritz et al., 2005, p. 234).

Finally, organizational employees need to be aware that, while competence and technical ability are important for every job, other influential factors will affect their careers. Employees need to constantly assess the value their jobs bring to the organization and their importance to the business's core proposition and mission.

REFERENCES

Abele, A. E., & Wojciszke, B. (2007). Agency and communion from the perspective of self versus others. *Journal of Personality and Social Psychology*, *93*(5), 751–763. doi:10.1037/0022-3514.93.5.751 PMID:17983298

Adams, S. M., Gupta, A., & Leeth, J. D. (2009). Are female executives over-represented in precarious leadership positions? *British Journal of Management*, *20*(1), 1–12. doi:10.1111/j.1467-8551.2007.00549.x

Bedian, A. J., & Zamnuto, R. F. (1991). *Organization: theory and design*. Dryden Press.

Bogle, J. C. (2008, May). Reflections on CEO compensation. *The Academy of Management Perspectives*, *22*(2), 21–25. doi:10.5465/amp.2008.32739756

Brass, D. J. (1985). Men's and women's networks: A study of interaction patterns and influence in an organization. *Academy of Management Journal*, *28*(2), 327–343.

Bunge, J. (2020, January 21). Tyson scion to lead sustainability push. *The Wall Street Journal*. https://www.wsj.com/articles/tyson-scion-to-lead-sustainability-push-11579606201

Burns, J. M. (1978). *Leadership*. Harper & Row.

Burris, K., Ayman, R., Che, Y., & Min, H. (2013). Asian Americans' and Caucasians' implicit leadership theories: Asian stereotypes, transformational, and authentic leadership. *Asian American Journal of Psychology*, *4*(4), 258–266. doi:10.1037/a0035229

Carson, T. L. (1993, April). Does the stakeholder theory constitute a new kind of theory of social responsibility? *Business Ethics Quarterly*, *3*(2), 171–176. doi:10.2307/3857371

Chandan, J. S., & Lakshminarayanan, S. (2006). *Fundamentals of management*. Houghton Mifflin.

Dessler, G. (1986). *Organization theory: Integrating structure and behavior* (2nd ed.). Prentice-Hall.

Donaldson, T., & Preston, L. E. (1995). The stakeholder theory of the corporation: Concepts, evidence, and implications. *Academy of Management Review*, *20*(1), 65–91. doi:10.5465/amr.1995.9503271992

Eisenstadt, S. (1958). Bureaucracy and bureaucratization. *Current Sociology*, *6*(2), 99–124. doi:10.1177/001139215800700201

Granovetter, M. S. (1983). The strength of weak ties: A network theory revisited. *Sociological Theory*, *1*, 201–233. doi:10.2307/202051

Gündemir, S., Carton, A. M., & Homan, A. C. (2019). The impact of organizational performance on the emergence of Asian American leaders. *The Journal of Applied Psychology*, *104*(1), 107–122. doi:10.1037/apl0000347 PMID:30247048

Heilman, M. E. (2012). Gender stereotypes and workplace bias. *Research in Organizational Behavior*, *32*, 113–135. doi:10.1016/j.riob.2012.11.003

Ibarra, H. (1993). Network centrality, power, and innovation involvement: Determinants of technical and administrative roles. *Academy of Management Journal*, *36*(3), 471–501.

Ibarra, H. (2019). A lack of sponsorship is keeping women from advancing into leadership. *Harvard Business Review Digital Article*. https://herminiaibarra.com/a-lack-of-sponsorship-is-keeping-women-from-advancing-into-leadership/

Kanter, R. M. (1980, Summer). Power failure in management circuits. *The McKinsey Quarterly*, 68–87.

Keller, G. F. (2013). Evaluating if a linkage exists between CEO compensation and the net income and stock price of their firm: A micro study. *3rd Annual International Conference on Business Strategy and Organizational Behavior*, 81–86. 10.5176/2251-1970_BizStrategy13.08

Lawrence, A. T., & Webber, J. (2015). *Business and society: Stakeholders, ethics, public policy* (15th ed.). McGraw Hill Education.

Lussier, R. N., & Hendon, J. R. (2013). *Human resource management: Functions, application, skill development*. Sage Publications.

McShane, S. L., & Von Glinow, M. A. (2019). *Organizational behavior* (4th ed.). McGraw Hill.

Oxman, J. A., & Smith, B. D. (2003). The limits of structural change. *MIT Sloan Management Review*, *45*(1), 77–82.

Patel, C., Budhwar, P., Witzemann, A., & Katoud, A. (2019, October). HR outsourcing: The impact on HR's strategic role and remaining in-house HR function. *Journal of Business Research*, *103*, 397–406. doi:10.1016/j.jbusres.2017.11.007

Prendergast, C., & Topel, R. (1993). Discretion and bias in performance evaluation. *European Economic Review*, *37*(2-3), 355–365. doi:10.1016/0014-2921(93)90024-5

Ramaswami, A., Dreher, G. F., Bretz, R., & Wiethoff, C. (2010). Gender, mentoring, and career success: The importance of organizational context. *Personnel Psychology*, *63*(2), 385–405. doi:10.1111/j.1744-6570.2010.01174.x

Ryan, M. K., & Haslam, A. S. (2007). The Glass Cliff: Exploring the dynamics surrounding the appointment of women to precarious leadership positions. *Academy of Management Review*, *32*(2), 549–572. doi:10.5465/amr.2007.24351856

Ryan, M. K., & Haslam, A. S. (2009). Glass cliffs are not so easily scaled: On the precariousness of female CEOs' positions. *British Journal of Management*, *20*(1), 13–16. doi:10.1111/j.1467-8551.2008.00598.x

Safdar, K. (2020, February 8). Meet the new Nike boss: Trading tech for Air Jordans. *The Wall Street Journal*. https://www.wsj.com/articles/meet-the-new-Nike-boss-trading-tech-for-air-jordans-11581166802

Sandhu, S., & Kulik, C. T. (2019). Shaping and being shaped: How organizational structure and managerial discretion co-evolve in new managerial roles. *Administrative Science Quarterly*, *64*(3), 619–658. doi:10.1177/0001839218778018

Schein, V. E. (1978). Sex role stereotyping, ability and performance: Prior research and new directions. *Personnel Psychology*, *31*(2), 259–268. doi:10.1111/j.1744-6570.1978.tb00445.x

Schermerhorn, J. R. Jr, & Bachrach, D. G. (2015). *Management* (13th ed.). Wiley.

Shafritz, J. M., Ott, S. J., & Jang, Y. S. (2005). *Classics of organization theory* (6th ed.). Wadsworth Thomson.

Sorkin, A. R. (2018, January 15). BlackRock's message: Contribute to society or risk losing our support. *The New York Times*. https://www.nytimes.com/2018/01/15/business/dealbook/blackrock-laurence-fink-letter.html

Stoll, J. D. (2020, January 18). Airbnb's new compensation plan asks shareholders to share with other stakeholders. *The Wall Street Journal*. https://www.wsj.com/articles/airbnbs-new-compensation-plan-asks-shareholders-to-share-with-other-stakeholders-11579358335

Uhl-Bien, M., Schermerhorn, J. R. Jr, & Osborn, R. N. (2014). *Organizational behavior* (12th ed.). John Wiley.

Warner, F. (2002, October 31). Finbarr O'Neill is not a car guy. *Fast Company*. https://www.fastcompany.com/45557/finbarr-oneill-not-car-guy

Wosinska, W., Dabul, A. J., Whetstone-Dion, R., & Cialdini, R. B. (1996). Self-presentational responses to success in the organization: The costs and benefits of modesty. *Basic and Applied Social Psychology*, *18*(2), 229–242. doi:10.120715324834basp1802_8

Wrzesniewski, A., & Dutton, J. E. (2001). Crafting a job: Revisioning employees as active crafters of their work. *Academy of Management Review*, *26*(2), 179–201. doi:10.5465/amr.2001.4378011

APPENDIX

Figure 1. Partial (Generic) Organizational Chart

Chapter 3
Organizational Diversity and Culture

ABSTRACT

An organizational workforce is not a monolith. Organizational diversity is a catch-all term that implies that employees are different in ways that impact their interaction with, and their experience of, working in the organization. It also suggests that the organization is cognizant of these differences. Diversity is widely accepted as a growing and integral part of the workplace. This diversity does not detract from organizations' reliance on their employees to perform their roles and work with others. Thus, organizations strive to find effective and efficient means to address employee concerns and respond to employee needs related to diversity. Workplace culture is important in this context and plays a key role in influencing all employees. The understanding of what differentiates employees from each other changes with social perceptions and as the composition of the workforce itself alters over time. In the current social environment, Asian women are understood to be a group that represents workplace diversity.

INTRODUCTION

An organization is defined as a group of people working together towards a common goal (Uhl-Bien et al., 2014). In Chapter 2 we discussed how organizations are structured and how they function through the mechanisms

DOI: 10.4018/978-1-7998-4384-9.ch003

of the division of work, specialization, and coordination. Now we turn our attention to the "group of people" in an organization.

The people working in an organization reflect the larger society in which the organization is situated. Workplaces often mirror the sociocultural dynamics of social lives (Eswaran, 2019). The gender, racial, and ethnic diversity of corporate workforces has increased since the 1960s (Dobbin et al., 2007). Technological changes have made it possible for people with disabilities to do certain kinds of work that might have been unavailable to them before. Along with the ADA (Americans with Disabilities Act), this introduced another type of diversity in the workforce. Recognition of other factors that influence the work environment, such as age, sexual orientation, and religion, have been gaining prominence as well. These demographic and cultural shifts, along with changes in the legal environment, have contributed to increased workforce diversity. At the same time, the competitive environment for U.S. corporations has become increasingly dynamic and complex. Customers, suppliers, franchisees, and business partners have become diverse in different ways. Thus, organizations can view a diverse workforce in multiple ways—as an unavoidable challenge, as a means to gain market share, as providing access to bigger pools of talent, or as a "socially acceptable way to address race and gender issues" (Jayne & Dipboye, 2004, p. 410).

In this chapter, we discuss corporate motivations for and approaches to managing workplace diversity. Organizational culture is an important aspect of organizational functioning that has a significant impact on diversity. While diversity programs can be designed and implemented, their efficacy is determined by the attitudes and responses of organizational members. Culture plays a key role in influencing these reactions. Organizational culture is not static. It is linked to the company's key values and to environmental changes, both internal and external. Asian women's experiences are affected by workplace cultures as well as the diversity policies and practices implemented by organizations.

The discussion in the chapter about diversity and culture is broad and general because there has been no research published on programs and initiatives in the specific context of Asian women. However, it is relevant to examine these general organizational motivations and actions towards diversity since they are predictors of what Asian women can expect in workplaces. One such program that could be particularly relevant to this group is Employee Resource Groups.

Diversity in Organizations

In general, diversity refers to differences between individuals in the workplace, due to either individual, group, or cultural characteristics. While diversity is understood in general terms, it is difficult to define precisely. However, for research purposes a definition is required, even a broad one. A workable definition holds that diversity is the "degree of intra-organizational representation of people with different group affiliations of cultural significance" (Herdman & McMillan-Capehart, 2010, p. 39).

Diversity in business organizations is understood as having a workforce composed of various groups or social categories. This conception allows the measurement of diversity through a count of the number of employees belonging to each group. In addressing diversity, organizations initially focused on legally protected categories such as race and gender. However, the focus has since broadened to include a wider range of differences (Jayne & Dipboye, 2004, p. 410). Both the kinds and amount of workplace diversity have increased over the last few decades.

Social changes, such as an increase in the percentage of women participating in the labor force, have contributed to an increase in gender diversity. As noted in Chapter 2, immigration policy changes in the 1960s led to demographic shifts in the U.S. labor pool (Jayne & Dipboye, 2004, p. 409). Another change has been the globalization of U.S. corporations, whereby these businesses intentionally sought to make their U.S.-based workforces more international. These factors have resulted in increased racial and ethnic diversity in workplaces. Technological advances and other socio-cultural changes have also led to American workplaces diversifying on the basis of ability-status, sexual orientation, and religion (Eswaran, 2019; Konrad, 2006). This list is not exhaustive; it merely indicates that diversity itself has become more diverse.

Corporate America has consequently experienced an increase in diversity awareness, perhaps born of necessity. For example, executives at a large financial services company were often asked about the makeup of their workforce. For several years they had no ready answer. At one corporation, there is now a 23-page answer detailing the workforce composition based on various dimensions of diversity (Nguyen, 2019). This document was created in response to the CEO's stance that big companies need to be intentional in building a diverse workforce (Nguyen, 2019). Companies have been implementing various diversity responses in recent years, even if some do so without much fanfare. For instance, very few businesses (about 3% of

Fortune 500 companies) shared detailed diversity-related information (Jones & Donnelly, 2017) even if they had programs aimed at increasing diversity. Interestingly, those that are transparent in implementing such programs are not necessarily those ranked by employees as the best places to work, in terms of the workplace's diversity (Bush & Peters, 2016).

Employee conception of diversity is changing as well, varying most dramatically along generational divides. Prior generations had (traditionally) viewed diversity through the perspectives of demographics, equality, and representation. In contrast, millennials view diversity as a "melding of varying experiences, different backgrounds, and individual perspectives" (Eswaran, 2019). This is an important difference for companies to consider since millennials are projected to comprise 75% of the global workforce by 2025 (Eswaran, 2019), and some companies have thus already factored it into their strategy. For instance, one large U.S. corporation redesigned its entire approach, shutting down long-standing diversity programs that were structured around demographic groupings and beginning new programs that were more inclusive. The company stated that this decision was a response to changing times, specifically since "millennial employees don't like pigeonholes" (Green, 2017).

Researchers have been interested in diversity representation at various levels of the organization. One important data point in this research is the composition of the overall workforce. Another area of interest has been the higher organizational levels—the board of directors, the CEO, top executives (3–5 levels from the CEO), middle-management, and first-level management. The nature of business competitiveness and investor pressure has focused interest on board representation (Harvard Law Forum, 2018). Further, board diversity has been linked positively to improved organizational performance, even on financial measures (Deloitte, 2018). In the U.S., board diversity has been steadily increasing. Among Fortune 500 companies, the number of organizations with more than 40% diversity on their boards doubled over the last two decades (Harvard Law Forum, 2018). Asian representation, although still low, has increased as well. Data from 2018 showed that Asians held 3.8% of board seats and Asian women had 17 seats (Harvard Law Forum, 2018). An interesting delineation between board and CEO diversity was made by Cook and Glass (2015). They found that diverse boards were effective in raising the levels of diversity in the organization, particularly by influencing (non-minority) CEOs. However, individual minority CEOs had a limited impact on diversity in their organizations.

Diversity of all kinds is thus the most likely future for American corporate workplaces. This includes diversity not only in employees, but also in customers, suppliers, investors, and boards. However, an important caveat in this discussion of diversity is that its mere presence does not imply that the organization has been able to accrue all the benefits of diversity and avoid the pitfalls. Diversity can affect an organization in a multitude of positive ways. At the same time, there are many challenges associated with workplace diversity. For instance, researchers have found both positive and negative effects of demographic diversity on organizational outcomes (Olsen & Martins, 2012, p. 1168). Negative effects might include "increased relationship conflict, decreased productivity, intent to quit, and lower organizational commitment" (Herdman & McMillan-Capehart, 2010, p. 40). These challenges can be compounded by organizations wanting to take an easy way out when addressing diversity-related issues by choosing to "recycle costly and ineffectual initiatives" (Newkirk, 2019).

Business Case or Ethical Imperative?

Organizational approaches to diversity have been affected by changes in the legal environment over the last few decades. During the 1960s, President Kennedy signed an affirmative action order whose intent was to attempt to redress past discrimination. This legislation affected certain employers, specifically those with federal government contracts. Further, the Civil Rights Act of 1964 induced businesses to implement diversity programs, including training, mentoring, affinity groups, and cultural workplace celebrations (Dobbin et al., 2007). In principle, the affirmative action order and the Civil Rights Act should have made discrimination illegal in the private sector (Dobbin et al., 2007). However, in practice, employers at that time did not think these laws would require them to make drastic changes.

Another legislative initiative was the Equal Employment Opportunity Commission (EEOC). It was established during that period with the purpose of investigating employment-related discrimination. Over time, the EEOC has had a presence in organizational hiring processes.

While legal imperatives made it mandatory for businesses to act in certain ways, other environmental changes have had a deep impact as well. Social, cultural, and technological factors have affected how businesses view and manage diversity. Diversity management refers to the collection of a business's responses directed internally towards its employees. This includes selection and hiring, development and promotion, and even final parting with employees. Diversity management is more than merely complying with legal frameworks; it "goes beyond meeting legal standards of nondiscrimination and nudges organizations toward proactive and voluntary action" (Fisk et al., 2019, p. 287).

Since diversity management mostly refers to voluntary and self-chosen organizational actions, these initiatives need to have staying power. Otherwise, they are likely to fall into the "flavor of the month" trap. Thus, businesses' motivations for putting resources into diversity management are critical. Management scholars have distinguished two main motivations of businesses in this domain. The first arises from a resource utilization viewpoint and is referred to as the business case. The second, which comes from a social justice perspective, is called the ethical imperative.

The business case for diversity states that organizations "devote resources to diversity initiatives because they believe diversity is a business imperative and good for the bottom line" (Jayne & Dipboye, 2004, p. 409). This motivation represents diversity as an asset to be leveraged. Under this perception, diverse workplaces should attract larger talent pools and be better positioned to appeal to diverse customer groups. Further, diverse workplaces should be better at innovating and problem-solving since their employees have a wider range of experiences and perspectives (Konrad, 2006). These arguments suggest that a diverse workforce could help with, if not ensure, business success. However, this reasoning appeared to be aimed at persuading those businesses that were reluctant to change. Additionally, in this situation the onus for delivering all these advantages is placed on the employees representing diversity. As noted by Jones et al. (2013, p. 56), the "sole reliance on the business case for diversity can minimize or ignore the historical experience of disadvantaged people and the genuine intergroup tensions that persist."

The ethical imperative stance holds that businesses need to address organizational diversity since it is a basic "human rights issue" (Lozano & Escrich, 2017). Diversity represents different values, beliefs, and customs. Organizations thus need to take all these represented aspects of individual identity into account in their functioning. In this context, Lozano and Escrich (2017) differentiated between organizational indifference, tolerance, and respect. In "indifferent" organizations, there was exclusion, and employees who did not fit the norm were viewed as mere labor. Tolerance in this context had the goal of peaceful co-existence, yet it was closely linked to cultural and group identities. In "tolerant" organizations, there could be active antidiscrimination policies in place and employee diversity could be viewed as adding value to the business.

Diversity could be used to gain business advantages, yet there could also be asymmetry and distinct differences between majority and minority employees. Respect went beyond tolerance by requiring judgment and reflection. In "respect" organizations, the environment encouraged learning. There would be attempts to ensure parity between all members and to integrate employees from different backgrounds. Based on the literature, it appears that organizations often followed the "tolerance" strategy. In those workplaces, employees were "not insulted," but they were not granted recognition either. They were simply not seen as persons with a meaningful and important presence (Lozano & Escrich, 2017). Minorities, including Asian women, have reported feelings of invisibility in organizations (Rosette, et al., 2016), which would align with an organizational attitude of tolerance.

These two main motivations have been linked to the underlying values of the organization. The business case advocates leveraging diversity to achieve business-related outcomes. It presents diversity as a means to an end: it has an instrumental value. In contrast, the ethical imperative view has a functioning, diverse workforce as its final objective. This was true regardless of the implications for business outcomes and could thus be considered a terminal value (Olsen & Martins, 2012, p. 1171).

Some researchers suggested that the instrumental view justifying diversity as "good for the company's bottom line" (Jones et al., 2013, p. 56) can lead to negative effects, such as discrimination being justified as economically necessary. Conversely, such an instrumental view could also lead to positive outcomes. It emphasizes organizational decisions being made for performance benefits rather than individual characteristics. This might lead to diversity programs being viewed by minority group members "as less stigmatizing" and by majority members as "more just" (Olsen & Martins, 2012, p. 1172).

The reality is that business organizations exist by meeting business goals through the efforts of all organizational members. Hence, the most effective way to manage diversity might be to appeal to both economic and ethical motives (Jones et al., 2013, p. 57; Rabl et al., 2020, p. 531). Co-mingling business and ethical motivations would make diversity programs appear more authentic and likely to gain acceptance by participants (Jones et al., 2013).

An important dimension to consider is the self-identification of employees. Employees share a degree of similarity as organizational members. However, they can differ in demographic attributes such as gender, ethnicity, and age (Konrad, 2006). Apart from these group-related similarities and differences, each employee is unique in his or her own way. The "ontological approach" identifies this duality by presenting diversity as social or individual. On the one hand, diversity can be considered as a "social phenomenon explained by individual differences." This implies that appropriate approaches are those focused on the individual and the individual's relationships. On the other hand, diversity can be viewed as "societist" and linked to categories, which would imply that organizational approaches should be "extrapersonal" and focused on groups (Janssens & Steyaert, 2019, p. 518). Employee experiences in the workplace include both perspectives on diversity. Hence, organizations are challenged to strike a balance between focusing on individuals and focusing on groups.

Diversity Management

Organizational motivations towards diversity are often articulated as mission and values. These are translated into actions through the implementation of structural changes, policies, procedures, guidelines, and practices.

"Diversity management" refers to organizational actions directed towards employees and includes the collection of communications and actions related to diversity. Yang and Konrad (2011, p. 6) described it as "formalized practices developed and implemented by organizations to manage diversity effectively." Organizations have utilized a variety of diversity management approaches. In the 1970s, companies began hosting workshops to educate managers on race relations. By the 1980s, these workshops expanded to include broader sensitivity training programs aimed at reducing stereotyping (Dobbin et al., 2007). Some companies went further in establishing direct interventions through formal mentoring programs matching senior management with aspiring junior employees in diversity categories.

Over the last five decades, many large corporations have engaged in some form of diversity management. Training has been among the most popular of these strategies. Surveys of businesses showed that more than two-thirds of U.S. corporations, and 74% of Fortune 500 companies, have implemented diversity training programs, although such initiatives are not cheap (Jones et al., 2013, p. 55). On average, large organizations spend upwards of $1 million per year for diversity training (Jones et al., 2013, p. 55). The popularity of these formal training programs has led to the creation of a service industry of diversity trainers and diversity consultants.

The main aim of most training programs is to create awareness of bias, to educate employees on factors behind bias such as stereotyping, and to develop skills in preventing and managing biases. Training can be delivered in varied ways, including face-to-face discussions, online self-paced programs, "classroom-based training, videos, discussions, role-plays, simulations, and exercises" (Jones et al., 2013, p. 57). Jones et al. found that each of these methods was effective in a different way. For instance, role-playing techniques simulated situations and challenged participants to examine how to address them (Jones et al., 2013, p. 65). Several variables affected the efficacy of diversity training programs, including the method used, participant characteristics, and organizational culture. Lindsey et al. (2017) recommended two methods to be effective—perspective-taking, where employees are asked to assume a different identity, and goal setting, where employees set specific diversity-related goals.

Corporate diversity initiatives have received mixed reviews. Some have been critiqued for having a focus on demographic characteristics that is too narrow, arguing that diversity should refer to any difference related to any characteristic (Olsen & Martins, 2012, p. 1168). Harsh criticisms have also been leveled at the actual means and methods used in implementing diversity initiatives, including that businesses were seeking easy answers and avoiding difficult choices. Newkirk (2019) commented, "Everybody is quick to do unconscious-bias training and not interventions" and that simply offering many programs, none of which create actual change, only served to intentionally block change. Bush and Peters (2016, n.p.) observed the effects of flawed implementation: "Many companies invest in diversity efforts and appoint chief diversity officers yet are disappointed with the meager results."

Even when businesses appeared well-intentioned in allocating resources to diversity efforts, it seemed that they were not doing so optimally. Dobbin et al. (2007, p. 26) concluded that three of the most popular diversity management programs—diversity training, evaluations, and network programs—have had no positive impact on workplaces. In contrast, the two least popular approaches (mentoring and appointing diversity managers) had the most potential to be impactful. They added that "programs designed to reduce bias among managers responsible for hiring and promoting have not worked" on average, which was not surprising since research has established the persistent nature of stereotypes.

Training was singled out as being ineffective, overvalued, or even harmful. Jones et al. (2013, p. 55) stated that the "extant literature on diversity training programs continues to yield little evidence of their overall effectiveness."

Even worse, these programs could lead to negative outcomes (Jones et al., 2013, p. 56) such as triggering a backlash against minority group members (Lindsey et al., 2017).

Analysis of diversity initiatives and organizational outcomes has indicated that it is highly unlikely for there to be "one-best way" when it came to managing diversity (Jayne & Dipboye, 2004, p. 413). Some general conclusions can be surmised from past data, however. For instance, voluntary diversity programs and those that focus on cultural awareness can be effective, whereas mandatory training or threats of lawsuits are likely to be ineffective (Dobbin et al., 2007).

Despite these findings, the overall relationship between diversity and organizational outcomes continues to be complex. Multiple studies in the field have indicated that various contingent factors need to be considered in attempting to establish connections between the diversity of an organization and its outcomes (Yang & Konrad, 2011, p. 7). In particular, Jones et al. (2013) recommended a targeted rather than general approach through performing a needs assessment before launching a diversity program.

The success of diversity programs directed at employees could depend to a large extent on how the programs are framed (Jayne & Dipboye, 2004, p. 414). Diversity can be a controversial, even contentious, issue. Proponents of diversity argue that it "increases the knowledge, perspectives, and ideas that are available as inputs into creative processes and decision making, thus enhancing performance" (Olsen & Martins, 2012). Opponents highlight negatives, such as an increase in interpersonal conflict and a reduced sense of cohesion among organizational members. While employees routinely participate in various kinds of training in an organization, research has shown that diversity training appeared different than other types. Jones at al. (2013, p. 56) noted that it faced "a number of unique challenges, including backlash, a negative response to diversity training that other training programs may not encounter."

In some organizations, there was less backlash when diversity was presented as a means to gain a competitive advantage rather than to redress societal injustices (Jones et al., 2013, p. 63). That is, it was helpful in these situations to present diversity as a business case to persuade detractors rather than as an ethical imperative required of them. However, as noted in the previous section, the best approach might be a combination of business and ethical motivations.

Jayne and Dipboye (2004, p. 414) suggested three different framings for diversity training: "integration and learning; access and legitimacy;

discrimination and fairness." Integration and learning focus on developing functional effectiveness by encouraging employees to find ways to rethink primary tasks and processes. The "access and legitimacy" framing was effective when the firm was looking to enter new and diverse markets. The "discrimination and fairness" approach builds cohesiveness by appealing to employees' inner sense of right and wrong. The authors noted that the most effective framing was the first one, "integration and learning," which has also been referred to as the "learning and effectiveness paradigm" by Thomas and Ely (1996, p. 85) and the "learning perspective" by Dass and Parker (1999, p. 71). This perspective reflects a proactive business strategy under the assumption that diversity "creates a learning environment where everybody within the organization can benefit from a diverse work context" (Podsiadlowski et al. 2013, p. 161). Thus, this approach signals the inclusion of all employees and attempts to disperse the perception that only "diverse" employees are the intended beneficiaries of programs and resources (Rabl et al., 2020, p. 532). This approach also encourages employees to utilize their diversity and related knowledge in addressing organizational issues. The intended goals were threefold: to promote feelings of justice and inclusion, to reduce discriminatory practices, and to improve the firm's competitive financial positioning (Yang & Konrad, 2011). "Learning and integration" (Ely & Thomas, 2001) organizations encouraged employees to utilize aspects of their identities in the form of demographic and cultural knowledge and experience for organizational purposes (Yang & Konrad, 2011, p. 7).

Organizations have taken various actions in response to increasing diversity in their workplaces, even if they could not or did not articulate framings or philosophies of diversity. These actions could be broadly categorized as one of three types (Dobbin et al., 2007; Kalev et al., 2006, p. 589). The first type focuses on moderating managerial bias and attempts to influence and change employee attitudes and behaviors. The second type focuses on improving the experience of individual minority employees who feel isolated and to attempt to improve their workplace social networks. The third type focuses on achieving outcomes by establishing diversity goals and assigning responsibility for meeting those goals to specific organizational members.

As mentioned previously, past efforts of organizations to manage their diversity have been only partially successful. Recommendations for the future attempt to overcome some of those limitations. Olsen and Martins (2012, p. 1169), for example, suggested adopting a broad definition of diversity management that encompasses all differences yet retains a commitment to business success. They described this practice as the "utilization of human resource (HR) management practices to (i) increase or maintain the variation in human capital on some given dimension(s), and/or (ii) ensure that variation in human capital on some given dimension(s) does not hinder the achievement of organizational objectives, and/or (iii) ensure that variation in human capital on some given dimension(s) facilitates the achievement of organizational objectives."

Yang and Konrad (2011, p. 8) suggested that the aim should be to impact a broader group than employees and that effective diversity management should "create a more diverse set of stakeholders; develop a positive working relationship among diverse stakeholders; create value from diversity." Fisk et al. (2019, p. 287) recommended that organizations delineate three ways to assess diversity programs, specifically "how and to what extent minorities are integrated and included; efficacy of organizational policies and priorities aimed at diversity and inclusion; impact on long-term outcomes related to leadership quality, employee satisfaction, and employee conflict." Yang and Konrad (2011, p. 7) suggested a slightly different focus on efforts attempting to "promote perceptions of organizational justice and inclusion; reduce discrimination; improve financial competitiveness."

Scholars have recommended a measured and multi-phased approach to diversity management. Jones et al. (2013, p. 59) listed possible phases as: performing a diversity needs assessment, developing an approach, implementing training and development initiatives, and evaluation. Organizational approaches must fit the company's specific needs, and thus these approaches vary. Jayne and Dipboye (2004, p. 412) identified several types of approaches, including changing workforce composition through recruiting, retention, and leadership development; developing external relationships by including minority communities and suppliers in business efforts; communicating the rationale for diversity programs and rewards; implementing training programs for both awareness building and issue-based preventative actions; and creating internal structures such as diversity officers.

Olsen and Martins (2012) noted the complexities of diversity management beyond specific initiatives and programs. Different organizational units can have distinct diversity management approaches (Olsen & Martins, 2012, p. 1170). Such differences should align with concepts such as occupational cultures. Further, diversity management also functions as a signal; members understand the unstated meanings behind organizational actions. Herdman and McMillan-Capehart (2010, p. 41) pointed out that employees rely on "organizational cues and signals in interpretation of an organization's commitments and goals." Olsen and Martins (2012) stated that, more than "explicit diversity statements and HR practices," it is "organizational norms or general codes of conduct" that affected diversity outcomes. Hence, if what an organization says and what it does are different, diversity initiatives are likely to fail.

The concept of organizational diversity climate includes both explicit and implicit aspects. The diversity climate also encompasses more than just programs and practices. Herdman and McMillan-Capehart (2010, p. 2) described the diversity climate as "aggregate perceptions about the organization's diversity-related formal structure characteristics and informal values." They commented that the launch of diversity initiatives can start building an organization's diversity climate. Other factors, such as minority representation in positions of leadership, further strengthened this climate. Organizational experiences that are shared by employees and interpreted consistently, such as teamwork or performance evaluations, also contribute to climate.

Diversity climate thus reflects the collective perceptions among employees as to what the organization considers as acceptable practices and procedures, and what behaviors it values, supports, and rewards (Herdman & McMillan-Capehart, 2010, p. 41). Multicultural organizations (Cox, 1994) encourage employees to express their unique identities rather than requiring them to assimilate into an organizational culture. Jayne and Dipboye (2004, p. 414) commented, "Diversity programs are more likely to be accepted in multicultural organizations with diversity climates and in firms that are growth-oriented rather than engaged in downsizing."

Organizational Culture

Workforce diversity is the present and future reality for organizations. The challenge for organizations is to manage individual differences between employees while still creating a sense of cohesion among them. It might be easier to develop effective communications and working relationships when workplaces are largely homogenous rather than when they are heterogenous (Yang & Konrad, 2011, p. 9). However, to paraphrase Donham (1929, p. 385), "Since our environment is constantly changing, the art of working (living) together must constantly change with it."

Diversity management has two mirroring aspects—individual employees and organizational environment. It is important to understand how and to what extent employees are required to change. This same is true for organizations.

Individual aspects for employees include behaviors, attitudes, identities (sense of self), values, impressions (including stereotypes), and motivations. Environmental aspects, on the other hand, include policies, procedures, practices, and structures.

Organizational culture plays an important role in tying together the individual and the collective. This culture has a great impact across all aspects of functioning, and it is both affected by and in turn affects employees. Management scholars have long recognized that the collective of people working together "differs from the individuals of whom it is constituted" (Laski, 1916) and that "we are compelled to personalize these associations" (Laski, 1916, p. 404). Thus, an organization exists as an entity separate from, although constituted of, its individually distinct members. Since organizations take actions, make decisions, and otherwise are functional, Baty (1920, p. 360) commented on "the attribution of personality to business corporations." One way to understand a business's "personality" is through the culture of the organization.

Organizational culture has been the subject of much study and analysis (van Vianen & Fischer, 2002, p. 316). There has been general agreement that culture refers to learned behaviors but little agreement on a definition or description of organizational culture. Pettigrew (1979, p. 574), in the context of organizational growth and evolution, referred to organizational culture as "symbol, language, ideology, belief, ritual, and myth." Hofstede et al. (1990, p. 286) described an organizational culture construct as being "holistic, historically determined, related to anthropological concepts, socially constructed, soft, and difficult to change." Schein (1990, p. 111), in the context of group learning, described it as "a pattern of basic assumptions, invented, discovered or developed by the group, as it learned to cope with external and internal, that has worked well enough to be considered valid, and so taught to new members, as the correct way to perceive, think and feel in relation to those problems."

Some researchers have attempted to differentiate between culture and manifestations of culture. A value can be thought of as "an enduring belief that a specific mode of conduct or end-state of existence is personally or socially preferable to an opposite or converse one" (Olsen & Martins, 2012, p. 1171). Values can be considered as the core of corporate culture. However, Hofstede et al. (1990, p. 311) proposed that, rather than seemingly abstract values, it was the "shared perceptions of daily practices" that constituted the core of corporate culture. Culture has to be manifest to have any impact. Typically, culture becomes visible through various practices running through symbols, heroes, rituals, and values (Hofstede et al., 1990, fig. 1, p. 291). Schein proposed a model where culture exists at different levels ranging from shallow to deep. At the surface are artifacts, including symbols, myths, and heroes; at a deeper level were values; and at the core was a set of unquestioningly accepted beliefs (Hatch, 1993, p. 657). Schein's model could be made dynamic by adding interpersonal relationships to the mix (Hatch, 1993, p. 660).

Thus, corporate culture, while related to what the organizational members hold as good or ethically right, is complex and can exist in various forms and at different levels in the organization. This culture becomes apparent, or manifest, through the actions and interactions of organizational members. Organizational culture can, and often does, change in response to variations in internal and external environments.

Interestingly, culture is not consistent across an organization. Occupational and national cultures are mutually independent factors that can alter organizational sub-cultures. Occupational cultures are related to organizational structures containing specializations. National cultures exist within organizations due to the U.S. workforce having significant diversity in terms of employees' national origins and ethnicities.

Occupational, or professional, culture is specific to an occupation. Common occupations found in most corporations, across industries, include accounting, sales, information technology, finance, and business law. Some occupations might be more industry-specific, such as chemical engineer or research biologist. Occupational culture can be broadly defined as the values, norms, and symbols that people working in a specific occupation share (Jacks & Palvia, 2014, p. 20). This culture is informed by common educational, training, or work experiences. For instance, information technology professionals have been found to share six common values: "Structure of Power, Control, Open Communication, Risk, Reverence for Knowledge, and Enjoyment" (Jacks & Palvia, 2014, p. 33). Occupational cultures point to commonalities across organizational boundaries.

Schein (1990) proposed an explanation of the variations found between national cultures. He suggested that cultures arise when people in a particular group encounter specific or even unique problems. In the national or ethical context, these problems are a mix of survival challenges arising from their external environment and cohesiveness challenges in internal structures. The resultant learning establishes the culture, which is "simultaneously a behavioral, cognitive and emotional process" (Schein, 1990, p. 111). The effects of national cultures can linger within an organizational environment when individuals from different countries of origin work together.

The impact of national cultures on organizational environments has been studied by Hofstede (1991). According to Hofstede, culture is learned behavior, differentiated from both general human nature and specific individual personality. Hofstede's model is based on surveys of employees of varied national origins working in the same organization at different locations. Using this research, Hofstede proposed four key dimensions on which national cultures differ: Power distance (small to large), Uncertainty avoidance (weak to strong), Collectivism vs individualism, and Femininity vs masculinity (Hofstede, 1991, p. 14). Power distance is the extent to which individuals in the society accept that power is distributed unequally within any organization (Moran et al., 2011, p. 19). Uncertainty avoidance refers to the extent to which an individual feels threatened or discomforted by uncertain or ambiguous situations. Individualist societies consider the individual as the basic social unit; each person is expected to take care of himself or herself, and perhaps their immediate family members. In contrast, collectivist societies have tight social frameworks with(in) groups as the basic social unit; ingroup members are expected to take care of each other. In masculine cultures, dominant societal values include assertiveness and material things, whereas feminine cultures stresses other aspects such as quality of life and taking care of others (Moran et al., 2011). Hofstede's model has been highly influential and has been studied in many different contexts since it was published.

Schein (1984, p. 71) linked national and ethical cultures to careers. He stated that the very notion of a "career" changes depending on the cultural context, and that culture influences career patterns. According to Schein (1984, p. 74), cultures differ by how they "separate self, work and family" (Schein, 1984, p. 74). These divisions affect employees' commitment and motivations, as well as the time and resources they are willing to devote to their careers. Thus, rather than assuming that organizational culture is uniform and overwhelming, it might be important for managers to learn "how to decipher the cultures in which their employees are operating" (Schein, 1984, p. 80).

National cultures are different from, and independent of, organizational cultures. Specifically, "national culture differences" (Hofstede et al., 1990, p. 312) play a significant role in the value that people hold, even in workplaces. Hofstede et al. (1990) noted that employees within the same company, while espousing similar organizational practices, differed in terms of values, which were in turn influenced by national cultures. As a contrast, even among people holding the same values, there was a difference in organizational practices. Hofstede et al. (1990) concluded that while national cultures can be differentiated through values, organizational cultures are distinguished by practices.

Employee Resource Groups

Workforce composition is a factor to be considered when choosing diversity initiatives. Different employee groups face different challenges in the workplace. Some organizations have developed initiatives in recognition of these differences. For instance, IBM created task forces as part of its diversity strategy. Each taskforce was focused on a different group, such as Asians, gays and lesbians, and women, and each taskforce included senior executives (Thomas, 2004, p. 98). Thomas found that groups could differ in terms of their needs. For instance, in a survey of Asian employees, Thomas (2004, p. 102) found that their main concerns were being stereotyped, a lack of networking opportunities, a lack of mentors, and unclear development pipelines. In contrast, the main concerns of women were a lack of networking opportunities, difficulty in career advancement, difficulty in maintaining work/life balance, and executive commitment to advancing women.

One popular diversity initiative in organizations for the last few decades has been employee groups. While these are not direct interventions like recruitment strategies or mentoring programs, employee groups do exist within the organizational parameters and are subject to certain rules. Originally, such groups were based on identity-related characteristics. Organizational support for such groups permitted employees to bring their personal concepts of identity to the workplace, which would presumably help organizations understand them better (Welbourne & McLaughlin, 2013, p. 36). Such groups have existed under various names, including "affinity groups," "employee resource groups," and "employee professional networks." Welbourne et al. (2015, p. 3) noted that the first such affinity group was formed at Xerox as the "Black Employees Caucus in 1964." Later, the term "caucus" was replaced by other terms like group, council, forum, or network.

An Employee Resource Group (ERG) is formally supported by the organization but run by volunteer employees. The intent is for these groups to serve as resources for both employees and their organizations. ERG sizes can vary, depending on the organization and the basis for forming the ERG; they could have "a few members or a few thousand (Welbourne et al. 2015, p. 4). An effective ERG would help develop a "diverse and inclusive work environment within the context of the organization's mission, values, goals, business practices and objectives" (Welbourne et al. 2015, p. 4).

ERGs have become popular over time and appear almost ubiquitous in large organizations. About 90% of Fortune 500 companies have ERGs, sometimes referred to as "affinity groups" or "professional networks" (Cenkci et al., 2019, p. 2; Gutiérrez & Saint Clair, 2018, p. 110; Welbourne et al., 2015). It is predicted that as ERGs become more closely linked to organizational goals, their support is likely to grow and their influence to expand.

Having started as support networks for employees based on "Equal Employment Opportunity protected characteristics" (Gutiérrez & Saint Clair, 2018, p. 110), ERGs have branched out in many directions. Welbourne and McLaughlin (2013, p. 38) identified three types of ERGs: social cause, professional, and attribute (characteristic). Employees joined social cause centered ERGs, such as cancer support and environment awareness, when they wanted to be part of a bigger cause and identified strongly with the group. Professional ERGs, such as adoptive parents and wellness groups, were mostly for socializing and relaxing purposes but also simultaneously built connections. Attribute-based ERGs, such as gender and race/ethnicity-based groups, were the most traditional ones, where members joined on the basis of shared characteristics. Their motivations were to interact with other members of the organization with whom they had something in common and to gain opportunities for professional advancement.

Cenkci et al. (2019, p. 1) commented that ERGs served as internal communities for employees. As noted above, different employees accrue different benefits from ERGs. Organizations have found them useful as well. For instance, they can serve as tools to "attract and retain a diverse workforce" (Welch et al., 2018, p. 110). Goode (Goode & Dixon, 2016) noted that companies with well-developed diversity strategies used ERGs as an asset in improving overall business functioning.

Despite their apparent popularity, ERGs have been critiqued. For one, they might simply not be considered an attractive option by some intended members. Gutiérrez and Saint Clair (2018, p. 117) found that some ethnic minority members did not perceive the benefits of such employee groups. In particular, these employees had "high social dominance orientation" and a deep belief in inherent group hierarchies. Another criticism was that, by their very nature, ERGs can be limiting. This would seem contradictory with the ultimate purpose of these groups to create an atmosphere of inclusion in the organization. Employees who were not, and could not, be members of an ERG might resent the organizational resources and support given to it. One option to mitigate such negative reactions was by welcoming and including "allies" (Cenkci et al., 2019, p. 3) in the group.

Sometimes affinity groups have themselves been accused of discrimination in professional settings, which raises the question of whether the organization was responsible for the actions of a group it sponsored (Welch et al., 2018). Another criticism of ERGs is that by permitting a large number of varied ERGs to form, organizations have broadened the focus too much. The groups that the original ERGs were intended to serve continued to face challenges while new groups took resources away from them.

Dixon (Goode & Dixon, 2016) did not argue that ERGs are necessary, merely stating that they are a necessary step for organizations on their journey to creating more inclusive workplaces. In some organizations, ERGs have been replaced by more effective and more powerful organizational structures like diversity, equity, and inclusion committees. Indeed, Green (2017) described one large company that systematically phased out all the ERGs. Some of these, such as the women's affinity group, had lasted for more than 20 years. It appeared that employees in these groups thought it was time to replace them with groups referred to as "inclusion councils." Such inclusion councils included senior executives and were held accountable to provide outcomes.

Despite these challenges and criticisms, ERGs will likely continue to exist in some form in organizations. This is particularly true if ERGs function effectively and provide organizational value. Welbourne and McLaughlin (2013, p. 39) found that the "only factors differentiating high versus low performing ERG's were ERG related issues, whereas ERG leaders thought management was [the] key deterrent." This points to the power that ERG leaders have in influencing both their members and other organizational constituents. Effective ERGs drive innovation and organizational change, both within their group and in the larger organization.

As workplaces continue to change and evolve, corporations have changed the playing field for ERGs. Some companies now encourage or even require high-functioning groups to express a value proposition, describe how performance will be measured, have more executive sponsorship and interaction, and work with corporate governance (U.S. Black Engineer, p. 18).

Notes in Conclusion

Organizational workplaces have become increasingly diverse over the last few decades. Two factors contributed to this increase: first, members belonging to groups that had not been represented in significant numbers in the past entered the workplace. This includes women in general and Asian women as a sub-group. The second factor is the recognition that certain personal characteristics have an impact on the workplace, such as age and sexual orientation.

For businesses today, managing diversity effectively has become a necessity, not an option. Jones et al. (2013, p. 55) noted, "today's increasingly diverse workplace requires employees to possess the relevant knowledge, skills, abilities, and attitudes to effectively interact with colleagues, customers, and clients who are different from themselves." Individual employees who experience differences between their workplace culture and home culture will need to reconcile those differences. This is important for organizations as well, hence their efforts to make it easier for employees to negotiate workplaces.

Currently, the focus has shifted from the goal of a multicultural workplace to an inclusive one. An inclusive workplace is both welcoming of differences and allows for employees to approach work in ways that encourage their best performance (Goerner, 2019, p. 549). Eswaran (2019) noted that millennials overwhelmingly believe that organizational innovation is linked to diversity and a related culture of inclusion.

While not mandated or legally required to do so, organizations have responded to the increase in diversity. A business's attitude might be that responding to diversity is a business imperative (i.e. diversity is an asset to be leveraged) or the business might be motivated by an ethical imperative (i.e. valuing a culture of equity and fairness). In most cases, it is likely a mix of both. Organizational responses to increasing diversity have included programs, structural changes, and organizational activities. The most common approach has been diversity training; however, this method has been critiqued as being moderately effective at best.

Diversity-related changes in workplaces can occur at the individual level (such as specialized mentoring) or the organizational level (such as hiring policy). They can be driven by individual employees or by organizational units (such as the board of directors). Individual employees typically bring to attention disparate treatment (such as biased evaluation of women) or environmental inconsistencies (such as receiving a paid day off for religious observances related to some religions and not others). Diversity inevitably affects organizational culture and functioning, and occasionally structure as well.

Two organizational approaches that are likely to be directly impactful for Asian women are employee resource groups (ERGs) and mentoring.

ERGs have existed in organizations under different names and formats for several years. They are an informal structure supported by the organization for members of a group sharing a specific characteristic or identity. The members can determine whether the group exists to provide support of various kinds to members, to build networks, or to attempt to play an active role in organizational functioning. A caveat regarding these groups is that for an ERG to be effective, the organization should be willing to consider its recommendations for change, and the ERG should attract membership across organizational levels. (Mentoring will be discussed in Chapter 4.)

REFERENCES

Baty, T. (1920). The rights of ideas: And of corporations. *Harvard Law Review*, *33*(3), 358–375. doi:10.2307/1327477

Bush, M., & Peters, K. (2016, December 5). How the best companies do diversity right. *Fortune*. https://fortune.com/2016/12/05/diversity-inclusion-workplaces/

Cenkci, A. T., Zimmerman, J., & Bircan, T. (2019). The effects of employee resource groups on work engagement and workplace inclusion. *International Journal of Organizational Diversity*, *19*(2), 1–19. doi:10.18848/2328-6261/CGP/v19i02/1-19

Cook, A., & Glass, C. (2015). The power of one or power in numbers? Analyzing the effect of minority leaders on diversity policy and practice. *Work and Occupations*, *42*(2), 183–215. doi:10.1177/0730888414557292

Cox, T. J. (1994). *Cultural diversity in organizations*. Berrett-Koehler Publishers.

Dass, P., & Parker, B. (1999). Strategies for managing human resource diversity: From resistance to learning. *The Academy of Management Executive*, *13*(2), 68–80. doi:10.5465/ame.1999.1899550

Deloitte. (2018). *Missing pieces report: The 2018 board diversity census of women and minorities on Fortune 500 boards*. https://www2.deloitte.com/us/en/pages/center-for-board-effectiveness/articles/missing-pieces-report-industry-view.html. https://www2.deloitte.com/us/en/pages/center-for-board-effectiveness/articles/missing-pieces-report-industry-view.html

Dobbin, F., Kalev, A., & Kelly, E. (2007). Diversity management in corporate America. *Contexts*, *6*(4), 21–27. doi:10.1525/ctx.2007.6.4.21

Donham, W. B. (1929). Business ethics: A general survey. *Harvard Business Review*, *7*(4), 385–394.

Ely, R. J., & Thomas, D. A. (2001, June). Cultural diversity at work: The effects of diversity perspectives on work group processes and outcomes. *Administrative Science Quarterly*, *46*(2), 229–273. doi:10.2307/2667087

Eswaran, V. (2019, April 29). The business case for diversity in the workplace is overwhelming. *World Economic Forum (Davos).* https://www.weforum.org/agenda/2019/04/business-case-for-diversity-in-the-workplace/

Fisk, J. M., Silvera, G. A., & Haun, C. N. (2019). Developing and defining diversity. *Public Integrity*, *21*(3), 286–300. doi:10.1080/10999922.2018.1471324

Goerner, C. (2019). Creating companies where women can thrive. *Business Horizons*, *62*(5), 549–551. doi:10.1016/j.bushor.2019.04.001

Goode, S., & Dixon, I. (2016, September). Are employee resource groups good for business? *HRMagazine*, *61*(7), 24–25.

Green, J. (2017, July 19). Deloitte thinks diversity groups are passe. *Bloomberg*. https://www.bloomberg.com/news/articles/2017-07-19/deloitte-thinks-diversity-groups-are-pass

Gutiérrez, A. S., & Saint Clair, J. K. (2018). Do organizations' diversity signals threaten members of the majority group? The case of employee professional networks. *Journal of Business Research*, *89*, 110–120. doi:10.1016/j.jbusres.2018.04.003

Harvard Law Forum. (2018). Missing pieces report 2018: Corporate board. *Harvard University*. https://corpgov.law.harvard.edu/2019/02/05/missing-pieces-report-the-2018-board-diversity-census-of-womenand-minorities-on-fortune-500-boards/

Hatch, M. J. (1993). The dynamics of organizational culture. *Academy of Management Review*, *18*(4), 657–693. doi:10.5465/amr.1993.9402210154

Herdman, A. O., & McMillan-Capehart, A. (2010). Establishing a diversity program is not enough: Exploring the determinants of diversity climate. *Journal of Business and Psychology*, *25*(1), 39–53. doi:10.100710869-009-9133-1

Hofstede, G. (1991). *Cultures and organizations: Software of the mind.* McGraw Hill.

Hofstede, G., Neuijen, B., Ohayv, D. D., & Sanders, G. (1990, June). Measuring organizational cultures: A qualitative and quantitative study across twenty cases. *Administrative Science Quarterly*, *35*(2), 286–316. doi:10.2307/2393392

Jacks, T., & Palvia, P. (2014). Measuring value dimensions of IT occupational culture: An exploratory analysis. *Information Technology Management*, *15*(1), 19–35. doi:10.100710799-013-0170-0

Janssens, M., & Steyaert, C. (2019). A practice-based theory of diversity: Respecifying (in)equality in organizations. *Academy of Management Review*, *44*(3), 518–537. doi:10.5465/amr.2017.0062

Jayne, M. E. A., & Dipboye, R. L. (2004, November 17). Leveraging diversity to improve business performance: Research findings and recommendations for organizations. *Human Resource Management*, *43*(4), 409–424. doi:10.1002/hrm.20033

Jones, K. P., King, E. B., Nelson, J., Geller, D. S., & Bowes-Sperry, L. (2013). Beyond the business case: An ethical perspective of diversity training. *Human Resource Management*, *52*(1), 55–74. doi:10.1002/hrm.21517

Jones, S., & Donnelly, G. (2017, June 16). Why we logged every Fortune 500 company's diversity data, or lack thereof. *Fortune*. https://fortune.com/2017/06/16/why-we-logged-every-fortune-500-companys-diversity-data-or-lack-thereof/

Kalev, A., Kelly, E., & Dobbin, F. (2006). Best practices or best guesses? Assessing the efficacy of corporate affirmative action and diversity policies. *American Sociological Review*, *71*(4), 589–617. doi:10.1177/000312240607100404

Konrad, A. M. (2006). Leveraging workplace diversity in organizations. *Organizational Management Journal*, *3*(3), 164–189. doi:10.1057/omj.2006.18

Laski, H. J. (1916, February). The personality of associations. *Harvard Law Review*, *29*(4), 404–426. doi:10.2307/1326689

Lindsey, A., King, E., Membere, A., & Cheung, H. K. (2017). Two types of diversity training that really work. *Harvard Business Review*. https://hbr.org/2017/07/Two-types-of-diversity-training-that-really-work

Lozano, J. F., & Escrich, T. (2017). Cultural diversity in business: A critical reflection on the ideology of tolerance. *Journal of Business Ethics*, *142*(4), 679–696. doi:10.100710551-016-3113-y

Moran, R. T., Abramson, N. R., & Moran, S. V. (2011). *Managing cultural differences* (9th ed.). Routledge Publishing.

Newkirk, P. (2019, October 21–28). Diversity has become a booming business. So where are the results? *Time*, *194*(16), 38–39.

Nguyen, L. (2019, November 20). Bank of America touts diverse staff in new trove of employee statistics. *Bloomberg*. https://www.bloomberg.com/news/articles/2019-11-20/bofa-touts-diverse-staff-in-new-trove-of-workplace-statistics

Olsen, J. E., & Martins, L. L. (2012, February 28). Understanding organizational diversity management programs: A theoretical framework and directions for future research. *Journal of Organizational Behavior*, *33*(8), 1168–1187. doi:10.1002/job.1792

Pettigrew, A. M. (1979). On studying organizational cultures. *Administrative Science Quarterly*, *24*(4), 570–581. doi:10.2307/2392363

Podsiadlowski, A., Groschke, D., Kogler, M., Springer, C., & van der Zee, K. (2013). Managing a culturally diverse workforce: Diversity perspectives in organizations. *International Journal of Intercultural Relations*, *37*(2), 159–175. doi:10.1016/j.ijintrel.2012.09.001

Rabl, T., Triana, M., Byun, S., & Bosch, L. (2020). Diversity management efforts as an ethical responsibility: How employees' perceptions of an organizational integration and learning approach to diversity affect employee behavior. *Journal of Business Ethics*, *161*(3), 531–550. doi:10.100710551-018-3849-7

Rosette, A. S., Koval, C. Z., Ma, A., & Livingston, R. (2016). Race matters for women leaders: Intersectional effects on agentic deficiencies and penalties. *The Leadership Quarterly*, *27*(3), 429–445. doi:10.1016/j.leaqua.2016.01.008

Schein, E. H. (1984). Culture as environmental context for careers. *Journal of Occupational Behaviour*, *5*(1), 71–81. doi:10.1002/job.4030050107

Schein, E. H. (1990). Organizational culture. *The American Psychologist*, *45*(2), 109–119. doi:10.1037/0003-066X.45.2.109

Thomas, D. A. (2004, September). Diversity as strategy. *Harvard Business Review*, *82*(9), 98–108. PMID:15449859

Thomas, D. A., & Ely, R. J. (1996, September-October). Making differences matter: A new paradigm for managing diversity. *Harvard Business Review*, 79–90.

Uhl-Bien, M., Schermerhorn, J. R. Jr, & Osborn, R. N. (2014). *Organizational behavior* (12th ed.). John Wiley.

U.S. Black Engineer. (2018). ERG= Diversity top companies share the value of their employee resource groups. *U.S. Black Engineer and Information Technology*, *42*(3), 18–20.

van Vianen, A. E. M., & Fischer, A. H. (2002). Illuminating the Glass Ceiling: The role of organizational culture preferences. *Journal of Occupational and Organizational Psychology*, *75*(3), 315–337. doi:10.1348/096317902320369730

Welbourne, T. M., & McLaughlin, L. L. (2013). Making the business case for employee resource groups. *Employment Relations Today*, *40*(2), 35–44. doi:10.1002/ert.21409

Welbourne, T. M., Rolf, S., & Schlachter, S. (2015). *Employee resource groups: Introduction, review research agenda.* CEO Publication Center for Effective Organization, Marshall School of Business, University of Southern California. https://ceo.usc.edu/wp-content/uploads/2015/05/2015-13-G15-13-660-ERG_Introduction_Review_Research.pdf

Welch, A. M. V., Moore, E. D., Kroll, J., & Sharp, H. (2018). Legal traps associated with affinity groups. *ABA Journal of Labor & Employment Law*, *33*(3), 110.

Yang, Y., & Konrad, A. M. (2011). Understanding diversity management practices: Implications of institutional theory and resource-based theory. *Group & Organization Management*, *36*(1), 6–38. doi:10.1177/1059601110390997

Chapter 4
Mentoring, Networks, and Leadership

ABSTRACT

Relationships of many kinds exist within organizations. They can be related to reporting structures, such as those with supervisors and direct reports, or they can result from work overlaps, such as relationships with co-workers in the department or colleagues on committees. Mentorship is a special kind of work relationship that is often tied to professional outcomes. Workplace friendships, both deep and casual, that cut across structural boundaries are not uncommon. These workplace relationships vary widely in terms of the benefits that accrue from them as well as the effort required in maintaining them. At the same time, managing work relationships has a critical impact on career experiences and career progress. In this chapter, the authors discuss research on various types of organizational relationships and their implications for Asian women.

INTRODUCTION

As noted in earlier chapters, an organization is defined as a group of people working together towards a common goal (Uhl-Bien et al., 2014). In Chapter 2, we discussed how organizations function through the processes of division of work, specialization, and coordination. Chapter 3 focused on the workforce characteristics (diversity) and functioning (culture) of the people within an organization. In this chapter we consider the "working together" facet of

DOI: 10.4018/978-1-7998-4384-9.ch004

organizations. This includes important relationship-based aspects such as mentoring, networks, and leadership.

Organizational work is more than simply a collection of designated jobs being performed by employees. At lower organizational levels, jobs consist of specified tasks, and the main responsibility of employees is to complete work assigned to them (Ibarra, 1993b). Each job in the organization is linked to other jobs through explicit reporting structures. At higher levels, jobs and their connections become more complex. Managers might have to plan a large portion of their work and that of their subordinates. They might also need to interact with others in the organization for various reasons. Interactions typically occur with peers, coworkers, bosses, subordinates, and cross-departmental colleagues in team structures or for specific pieces of work. The impact of interpersonal interactions is likely to increase with the level of the employees concerned. Hence, working together becomes more complicated than a simple coordination of tasks. Jobs become less well-defined and performance evaluation becomes complex in these situations. As Akutagawa (2013, p. 281) commented, rather than technical expertise, soft skills such as developing a personal brand and networks become "the differentiator at mid-senior levels."

Connections and relationships of various kinds exist in the workplace. Some are attached to an employee's position, such as links with the supervisor and with coworkers. Other relationships might be work-related but are not connected via reporting relationships. These include cross-functional teams or groups and special committees. Yet other relationships might be indirectly work-related and more inter-personal or developmental, such as those with mentors or sponsors. Workplace relationships can have short-term or long-term impacts. Short-term impacts affect the employee's performance and work output, whereas long-term impacts affect career pathways and progression. Ibarra (1993a, p. 494) noted that workplace connections have the "potential to mobilize, through direct and indirect links, a much broader base of support than that implied by the reporting relationships or functional requirements of the organizational chart." In a similar vein, Schein (1978, p. 265) noted that "one of the most significant components of successful power acquisition is the development of informal/influence relationships." Employees who are skilled in developing and managing relationships are likely to accrue career benefits in tangible ways.

Organizations have a vested interest in developing leadership characteristics in their employees. Employees in key leadership positions have significant power to influence changes and are responsible for making important decisions with immediate and long-term impacts (Hoyt, 2005, p. 2). Managers at higher levels of the organization are required to exhibit greater levels of leadership qualities. This includes taking ownership and responsibility for specific work outputs, decision making with high levels of uncertainty, and managing a greater number and variety of employees.

Individuals need to know how to cultivate, maintain, and utilize workplace relationships. Managing these relationships affects not only their work performance and work experience but their career progress as well. Employees who are interested in ascending the organizational hierarchy also need to understand leadership and how it manifests in the workplace. This chapter describes different types of networks and ties, including the special workplace relationship of mentoring. It also discusses leadership from the perspective of models and types of organizational leadership.

Mentors and Sponsors

Most people would be able to name a person they consider as a mentor in their personal or professional life. These relationships mean different things to different people. The benefits of these relationships also vary across people, situations, and time.

Organizational mentoring is a specific relationship whose purpose is to aid the professional, and sometimes personal, development of an employee. Mentoring relationships can be initiated through formal matching programs or informal employee initiatives. Eby et al. (2010, p. 81) described workplace mentoring as "a developmentally oriented relationship between a less experienced, junior employee (protégé) and a more experienced, seasoned employee (mentor) where the goal is personal and professional development of the protégé." Higgins and Kram (2001, p. 264) added that mentoring is typically "a dyadic relationship," that is, a one-to-one interpersonal relationship.

Mentoring can be an intensely personal relationship (Eby et al., 2000). So, it would not be surprising that mentoring was found to be particularly effective in organizations that "culturally endorsed a high focus on relationships" (Kossek et al., 2017, p. 228). Organizational culture, in particular, was found to have a significant impact on encouraging or discouraging mentoring relationships (Eby et al., 2006, p. 269). For instance, a highly competitive or political workplace was found to be inimical to mentoring relationships, whereas one that placed a high value on individual development was conducive to them (Aryee et al., 1999).

Mentoring is manifest in two independent ways in organizations, although both contribute to individual employee development. One manifestation is in the form of direct career-related support to the protégé and help in the development of their professional skills (Eby et al., 2010). Typically, the mentor helps increase the protégé's organizational visibility and provides opportunities for challenging assignments of significant business value (Kram, 1983, p. 614). Such support can also include active advocacy and sponsoring protégés, as well as protecting them as needed. This support can directly affect the protégé's career movement in the organizational hierarchy (Tharenou, 2005, p. 78). Mentoring also manifests in the form of psychological support, which helps in building personal skills (Eby et al., 2010). In this role, the mentor signals acceptance and confirmation, provides counsel as needed, and acts as a friend (Kram, 1983, p. 614). Such support primarily helps foster the protégé's feelings of self-worth, "emotional well-being," and "personal growth" (Tharenou, 2005, p. 78). Any career advancement effects are only secondary.

Mentoring relationships can and do change dynamically over time. Kram (1983, p. 609) noted that "in order to understand the nature and impact of mentoring, it is necessary to examine how it changes over time." Further, Kram (1983, p. 614) identified the four phases of a mentoring relationship as initiation, cultivation, separation, and redefinition. Initiation can occur at the formal behest of the organization, or it can be broached informally by either party. The cultivation phase is related to the mutual benefits that both parties accrue. Separation can occur for different reasons. In successful mentoring relations, the protégé might advance professionally and personally to a state where the existing relationship has outlived its purpose. In unsuccessful cases, there might be pulling away by either party or a mutual decision to terminate the relationship. Finally, in some situations, the interpersonal relationship could be resurrected differently. For instance, the parties might not be mentor and protégé but professional peers and allies.

Higgins and Kram (2001) identified factors that affected the success of a mentoring relationship, namely the protégé's locus of control, the race and gender of both the protégé and the mentor, and the organizational environment. Eby et al. (2006, p. 268) found that when organizations required mentor accountability, there was "reduced willingness to mentor." When the onus of outcomes is placed on the mentors, they might feel that they are being held accountable with no acknowledged reward (benefit). Kram and Isabella (1985, p. 111) noted that "both individuals in the mentoring relationship should benefit," or at least they should have the perception that they did. Eby et al. (2010) recommended that organizations provide guidance to mentors and protégés in setting realistic expectations regarding mentoring.

Researchers have cautioned that organizations might offer mentoring as a ready solution when employees raise issues regarding (a lack of) developmental opportunities and activities. As with all interpersonal relationships, mentoring is "likely to have both positive and negative aspects" (Eby et al., 2010, p. 81). In some cases, both parties might take it as a learning opportunity so that the relationship is viewed as beneficial to both the mentor and the mentee. However, it is possible for mentoring to fail to meet its goals and even impact participants negatively. According to Kram (1983, p. 609), "More often than not, a mentoring relationship ends with ambivalence and anger." While this assessment might appear unduly harsh, researchers have noted that mentoring relations face challenges for a variety of reasons. Both the mentor and the protégé might experience discomfort. For instance, the mentor might have the means to get the protégé important work or contacts but might have a brusque style or an unwelcoming attitude. Conversely, the protégé could be highly skilled and able but could react badly to criticism (Eby et al., 2010). In some situations, the mentor and protégé could have unsurmountable differences of opinion on the importance of certain values, beliefs, and attitudes, or could have different visions of how professional relationships should be (Eby et al., 2000, p. 7). In negative mentoring relationships, either the mentor or the protégé (more often the former) might begin distancing themselves to signal disengagement in the relationship. Such behavior has occurred often and has a long-term impact even if the parties seemed to accept it at the time (Eby et al., 2000). Protégés identified manipulative behavior, taking credit, and inappropriate delegation of work as unsatisfactory mentor behaviors.

An employee can be assigned mentors through formal programs or acquire one when a senior employee makes an offer of mentorship. However, it is not unusual for employees to seek out mentors on their own. Aryee et al. (1999) studied mentoring relationships where the protégé initiated the contact. This study is relevant to the context of Asian women since women have often been told that they needed to be more proactive in signaling interest in career growth, and because Asians have been stereotyped as more focused on technical aspects of work rather than relationships. The study considered the impact of protégé personality traits as well as situational characteristics of the organization, such as culture and opportunities for interaction. Aryee et al. (1999) concluded that extraversion was the only personality trait that affected the mentoring experience.

Sponsorship is another workplace relationship similar to mentoring in some ways. Sponsors are powerful and influential members of an organization who are willing to risk their organizational political capital on behalf of their protégés to obtain material gains for them. According to Ibarra (2019, p. 3), "while a mentor is someone who has knowledge and will share it with you, a sponsor is a person who has power and will use it for you." Like mentors, sponsors can provide general support and advice. Further, they are also willing to share important information, provide introductions to powerful insiders, make opportunities available, increase the protégé's organizational profile, and actively advocate for the protégé. Thus, sponsorship differs from general mentoring because of the intensity and organizational focus of the sponsor's efforts; senior employees actively advocate for protégés rather than merely providing support and guidance (Perera, 2019).

Sponsorship is more likely than mentoring to deliver direct career benefits to the protégé However, as a consequence, the sponsor's political capital is likely to get depleted. Hence, sponsorship is likely to be ineffective if it is organizationally mandated on senior executives (Ibarra, 2019). Even more than a mentor, a sponsor needs to have a clear sense of the benefit to themselves that will justify the risks to their own career. Women were especially likely to encounter challenges in getting sponsors. It appeared that some women, especially those with inadequate interpersonal skills, were viewed as "derailment risks" and that executives were unwilling to sponsor them for that reason (Perera, 2019, p. 67). Apart from dealing with such perceptions, women have also received conflicting messages about sponsoring. They have often been told that sponsors are important, even critical, to their career growth. Yet, they need to choose their sponsors carefully, since a sponsor's failure could affect their careers more than it would a man's (Perera, 2019).

Changes in the business environment have affected workplace mentoring experiences. Higgins and Kram (2001) identified some of these: a change in the social contract between organizations and employees such that frequent changes in career paths are now the norm; the advent of technological changes that have affected how and what kinds of work are done; patterns of frequent organizational structural changes that affect the availability of mentors; an increase in organizational diversity and recognition that mentoring approaches need to be diverse as well.

Relationships and Networks

The very nature of organizational functioning indicates the existence and importance of various relationships among an organization's members. An employee's network refers to other individuals with whom the employee has workplace relationships. In the literature, relationships have been referred to as "ties." Researchers have studied different kinds of ties and the benefits associated with each type.

Workplace networks are likely to differ for employees due to various reasons. Some relationships are built into the organization's structure. The organizational chart reflects both positions as well as some employee relationships, specifically those of reporting (Lincoln & Miller, 1979, p. 183). Since an employee is likely to have more peers than bosses, many network contacts might not be reflected in the organizational chart (Kram & Isabella, 1985, p. 112). The nature of the work done in organizations requires that individual employees depend on interaction, help, and support from many others (Higgins & Kram, 2001, p. 264). Thus, an employee's organizational position, with the responsibilities attached to it, is an important factor that affects the entire network. An employee can be part of certain formal and informal groups in the workplace and develop relationships through them. Finally, an employee's personality characteristics can play a role in determining how their network functions, although it appears that this was less significant for women than men (McNamara & Pitt-Catsouphes, 2014). Thus, employee networks can have different patterns and dynamics depending on the situations, environments, cultures, and personal characteristics of the people involved (Lincoln & Miller, 1979, p. 183).

Networks contribute to social capital (Rodrigues et al., 2019) and thus are important for employees. As noted, even for employees in similar positions, the networks they are involved in are likely to be different. Networks are differentiated from each other on several dimensions: the characteristics of contacts, the type of each connection, and the strength of each tie (Higgins & Kram, 2001; Schipani et al., 2009). The degree of similarity among contacts is a characteristic of interest. "Homophily" refers to the tendency of an individual to have contacts who have significant similarity to one another and to the individual. The opposite of homophily is diversity, where there is little similarity among individuals. Casciaro and Lobo (2006, p. 7) noted that "the role of similarity, or homophily, in generating interpersonal attraction, is one of the most solidly documented findings in social sciences." In other words, people tend to make connections with others like themselves. Many networks are typically "characterized by homophily" (Hanson & Blake, 2009, p. 140). The second dimension refers to the type of tie or connection between people. In workplace settings, ties are differentiated as instrumental or affective depending on their perceived or actual purpose. An instrumental tie is linked to work-related outcomes, and an affective tie is related to personal benefit. This is similar to the modeling of mentoring benefits as contributing to professional growth or providing personal support. The third dimension referring to the strength of each tie is an intuitive concept. It could be understood as a combination of "the amount of time, the emotional intensity and the intimacy which is mutual confiding and reciprocal services that characterize that tie" (Granovetter, 1973, p. 1360). Researchers have studied this aspect by differentiating relationship strength as weak or strong.

The implications of tie strength on networks have been researched extensively. Krackhardt (1992) noted that the emotional or affective element is critical in understanding the nature of a tie. Strong ties imply a great deal of interaction, with the exchange of possibly confidential information and needs being met mutually. This contrasts with the more casual nature of weak ties, where information exchanged could be beneficial but there might not be an expectation of either mutual benefit or continuity of the relationship. Further, Krackhardt (1992, p. 218) noted that "tie strength is not a continuous variable—there are types of ties." In other words, strong ties and weak ties are distinctly different in form and function. A successful sponsorship tie would likely be a strong one, while a formal mentoring tie could be weak.

A network with predominantly weak ties has been understood to be typically sparse and has sometimes been critiqued as isolating for individual employees. Sparsity is to be understood as contacts in a network not having connections between themselves. Granovetter (1983, p. 203) pointed out that weak ties might provide more freedom for an individual to present and express themselves differently in interactions with their contacts because their contacts did not interact with each other (i.e., to compare notes on the individual). Since a weak tie is relatively devoid of mutual expectation, it can bridge organizational distances, such as across units (Granovetter (1983). For instance, an employee in one department might discover a mutual interest with an employee in another department and maintain a low-key relationship on that basis. This mutual interest could be work-related, such as a tool or method, or personal, such as a hobby. This advantage of flexibility has been used to counter criticism about alienation in networks with weak ties. Granovetter (1973, p. 1378), a proponent of weak ties, noted that such seemingly casual contacts can provide means for an individual to enter and even integrate into a community. A disadvantage of weak ties is that due to low investment in the relationship, there might be little motivation for either party to exert influence and benefit the other in a concrete way (Ibarra, 1993b).

An advantage of weak ties, which is also associated with sparse networks, is the possibility of getting information from a range of non-overlapping contacts. Such information is likely to be more comprehensive and valuable in totality (Granovetter, 1983; Ibarra, 1993b). However, such information would need to be utilized in order for an employee to gain instrumental benefit. According to Granovetter (1983), an employee at a lower organizational level would only benefit through a weak tie, if at all, by cultivating a relationship with another employee at a higher status. Weak ties with employees of the same status were not useful in an instrumental way. Women, in particular, did not appear to benefit much from weak ties since the ties themselves might be viewed as lacking legitimacy (Hanson & Blake, 2009). Despite their drawbacks, weak ties are attractive because they are easy to develop and require less maintenance in terms of time and energy.

Strong ties need more effort to maintain and are characterized by high levels of emotional intensity, time investment, and some degree of mutual confiding (Casciaro & Lobo, 2006; Granovetter, 1983; Krackhardt, 1992). They are associated with higher levels of trust (Higgins & Kram, 2001) and greater motivations to assist (Krackhardt, 1992, p. 218). For example, an employee could avail of strong ties to help smooth their way in organizations (Ibarra, 1997, p. 99). Further, women might even require strong ties with powerful organizational partners to "signal their legitimacy and contribute to their advancement" (Ibarra, 1997, p. 93). Thus, strong ties can serve an important instrumental purpose. However, a drawback of networks with strong ties is that they tend to be homogenous, and thus the quality and quantity of information available through them is limited. Typically, it is difficult for an individual who is different from the network norm (women and minorities in many workplace environments) to enter existing networks (Ibarra, 1997, p. 93).

It might appear that relationship strength would be related to the degree of similarity (or dissimilarity) among contacts. Indeed, Granovetter (1973) associated weak ties with greater diversity in the group. However, this might not be true across workplace networks (as differentiated from social ones). Higgins and Kram (2001, p. 270) conceptualized different kinds of developmental networks based on the two independent dimensions of tie strength and degree of diversity in the contact group. The four groups they used were: receptive (weak ties, low diversity), traditional (strong ties, low diversity), opportunistic (weak ties, high diversity), and entrepreneurial (strong ties, high diversity). In general, networks with weak ties were not likely to be of great instrumental benefit; opportunistic networks had low reciprocity; and receptive ones had poor quality information. Networks with strong ties typically had high levels of trust and hence were likely to be of greater instrumental value, regardless of the diversity of contacts within them.

Organizations can be designed such that both formal and informal networks exist within its structure. Formal networks, such as a committee or team, are mostly designed to achieve a direct organizational outcome. Some of these networks, like a bowling team, can serve a more social purpose and even provide psychosocial support to employees. Informal relationships can be critical to the careers and socio-emotional well-being of employees. Lincoln and Miller (1979, p. 196) pointed to the importance of friendships in the workplace, noting that beyond social and emotional relationships, friendships are "systems of making decisions, mobilizing resources, concealing or transmitting information, and performing other functions closely allied with work." An informal network, consisting of "friends and influences" (Krackhardt, 1992, p. 223) can be the secret strength for some employees to advance in their career progress. Brass (1985, p. 339) considered informal interactions as important indicators of "influence and promotions in an organization." Krackhardt (1992, p. 223) commented that friendships give an employee a "competitive edge in any organizationally political endeavor." Some workplace networks can straddle the formal-informal divide. For instance, McNamara and Pitt-Catsouphes (2014, p. 368) identified "task advice" networks as pathways for the flow of information and knowledge "directly related to work task completion." They noted that these networks, which can contain both formal and informal aspects, can be very effective.

Organizational relationships and networks do not just materialize. Even if the framework for links is present in the organizational structure, relationships have to be built and maintained through intentional efforts. An individual employee's network is affected by the efforts of that employee, other employees, and the organization. Research on workplace networks has identified the importance of having ties beyond those built into the organizational structure. However, it is often difficult for employees who are in minority groups to be able to build such ties, despite their efforts. They might be accepted into certain organizational networks as a necessity and for instrumental reasons yet be excluded from social and friendship circles (Lincoln & Miller, 1979).

Affinity groups (Chapter 3) are one way that organizations help certain employees to develop networks (Chin et al., 2016, p. 61). Typically, members of an affinity group share a social identity (Gutiérrez & Saint Clair, 2018, p. 111). They "meet regularly to share information, capture opportunities, and solve problems that may arise for its members or the organization" (Gutiérrez & Saint Clair, 2018, p. 111). Over time, continual interaction can lead to the strengthening of ties within the group, which may include members at different organizational levels. As ties deepen, relationships move from "being instrumental, work-related purposes to having more affective/emotional elements" (Oh et al., 2004, p. 862). In other words, these relationships can move from being weak ties to strong ones.

Leadership in Organizations

As employees progress up the organizational hierarchy, their jobs become less defined, more complex, and include more aspects of personnel management that fall in the category of leadership. In short, the necessity for leaders is built into the structure. An employee in a position that has an attached leadership role must, of necessity, perform that role, regardless of their preferences. Hence, understanding leadership development and identity construction is important to organizations (DeRue & Ashford, 2010, p. 628). Conversely, an employee who would like to perform a leadership role needs to be in a position with the scope for leadership responsibilities. It is to the organization's advantage to ensure that leadership positions are occupied by employees who can meet the challenges intrinsic to those roles. As Ng et al. (2005, p. 367) commented, "career success is of concern not only to individuals but also to organizations." Thus, both management scholars and career researchers are interested in studying leadership in organizations.

A common question that arises is how, or even whether, leadership is different from management. According to Kreitner (2012), management is "working with and through others to achieve organizational objectives in a changing environment; central to this process is the effective and efficient use of limited resources." Other definitions of leadership echo this one, but with a variation in emphasis. According to Na (2017, p. 30), leadership is "a process of influencing others to action or to achieve a common goal." A more detailed description was provided by Burns (1978, p. 425): "leadership is the reciprocal process of mobilizing, by persons with certain motives and values, various economic, political, and other resources, in the context of competition and conflict, in order to realize goals independently or mutually held by both leaders and followers (nature of goals is crucial)." Certain broad concepts of leadership are commonly accepted across diverse groups in U.S. organizations. Chin et al. (2016, p. 50) reported that a diverse group of managers described leadership as a "process that involves influence occurring within a group context and which involves goal attainment" and as an "influence relationship among leaders and followers who intend real changes that reflect their mutual purposes."

Leadership in organizational environments has been researched extensively. These studies tend to focus on the characteristics of leaders and styles of leadership. Several proposed theories and models attempted to answer questions related to effective organizational leadership. Chin et al. (2016, p. 52) noted that these theories included Traits theories (universal personality characteristics of leaders, leader identity); the Situational Model (leader responses as directive or supportive); the Least Preferred Co-worker Scale (adaptability to different situations; cultural and cognitive flexibility); Transaction versus Transformative; and LMX (leader and follower relationship).

Traits theories focus on personality characteristics likely to be of help in exercising organizational leadership. However, there has been no consensus on a set of required and sufficient traits for leadership. The traits approach became entwined with theories on leader behaviors, dealing with basic questions as "What behaviors characterize leaders? Is it the firm execution of authority over subordinates or the capacity to support and inspire them?" (Eagly & Carli, 2003, p. 808). Traits appeared as related to the willingness and capability of individuals to exert authority and power.

The interpersonal aspect of leadership was emphasized by Conger and Kanungo (1987, p. 639): "an individual who exerts maximum influence over other members is perceived as a leader." Conger and Kanungo (1987, p. 639) noted that the leader is "validated when followers recognize and identify the leader on the basis of interaction with him or her." Similarly, Heilman (2001, p. 661) commented that "advancement in organizations depends not only on competence assessments but also social acceptance and approval." Thus, organizational leadership has been delineated into two distinct aspects—goal attainment and interpersonal influencing. These dimensions have been variously referred to as initiating structure and consideration in management (Anderson & Sun, 2017), and as agentic and communal aspects in sociology (Eagly & Carli, 2007).

Leadership Theories: The Leader as an Individual

The first few theories present leadership as either one- or two-dimensional models (Vecchio, 2002). Trait theories are one-dimensional; they attempt to identify leaders simply through personality characteristics. As noted above, trait theories could not conclusively show that any one set of characteristics captures leadership potential. The addition of another dimension, namely work management, also did not capture the complexity of leadership. Later theories added more variables, such as situational characteristics and the leader's relationship with followers. Each one is incomplete in addressing the need for both organizations and individuals to participate in leadership development. The search for descriptive models of organizational leadership continues.

In the more recent past, theories that focus on the leader as a person have gained attention. These theories are particularly apt for women and minorities because they raise issues (such as authenticity) that had not been considered relevant in earlier models. In this section, we present some theories that are likely to be particularly relevant to Asian women: transactional vs. transformational leadership (with charismatic and authentic offshoots), and implicit leadership theory.

The transactional vs. transformational model combines both the content and style of the leader. A transactional leader is typically focused on meeting current goals (Eagly & Carli, 2007) and mostly uses tactics such as "rewards, coercion, task clarification and appeals to self-interest" (Eagly & Carli, 2003, p. 816). Transactional leaders are typically group leaders who are used to giving opinions and are skilled in give-and-take negotiations (Burns, 1978U). Transaction leaders are likely to be good managers, focused on the near-term, and are capable in the execution of planned work. In contrast, transformational leaders are future-oriented, they articulate goals and make and convey plans to attain them, and they present themselves as innovators or reformers (Eagly & Carli, 2003; Eagly & Carli, 2007). Transformational leaders are comfortable presenting themselves as role models and like to gain followers' trust and confidence (Eagly & Carli, 2007). The characteristics of transformational leadership include charisma, idealizations, inspirations, intellectual stimulation, and consideration for individuals (Lim & Ployhart, 2004). Although transactional and transformational styles are often presented as contrasts, with the implication that every individual would follow one or the other, the more likely scenario is that corporate leaders would (need to) exhibit aspects of both styles depending on the situation (Eagly & Carli, 2007). A transformational leader is likely to be particularly effective in extreme situations (Lim & Ployhart, 2004, p. 617), while transactional leaders would be more appropriate and effective in stable environments.

Two offshoots of the transformational leadership model are "charismatic" and "authentic." More so than transformational leaders, charismatic leaders seek to (and do) influence followers in a profound manner through the sheer force of their personalities (Conger & Kanungo, 1987, p. 637). Finally, the model of an authentic transformational leader is one who has a more "realistic concept of self" and is "connected to friends, family and community" (Bass & Steidlmeier, 1999). This model is particularly relevant in the context of leaders with different cultural backgrounds and multiple identities.

Most leadership theories have paid little attention to a leader's personal identities beyond their identity as a leader. However, that aspect becomes particularly salient in the context of leaders from minority groups. Differences between leaders are not simply a matter of certain personality or situational characteristics; there are other factors at work. Individual factors can become driving forces behind certain leaders' motivations, decisions, and actions. Whereas transformational and authentic approaches give importance to "socially oriented skills" (Burris et al., 2013, p. 260), implicit leadership theory goes further in the consideration of the leader as an individual.

The implicit leadership theory has also been referred to as leader categorization theory. An underlying assumption of this theory is that individuals have their own prototypical and cognitive determination of "boundaries and characteristics of leaders and non-leaders" (Burris et al., 2013, p. 259) or even of an "average leader" (Lim, 2017, p. 22). Potential and proposed leaders are evaluated against these prototypes and accepted or rejected on that basis (Festekjian et al., 2014, p. 103). Thus, the acceptance of an individual as a leader goes beyond their work competence and behavioral style. It could be based on completely unrelated factors, such as unalterable characteristics and underlying perceptions. This viewpoint could explain why women and minorities in leadership positions often face challenges in having their authority respected and their leadership accepted.

Employees form conceptualizations of who is an appropriate workplace leader based on various perceptions (Offermann & Coats, 2018, p. 513). These perceptions develop over time and are influenced by employees' experiences as well as the influences of their networks (Lim, 2017, p. 23). Festekjian et al. (2014, p. 103) proposed that this process occurs when "interconnected cognitive units" are "activated." The implication is that employees' perceptions can be changed, even if the process behind that change is not clear. Researchers on implicit leadership have attempted to identify factors that employees consider important. Offermann and Coats (2018, p. 514) noted that these factors include sensitivity, dedication, tyranny, charisma, attractiveness, masculinity, intelligence, and strength. More recent studies have indicated that "attractiveness" has been replaced by "well-groomed" and "creative."

Researchers have noted that leadership theories had to change in response to changes in organizational composition and functioning. According to Offermann and Coats (2018), one influential change has been an increase in teamwork, partly attributable to the increased presence of women in the workforce. They also noted that these workforce changes influenced perceptions of leadership. Whereas employees might have had prototypical ideas based on prior understanding, they could change their perceptions based on what they observed in terms of performance and outcomes.

Women and Organizational Leadership

The challenges that women face in obtaining leadership positions and the differences (if any) between how women and men lead have been extensively researched in studies on women and organizational leadership. These topics have been of interest due to the stark difference in numbers of women and men employees when compared across organizational levels. Carli and Eagly (2001, p. 631) noted, "although aggregate statistics on labor force participation (of women) and education suggest gender equality, the distributions of men and women in elite leadership positions tell quite a different story."

The term "Glass Ceiling" made its way into the popular lexicon after being introduced by a *Wall Street Journal* article (Antoniou & Aggelou, 2019). It became a focus of attention due to the visible rarity of women at higher organizational levels, despite parity in lower levels and in "pipelines," such as college education (Eagly & Karau, 2002, p. 573). The concept of the Glass Ceiling was later extended into the "Glass Cliff" (Ryan & Haslam, 2007) and "Bamboo Ceiling" (Hyun, 2005). All these constructs explore possible structural reasons for challenges that women face in attaining top-level positions and succeeding in them.

The corresponding challenge that women faced in ascending to leadership positions was the resistance they faced once there. This resistance was reflected in performance evaluations. According to Carli and Eagly (2001, p. 631), biases in evaluations were widespread and occurred "across a wide variety of settings and contexts." They consistently upheld the notion that women were "less competent than men and less worthy to hold leadership positions." The twin challenges that women faced aligned with descriptive and prescriptive gender stereotyping, namely, that women should not aspire to leadership positions; and, if they were in such a position, they could not perform well. Two theories were proffered as an explanation for these biases—role incongruity and lack-of-fit.

The role incongruity theory was proposed by Eagly and Carli (2003). It stated that employees perceived leadership roles as incongruous for women because they required decisive action (agency). However, women were stereotypically viewed as being more people- and relationship-oriented (communal). Thus, there was an incongruence between the leader role and the gender role that female leaders were expected to play simultaneously (Rosette & Tost, 2010).

The lack-of-fit model is aligned with Implicit leadership theory in that it considers the prototype image that employees have of a manager and leader. Employees typically described a "good manager" in terms of qualities that are normatively identified as masculine (Vecchio, 2002, p. 652). Indeed, the "Think Manager, Think Male" (Schein, 1978) mindset was found across the world (Schein et al., 1996). Although attitudes are not directly discriminatory practices, they have an indirect impact by affecting evaluations and limiting access to career progress (Eagly, 2007, p. 8). Further, this conception was so ingrained that even when women progressed up the organizational hierarchy, they were viewed as having negative traits (Lim, 2017). Consequently, women were offered fewer opportunities for promotion and training (Schein et al., 1996, p. 34). These attitudes towards female leaders were pernicious because they could spill over and become a disadvantage for women in general in the organization (Eagly, 2007).

Women's challenges in attaining leadership roles have also been understood by focusing on women as individuals. General leadership theories recognize the importance of how leaders interact with followers, namely the leadership style. Faced with evidence of the under-representation of women in leadership positions, the question of whether women "lead differently than men" was debated (Eagly et al., 2014, p. 154). Some leadership theories consider differences based on whether leaders are work-oriented or people-centered. Others consider the style as being autocratic or democratic (Eagly & Carli, 2003, p. 814). Research indicated that men and women managers were not different in terms of work- or people-orientation (Eagly & Carli, 2003, p. 814). A meta-analysis of 162 studies in leadership style (Eagly et al., 2014) confirmed that these orientations did not differ significantly, but the study also noted that there appeared to be a difference in leadership style. Women had—or were perceived to have or chose to have—a more participative, democratic, and collaborative style (Eagly & Carli, 2007; Eagly & Johnson, 1990). In contrast, men appeared to "adopt a more autocratic or directive style" (Eagly & Johnson, 1990, p. 247). Men and women also differed in other behaviors associated with leadership. Men were more likely to be transactional leaders and to engage in both active and passive management by exception (Eagly & Carli, 2003, p. 817). That is, men would directly attend to employees' mistakes as well as try to prevent them. Men were also more likely to be laissez-faire leaders. In comparison, women were more likely to practice transformational leadership and engage in "contingent reward behavior" (Eagly & Carli, 2003, p. 817).

Female leaders have struggled with situational challenges associated with stereotypes. Women, even those in leadership positions, were expected to show communal qualities such as "niceness, friendliness, and warmth" (Eagly et al., 2014, p. 159). They were also expected to care more about the well-being of their group and the general welfare of all employees (Eagly et al., 2014, p. 158). At the same time, agentic, and not communal, characteristics were considered essential for leaders (Hoyt, 2005). Agentic tendencies included assertiveness, competitiveness, and ambition (Eagly et al., 2014, p. 159), which appeared to be at odds with communal qualities. Thus, women leaders had to be extremely competent, at the very least, yet also show warmth and convey reassurance in order to minimize resistance to their authority (Eagly & Carli, 2003, p. 825). Some women tried to split this difference by "exhibiting both Agentic and Communal behavior" (Eagly et al., 2014, p. 161) in response to the combined "masculine and feminine demands" they faced (Eagly, 2007, p. 4).

The picture seemed to be somewhat different at middle management and executive levels. Mid-level women managers appeared to be as successful and effective as their male colleagues (Eagly & Carli, 2003, p. 823). This could have been due to the importance of interpersonal skills at that level. At the same time, some research found that at higher levels of the organization, there was not much difference between men and women in terms of leadership characteristics. This lack of difference was explained as the result of "organizational socialization" (Eagly & Carli, 2003, p. 814). According to this view, organizations tend to reward certain behaviors and personality characteristics, which in turn motivates ambitious employees, both male and female, to develop those desirable qualities. Women who ascend to the highest levels would thus be similar to men who have done so. However, they might have had to change the way they presented themselves; namely, they might have had to underemphasize their gender and behave counter-stereotypically.

Some researchers have noted that corporations in the future will require leaders to exhibit qualities and outlooks typically associated with women. Eagly and Carli (2003, p. 825) commented that women have faced disadvantages as organizational leaders, but they also have advantages and could be well-positioned for the future. They proposed that qualities closely associated with women, such as cooperation and collaboration, could be critical to future leadership (Eagly & Carli, 2003, p. 808). Some researchers have noted that these advantages are emphasized in light of general changes in organizational structures and functioning. For instance, the dynamic nature of environmental changes points to a need for transformational leadership, which has been identified as women's preferred style (Eagly & Carli, 2003, p. 825; Eagly, 2007, p. 5). Women have shown more skill in being inclusive, "power sharing and nurturing followers" (Vecchio, 2002, p. 645), which is an ideal fit for the needs of increasingly diverse workplaces. Despite the lack of mentoring (Ibarra, 2019), and even with stereotypes working against them (Hoyt, 2005, p. 9), women have developed self-efficacy and ascended the hierarchy. This approach and outlook is likely to resonate among minority employees as well as those who have a lack of internal network support. Finally, changing social norms and environments might require all employees to take on more responsibilities in their personal lives. Women working in organizations have already shown how to manage these often conflicting demands (Eagly, 2007, p. 4).

Research on Asian American Leadership

Although organizational leadership has long been studied in the U.S., little research has been done on Asian American leaders (Kawahara et al., 2013, p. 240). Most published work is either broad and general or relates the career histories of specific individuals. In particular, there is a lack of research and information about the experiences of Asian Americans in corporate workplaces (Lim, 2017, p. 11). Such work would be the foundational basis for theory-building regarding leadership challenges and pathways for Asian women in corporate America.

Some researchers have proposed the concept of a "Bamboo Ceiling" to identify structural barriers to upward career progression for Asians, both men and women. This term referred to the common Asian experience of having unquestioned, high qualifications for the jobs they do yet gaining little managerial success (Burris et al., 2013, p. 258). Gündemir et al. (2019, p. 107) commented that "despite remarkable high levels of education and income, Asian Americans remain under-represented at the top of organizational hierarchy."

Hyun (2005, p. 40) noted that a typical corporate assessment of Asian employees was that they were technically proficient "but not management material." Kawahara et al. (2013, p. 241) similarly found that while Asian Americans were thought to have the requisite competencies, they were not perceived as "having qualities necessary for leadership" and further they were perceived as being "good at 'task-oriented, methodical jobs' that needed little social interaction (example: engineering, production), but not in jobs that need 'promotion and aggrandizement' (example: sales)."

Some of these findings were borne out in Burris et al. (2013). They cited studies exploring how Asians were viewed as leaders as well as how Asians viewed leaders in organizational settings. They concluded that the prototype of a successful manager for Caucasians was primarily Caucasian; Asian managers were viewed as competent but not sociable, transformational, or authentic by Caucasians and other Asian Americans. Additionally, Asian Americans viewed Caucasian managers as less authentic, less sociable, and less transformational as compared to their vision of successful managers. Burris et al. (2013, p. 263) commented that few Caucasians had Asian managers, and so might not have had an opportunity to gain sufficient understanding and appreciation of norms and behaviors that might be culturally different. Festekjian et al. (2014) noted that Asian leaders activated attributes related to competence, which were different from those activated by Caucasian leaders.

Thus, race was possibly a factor that affected leadership perceptions (Festekjian et al., 2014, p. 114). Asians have had to contend with various stereotypes associated with them in the workplace. The "Model Minority," discussed in earlier chapters, has been a general societal stereotype directed towards Asians. In the workplace, Lim (2017, p. 29) noted an ambivalent perception of Asian employees as "hard working, conscientious," yet also "antisocial, nerdy, cunning, quiet." Gee et al. (2015, p. 107) observed that there is likely a "mismatch between the prototypical characteristics of business leaders and stereotypes associated with Asian Americans" that would affect leadership opportunities for the latter. Gündemir et al. (2019) explored Asian leadership in the context of leaders appointed at failing organizations. As noted earlier, Ryan and Haslam (2007, p. 555) labeled a phenomenon of the "appointment of women in precarious leadership positions" as the "Glass Cliff." Gündemir et al. (2019) contended that while women were chosen in such situations for their perceived interpersonal and communal skills, Asians were chosen for their perceived competence and willingness to sacrifice their self-interests so others do not suffer. They noted that there might be a discrepancy between Asian perceptions of self-sacrificing behaviors as complying with collectivist values, which are likely to be viewed negatively when the organization is not in crisis.

Asian American leaders have had to reconcile their values and identities with organizational ones in their efforts to be effective in the workplace. Some Asian American leaders have succeeded by presenting themselves as unconventional and transformational leaders. They attempted to "intellectually stimulate and inspire" their followers and emphasize working towards "a higher collective purpose, mission or vision" (Kawahara et al., 2013, p. 240). For some, a constant struggle against stereotypes might be a strong discouragement from even seeking leadership positions (Lim, 2017, p. 7–8). However, on a more positive note, Festekjian et al. (2014, p. 114) suggested that if stereotypes are challenged "perceptions could become more positive."

Asian American Women Leaders

Asian women as leaders and executives in American corporations have been minimally studied and under-researched (Lim, 2017). The contrast to the substantial body of literature on women and leadership is striking. There has been a significant amount of research on women in the workplace and as leaders, but few studies focus on Asian women.

Na (2017) documented the experiences of eight Asian women leaders using a narrative inquiry framework. All women in the study were immigrants who had come to the U.S. as children. The themes that became prominent in their narratives included the ability to move fluidly between their American and Asian selves; using the best of both cultures; strategically displaying and using uniqueness (even tokenism) to attain objectives; having strong professional and academic drives; being authentic and not compromising integrity; and having family for support. They also expressed the importance of communication and compromise, and a few expressed disappointment at the lack of support from other Asian women in the workplace.

Asian women might face difficulty in proving that they have leadership abilities and potential (Eagly & Carli, 2003, p. 820), more so than women in general. Some Asian women might have emphasized excelling at their tasks under the assumption that hard work will automatically yield rewards. In employing this strategy, they might be under-estimating the critical importance of networking and explicitly demonstrating assertiveness and self-promotion in the workplace (Akutagawa, 2013, p. 281).

Others have found that stereotypes of Asian women differed from those of women in general. Women are usually perceived as being communal, warm, and caring. In contrast, Asian American women in the workplace were perceived as very competent but not warm (Lim, 2017). Additionally, while they were perceived as having the ability to do their job, they were also considered not to be agentic, in that they are reluctant to take initiative and act (Lim, 2017, p. 47).

Kawahara et al. (2013, p. 241) noted that Asian women preferred a collaborative style of leadership. They might exhibit transformational leadership since their interpretation of personality characteristics like assertiveness and personal influence through charisma might differ from what is typical in American workplaces.

However, there appears to be room for optimism. Despite the challenges posed by stereotypes, work environments might be improving for Asian women. A study found that there was no significant backlash or discrimination in the evaluation of job applications of Asian women when the evaluators were Caucasian men, the presumed decision-making group in organizations (Lim, 2017). In other words, the hurdles to being hired might be easing up. Additionally, workplace stereotypes of Asian women did have many positive aspects that showed them as being well suited for executive positions (Gee et al., 2015).

Notes in Conclusion

The two broad dimensions of organizational work are technical aspects and interpersonal aspects. Technical aspects relate to the completion of tasks and include activities such as planning, organizing, and executing. Interpersonal aspects relate to building and maintaining relationships. These two aspects overlap, often in the execution of complex tasks like a team project. Technical and interpersonal aspects can be differentiated based on whether the employee can complete the task on their own or whether the task itself requires others to be involved. Another way to differentiate these dimensions is that technical aspects of task completion are related to work products. Time spent on building relationships might not have an immediate or tangible work product result. The importance of considering not only technical, task-related competence and expertise but also interpersonal skills has been stressed in management and leadership theories, acknowledging the fact that organizational work is not a collection of free-standing tasks; every employee's work needs to be coordinated with that of others.

Employees can have workplace interactions and build workplace relationships with a variety of other employees. The organizational structure provides for and even requires certain relationships, the most of important of which is between an employee and their supervisor. Another common set of relationships is between an employee and their supervisor's other reports. An employee's work is likely to be most closely linked with the work of this group. Employees can also build other formal, structural relationships. For instance, they can cultivate relationships with other members of cross-functional teams or committees where the employee is the departmental representative. These relationships could be considered as extensions of the job.

Some organizational relationships might be non-structural and non-work related. For instance, the employee could be a member of a union or an Employee Resource Group (ERG) or a temporary group (such as for holiday party planning). In addition to using group membership as an opportunity to interact with others, employees can also take the initiative to build relationships on an individual basis.

Regardless of how a professional relationship starts, employees can benefit by managing their workplace relationships strategically. Every relationship requires maintenance, which could include time and degree and/or depth of interpersonal interaction. Some relationships might be strong and others weak; both kinds have advantages and drawbacks.

One important workplace relationship is that of mentor-protégé. Employees can benefit greatly from having an engaged and influential mentor. However, these relationships often do not deliver all the anticipated benefits. Employees need to have realistic expectations and skill in managing this type of relationship.

Interpersonal skills are critical to leadership because a leader needs to be voluntarily accepted as a leader by others. It is possible that an individual placed in an organizational leadership position will not be accepted as a leader, in which case the individual will be ineffective in getting results, leaving the organization with no choice but to remove them from that position. Leadership requires individuals to be proactive in seeking, building, and maintaining relationships with people who are important to achieving goals.

REFERENCES

Akutagawa, L. (2013). Breaking stereotypes: An Asian American's view of leadership development. *Asian American Journal of Psychology*, *4*(4), 277–284. doi:10.1037/a0035390

Anderson, M. H., & Sun, P. Y. T. (2017). Reviewing leadership styles: Overlaps and the need for a new 'Full-range' theory. *International Journal of Management Reviews*, *19*(1), 76–96. doi:10.1111/ijmr.12082

Antoniou, A., & Aggelou, V. (2019). Female managers with male-type behavior. In A. Antoniou, C. Cooper, & C. Gatrell (Eds.), *Women, business and leadership: Gender and organisations* (pp. 199–215). Edward Elgar Publishing. doi:10.4337/9781786432711.00019

Aryee, S., Lo, S., & Kang, I. (1999). Antecedents of early career stage mentoring among Chinese employees. *Journal of Organizational Behavior*, *20*(5), 563–576. doi:10.1002/(SICI)1099-1379(199909)20:5<563::AID-JOB890>3.0.CO;2-#

Bass, B. M., & Steidlmeier, P. (1999). Ethics, character, and authentic transformational leadership behavior. *The Leadership Quarterly*, *10*(2), 181–217. doi:10.1016/S1048-9843(99)00016-8

Brass, D. J. (1985). Men's and women's networks: A study of interaction patterns and influence in an organization. *Academy of Management Journal*, *28*(2), 327–343.

Burns, J. M. (1978). *Leadership*. Harper & Row.

Burris, K., Ayman, R., Che, Y., & Min, H. (2013). Asian Americans' and Caucasians' implicit leadership theories: Asian stereotypes, transformational, and authentic leadership. *Asian American Journal of Psychology*, *4*(4), 258–266. doi:10.1037/a0035229

Carli, L. L., & Eagly, A. H. (2001). Gender, hierarchy, and leadership: An introduction. *The Journal of Social Issues*, *57*(4), 629–636. doi:10.1111/0022-4537.00232

Casciaro, T., & Lobo, M. S. (2006). Affective microfoundations of instrumental ties in organizations. *Harvard Business Review*, *83*(6), 93–100.

Chin, J. L., Desormeaux, L., & Sawyer, K. (2016). Making way for paradigms of diversity leadership. *Consulting Psychology Journal, 68*(1), 49–71. doi:10.1037/cpb0000051

Conger, J. A., & Kanungo, R. N. (1987). Towards a behavioral theory of charismatic leadership in organizational settings. *Academy of Management Review, 12*(4), 637–647. doi:10.5465/amr.1987.4306715

DeRue, S. D., & Ashford, S. J. (2010). Who will lead and who will follow? A social process of leadership identity construction in organizations. *Academy of Management Review, 35*(4), 627–647.

Eagly, A. H. (2007). Female leadership advantage and disadvantage: Resolving the contradictions. *Psychology of Women Quarterly, 31*(1), 1–12. doi:10.1111/j.1471-6402.2007.00326.x

Eagly, A. H., & Carli, L. L. (2003). The female leadership advantage: An evaluation of the evidence. *The Leadership Quarterly, 14*(6), 807–834. doi:10.1016/j.leaqua.2003.09.004

Eagly, A. H., & Carli, L. L. (2007). Women and the labyrinth of leadership. *Harvard Business Review*. https://hbr.org/2007/09/women-and-the-labyrinth-of-leadership

Eagly, A. H., Gartzia, L., & Carli, L. L. (2014). Female advantage: Revisited. In S. Kumra, R. Simpson, & R. J. Burke (Eds.), *The Oxford handbook of gender in organizations* (pp. 153–174). Oxford University Press.

Eagly, A. H., & Johnson, B. T. (1990). Gender and leadership style: A meta-analysis. *Psychological Bulletin, 108*(2), 233–256. doi:10.1037/0033-2909.108.2.233

Eagly, A. H., & Karau, S. J. (2002). Role congruity theory of prejudice toward female leaders. *Psychological Review, 109*(3), 573–598. doi:10.1037/0033-295X.109.3.573 PMID:12088246

Eby, L. T., Butts, M. M., Durley, J., & Ragins, B. R. (2010). Are bad experiences stronger than good ones in mentoring relationships? Evidence from the protégé and mentor perspective. *Journal of Vocational Behavior, 77*(1), 81–92. doi:10.1016/j.jvb.2010.02.010

Eby, L. T., Lockwood, A. L., & Butts, M. (2006). Perceived support for mentoring: A multiple perspectives approach. *Journal of Vocational Behavior, 68*(2), 267–291. doi:10.1016/j.jvb.2005.07.003

Eby, L. T., McManus, S. E., Simon, S. A., & Russell, J. E. A. (2000). The protégé's perspective regarding negative mentoring experiences: The development of a taxonomy. *Journal of Vocational Behavior*, *57*(1), 1–21. doi:10.1006/jvbe.1999.1726

Festekjian, A., Tram, S., Murray, C. B., Sy, T., & Huynh, H. P. (2014). I see me the way you see me: The influence of race on interpersonal and intrapersonal leadership perceptions. *Journal of Leadership & Organizational Studies*, *21*(1), 102–119. doi:10.1177/1548051813486522

Gee, B., Peck, D., & Wong, J. (2015). *Hiding in plain sight: Asian American leaders in Silicon Valley.* Ascend Report. https://cdn.ymaws.com/www.ascendleadership.org/resource/resmgr/Research/HiddenInPlainSight_OnePager_.pdf

Granovetter, M. S. (1973, May). The strength of weak ties. *American Journal of Sociology*, *78*(6), 1360–1380. doi:10.1086/225469

Granovetter, M. S. (1983). The strength of weak ties: A network theory revisited. *Sociological Theory*, *1*, 201–233. doi:10.2307/202051

Gündemir, S., Carton, A. M., & Homan, A. C. (2019). The impact of organizational performance on the emergence of Asian American leaders. *The Journal of Applied Psychology*, *104*(1), 107–122. doi:10.1037/apl0000347 PMID:30247048

Gutiérrez, A. S., & Saint Clair, J. K. (2018). Do organizations' diversity signals threaten members of the majority group? The case of employee professional networks. *Journal of Business Research*, *89*, 110–120. doi:10.1016/j.jbusres.2018.04.003

Hanson, S., & Blake, M. (2009, February). Gender and entrepreneurial networks. *Regional Studies*, *43*(1), 135–149. doi:10.1080/00343400802251452

Heilman, M. E. (2001). Description and prescription: How gender stereotypes prevent women's ascent up the organizational ladder. *The Journal of Social Issues*, *57*(4), 657–674. doi:10.1111/0022-4537.00234

Higgins, M., & Kram, K. E. (2001). Reconceptualizing mentoring at work: A developmental network perspective. *Academy of Management Review*, *26*(2), 264–288. doi:10.5465/amr.2001.4378023

Hoyt, C. L. (2005). The role of leadership efficacy and stereotype activation in women's identification with leadership. *Journal of Leadership & Organizational Studies*, *11*(4), 2–14. doi:10.1177/107179190501100401

Hyun, J. (2005). *Breaking the Bamboo Ceiling*. Harper-Collins.

Ibarra, H. (1993a). Network centrality, power, and innovation involvement: Determinants of technical and administrative roles. *Academy of Management Journal*, *36*(3), 471–501.

Ibarra, H. (1993b). Personal networks of women and minorities in management: A conceptual framework. *Academy of Management Review*, *18*(1), 56–87. doi:10.5465/amr.1993.3997507

Ibarra, H. (1997, March). Paving an alternative route: Gender differences in managerial networks. *Social Psychology Quarterly*, *60*(1), 91–102. doi:10.2307/2787014

Ibarra, H. (2019). A lack of sponsorship is keeping women from advancing into leadership. *Harvard Business Review Digital Article*. https://herminiaibarra.com/a-lack-of-sponsorship-is-keeping-women-from-advancing-into-leadership/

Kawahara, D. M., Pal, M. S., & Chin, J. L. (2013). The leadership experiences of Asian Americans. *Asian American Journal of Psychology*, *4*(4), 240–248. doi:10.1037/a0035196

Kossek, E. E., Su, R., & Wu, L. (2017, January). "Opting Out" or "Pushed Out"? Integrating perspectives on women's career equality for gender inclusion and interventions. *Journal of Management*, *43*(1), 228–254. doi:10.1177/0149206316671582

Krackhardt, D. (1992). The strength of strong ties: The importance of *Philos* in organizations. In N. Nohria & R. G. Eccles (Eds.), *Networks and organizations: Structure, form, and action* (pp. 216–239). Harvard University Press.

Kram, K. E. (1983, December). Phases of the mentor relationship. *Academy of Management Journal*, *26*(4), 608–625.

Kram, K. E., & Isabella, L. A. (1985). Mentoring alternatives: The role of peer relationships in career development. *Academy of Management Journal*, *28*(1), 110–132.

Kreitner, R. (2012). *Management* (12th ed.). Southwest Cengage.

Lim, B., & Ployhart, R. E. (2004). Transformational leadership: Relations to the five-factor model and team performance in typical and maximum contexts. *The Journal of Applied Psychology*, *89*(4), 610–621. doi:10.1037/0021-9010.89.4.610 PMID:15327348

Lim, J. I. (2017). Perceptions of Asian American and Female Leadership Candidates: The Impact of Descriptive and Prescriptive Stereotyping. City University of New York, CUNY Academic Works. Dissertations, Theses and Capstone Projects: Graduate Center.

Lincoln, J. R., & Miller, J. (1979, June). Work and friendship ties in organizations: A comparative analysis of relational networks. *Administrative Science Quarterly*, *24*(2), 181–198. doi:10.2307/2392493

McNamara, T. K., & Pitt-Catsouphes, M. (2014). Gender variation in the antecedents of task advice network size: Organizational tenure and core self-evaluations. *The Social Science Journal*, *51*(3), 368–376. doi:10.1016/j.soscij.2013.09.006

Na, Y. (2017). *The experiences of Asian immigrant women: Journeys into corporate leadership* [Doctoral dissertation, Alliant International University]. ProQuest LLC.

Ng, T. W. H., Eby, L. T., Sorensen, K. L., & Feldman, D. C. (2005). Predictors of objective and subjective career success: A meta-analysis. *Personnel Psychology*, *58*(2), 367–408. doi:10.1111/j.1744-6570.2005.00515.x

Offermann, L. R., & Coats, M. R. (2018). Implicit theories of leadership: Stability and change over two decades. *The Leadership Quarterly*, *29*(4), 513–522. doi:10.1016/j.leaqua.2017.12.003

Oh, H., Chung, M., & Labianca, G. (2004). Group social capital and group effectiveness: The role of informal socializing ties. *Academy of Management Journal*, *47*(6), 860–875. doi:10.5465/20159627

Perera, S. (2019). For better or worse? Human resource practices and women in leadership. In A. Antoniou, C. Cooper, & C. Gatrell (Eds.), *Women, business and leadership: Gender and organisations* (p. 6176). Edward Elgar Publishing. doi:10.4337/9781786432711.00010

Rodrigues, R., Butler, C. L., & Guest, D. (2019). Antecedents of Protean and Boundaryless career orientations: The role of core self-evaluations, perceived employability and social capital. *Journal of Vocational Behavior, 110*, 1–11. doi:10.1016/j.jvb.2018.11.003

Rosette, A. S., & Tost, L. P. (2010). Agentic women and communal leadership: How role prescriptions confer advantage to top women leaders. *The Journal of Applied Psychology, 95*(2), 221–235. doi:10.1037/a0018204 PMID:20230065

Ryan, M. K., & Haslam, A. S. (2007). The Glass Cliff: Exploring the dynamics surrounding the appointment of women to precarious leadership positions. *Academy of Management Review, 32*(2), 549–572. doi:10.5465/amr.2007.24351856

Schein, V. E. (1978). Sex role stereotyping, ability and performance: Prior research and new directions. *Personnel Psychology, 31*(2), 259–268. doi:10.1111/j.1744-6570.1978.tb00445.x

Schein, V. E., Mueller, R., Lituchy, T., & Liu, J. (1996). Think manager – think male: A global phenomenon? *Journal of Organizational Behavior, 17*(1), 33–41. doi:10.1002/(SICI)1099-1379(199601)17:1<33::AID-JOB778>3.0.CO;2-F

Schipani, C. A., Dworkin, T. M., Kwolek-Folland, A., & Maurer, V. G. (2009). Pathways for women to obtain positions of organizational leadership: The significance of mentoring and networking. *Duke Journal of Gender Law & Policy, 16*, 89–136.

Tharenou, P. (2005, June). Does mentor support increase women's career advancement more than men's? The differential effects of career and psychosocial support. *Australian Journal of Management, 30*(1), 77–109. doi:10.1177/031289620503000105

Uhl-Bien, M., Schermerhorn, J. R. Jr, & Osborn, R. N. (2014). *Organizational behavior* (12th ed.). John Wiley.

Vecchio, R. P. (2002). Leadership and gender advantage. *The Leadership Quarterly, 13*(6), 643–671. doi:10.1016/S1048-9843(02)00156-X

Chapter 5
Socio-Cultural Factors and the Work Environment

ABSTRACT

Employees are affected not only by internal organizational environments but also by external ones such as family, community, and society. Social and cultural factors affect how employees are viewed by others in the organization as well as how they respond to their work environments. Immigrants, in particular, are affected by their acculturation processes. Thus, when employees negotiate organizational workplaces, they need to factor in the influence of socio-cultural forces. Stereotyping is one way in which the external environment is manifest in workplaces. It has been found to be persistent, influential, and deeply impactful on careers. Stereotypes are affected by social and cultural factors, and in turn, they affect workplaces by shaping employees' perceptions and experiences. At the same time, the external environment can also present positive attributes for employees, for instance by being a source of social and emotional capital.

INTRODUCTION

Asian women in U.S. corporate workplaces are employees, but they are also individuals living in American society. Their workplace experiences are informed and affected by their lives and experiences outside as well as inside the workplace. In the last few chapters, we discussed organizational environments. In this chapter and the next, we expand the focus to broader

DOI: 10.4018/978-1-7998-4384-9.ch005

society. In the present chapter, we discuss the socio-cultural environment of Asian women in the U.S.

As noted previously, the term "Asian" refers to a geographic categorization rather than to one ethnicity or culture. Asian countries include multiple ethnicities and their cultures vary widely. Nevertheless, due to the census categorization as well as a degree of commonality across sub-cultures, Asian Americans are treated as one, albeit complex, group. According to Dhingra (2007, p. 16), "Asian America is a social construction" and is "extremely heterogeneous." This "heterogeneity across Asian Americans" (Kim & Zhao, 2014) includes more than 24 countries of origin (Zhou & Lee, 2017, p. 8), each of which has a distinct culture and various ethnicities.

Some scholars have pointed out that Asian Americans represent a growing and influential constituency in the U.S. (Smith, 2013), yet this group has "received relatively little attention from organizational scholars" (Gündemir et al., 2019, p. 116). This mirrors the lack of recognition of advancements as well as impediments in careers of Asian Americans in corporate environments. Asian Americans comprise about 5% of the U.S. population and have high educational levels (50% have a college degree). Yet, their workforce participation rate is not reflected at management levels (Benson & Yukongdi, 2005, p. 285). For instance, Asian Americans have minimal representation, around 1.5% at executive levels of Fortune 500 companies (Festekjian et al., 2014, p. 102). Even among millennials, they have been the only group underrepresented at management levels and they are predicted to have the weakest chances of becoming executives (Gee & Peck, 2015, p. 11). Asians represent the "largest cohort of professionals" but are "least likely among all races" to progress to managerial and executive levels (Gee & Peck, 2015, p. 4). This is true even in an industry in which they have over-representation at the general employee level. Gee et al. (2015) found that in Silicon Valley technology firms, Asians comprised 27% of the professional workforce but only 14% of executives.

Asian women have been gaining a place in U.S. society as a distinct group. They are projected to increase to above 7% of the American female population by 2050, from about 5% in 2012 (Smith, 2013). As with Asians in general, the group of Asian women is comprised of many subgroups, each with a unique history. Immigration laws have shaped, and continue to affect, the ways in which Asian women enter the U.S. and participate in economic activities once they arrive (Yamanaka & McClelland, 1994, p. 83). Regardless of the cultures and traditions of their countries of origin, once in the U.S. most immigrant Asian women enter the workforce (Kurien, 1999).

Asian American women have made great strides towards preparing for the workplace, particularly in obtaining educational credentials. They have the highest college graduation rates among groups of women at 49.4%, which is even higher than the 45.8% of Caucasian women (Smith, 2013). Their rates of earning degrees in the sciences and engineering is equal to that of Asian men.

At the same time, Asian women have faced challenges. The impact of ethnicity and race on the socio-cultural environment, including in workplaces, seems to be accentuated for Asian women due to the interaction of race and ethnicity with gender effects. For instance, Asian American women are under-represented in Fortune 500 CEOs and board members, even in comparison to women in general. According to Gee et al. (2015), they have the least representation as executives among all groups studied in the cross-section of gender and ethnicity. The authors further posit that the racial (ethnic) effect is far more detrimental to the professional progress of Asian women than the gender effect. In the area of business ownership, there are more than half a million businesses (co)owned by Asian American women. This represents about 6.7% of women-owned businesses in the U.S. However, more than 80% of these businesses have no employees other than the owner (Smith, 2013). In other words, it appears that Asian women face challenges in succeeding in American organizational workplaces.

Asian women in the U.S. have thus had to manage the demands of two social cultures, in addition to a third culture in the organizational environment. It is widely acknowledged that women are given the responsibility of maintaining cultural traditions and are often subject to restrictive role expectations. Asian women are subject to stereotypes rooted in both gender and ethnicity, at home and in the workplace, and they have had to manage their way within these cultures that differ widely on certain key values. Their position is unique, but they are often categorized with either (majority or other minority) women or (male) Asians without accounting for the fact that they face entirely different challenges. However, due to the dearth of research on this group, it is difficult to develop approaches and strategies that they would find effective.

Stereotypes: General and Specific

Stereotypes are “consensually held” (Phelan & Rudman, 2010, p. 265) beliefs about an entire social group that are applied to individual members of the group, regardless of their individual characteristics. These beliefs can be either complimentary in nature and positive in intent, or derogatory and negative (Lavaysse & Probst, 2019, p. 347).

Stereotypes can serve as a means to categorize and build cognitive understanding. As such, they can increase the efficiency of the perception processes that necessarily occur in interpersonal interactions. Stereotypes are communicated explicitly and often reinforced explicitly as well. McGarty et al. (2002, p. 2) note that the three guiding principles in the study of stereotyping in social psychology hold that stereotypes are "aids to explanation, energy-saving devices, and shared group beliefs." A critical element of why stereotypes are effective is their group appeal: "stereotypes attract little attention if they are not shared by many people" (McGarty et al., 2002, p. 5). Because workplaces have become more complex and diverse, employees are called upon to process vast quantities of information quickly. However, human beings typically have limited capacity for processing large amounts of information in short timeframes. This could be offered as an explanation for the persistence of workplace stereotypes.

Categorization is a quick and effective technique that individuals use to process all kinds of new information. Despite the supposed efficiency of this technique, it appears that workplace stereotypes have not been effective in the intended, desirable way. Negative effects related to workplace stereotypes have become so widespread that stereotypes are now conventionally accepted as leading to bias and misunderstanding, rather than functioning as aids to useful understanding (McGarty et al., 2002, p. 3). Some group members use stereotypes to differentiate and build group cohesiveness, but in a manner detrimental to the greater organization. Such individuals distance themselves from others by accentuating their differences with less desirable groups while highlighting similarities within their own group. As per Tajfel, this behavior can be effective in enforcing the status quo (McGarty et al., 2002, p. 8).

Stereotypes have been studied in the context of the descriptive expectations associated with them. The descriptive expectations related to workplace-related stereotypes have two independent dimensions: competence and warmth (Fiske et al., 2002, p. 878). (These areas align with similar dimensions in leadership styles, where they are referred to as initiating-structure, or task-oriented, and consideration or people-oriented.) Different stereotypes occupy different positions along a two-dimensional chart where each axis ranges from high to low competence and warmth. Researchers attempt to link this placement with individuals' experiences with stereotypes. Stereotypes associated with Asian Americans, particularly the Model Minority, would place them as high on competence and low on warmth. Lin et al. (2005, p. 44) stated that "findings suggest that the low-sociability stereotype is more powerful than the high-competence stereotype in determining the amount of liking and attention" that the stereotyped group experienced. In other words, perceivers were likely to form an impression based on (lack of) warmth rather than on competence. This perceived lack in the "warmth" dimension would be critical because professional environments appeared to place a high value on interpersonal behaviors. Being portrayed as "socially awkward and isolated" could be used to downplay employees' achievements related to competence and rationalize the undervaluing of behaviors that would otherwise be considered worthy of reward.

Arguably, the Model Minority is the most common stereotype of Asians in America. The term was first used by a journalist writing for the *New York Times Magazine* in 1966 (Fong, 1997) to describe Japanese Americans. The term "model" was used to connotate that this group worked hard and achieved material success without seeking help from others. Many researchers have noted that the Model Minority tag developed other associated meanings over time. Dhingra (2007, p. 136) noted that, according to this stereotype, "Asian Americans appear as hardworking but deficient in communication skills, and as accommodating instead of aggressive." As per Nichols (2017), the stereotype implied that Asian Americans were academic, high achieving, and hardworking. Lin at al. (2005) inferred that it portrayed Asians as diligent and successful, but only in the limited sphere of economic and educational endeavors. Some facts do support aspects of the Model Minority descriptive. Asians in America do seem to have stressed educational and professional qualifications, as indicated by data on the percentage of the group with college degrees. Also, Asian Americans seemed to prefer careers in the sciences and engineering in greater numbers than other ethnic groups (Kim & Zhao, 2014).

Researchers have attempted to identify the content of stereotypes associated with Asians in organizational workplaces. According to Giscombe and Mattis (2002, p. 104), Asians have been stereotyped as "diligent, intelligent, passive and reserved." Akutagawa (2013, p. 277) noted that Asian Americans commonly receive performance feedback from non-Asian supervisors indicating that they are "quiet, respectful, highly technical, never says no, hard worker." Hyun (2005, p. 40) stated that a typical corporate assessment concluded that Asian professionals are "technical but not management material." This was echoed by Kim and Zhao (2014, p. 638): "it is often stated that Asian Americans are desirable employees but not managers."

However, some researchers cautioned Asians to be aware of how they were perceived stereotypically. The Model Minority stereotype, while seemingly complimentary in attributing desirable qualities, might also portray Asians as "too competent, too ambitious, too hardworking and, simultaneously, not sociable" (Fiske et al., 2002, p. 880). Developing an awareness of how others perceived them was one aspect of social interactions in the workplace. Asian Americans also had to understand how adhering to certain cultural values might be perceived by others. Akutagawa (2013, p. 280) noted that while a cultural value could be affirming to an individual employee, it could be perceived in a different, unintended way by others in the workplace. For instance, being (perceived as) good in math seemed to be an advantage in educational environments with fellow students, but not so in professional spaces with colleagues (Williams et al., 2014).

Some researchers also cautioned that, depending on the circumstances, a cultural value could help or hurt a career. Holding on to a value despite negative signals from others in the workplace, and when it becomes associated with negative aspects of a stereotype, could turn that value from "strength to weakness" (Akutagawa, 2013, p. 280). In turn, this could lead to individuals experiencing value-dissonance. Thus, some Asian employees could develop mixed feelings about strong Asian values like conformity, obedience, and humility (Nichols, 2017) if they experienced that these values were not rewarded at work. However, individuals who chose to behave counter to stereotypes could be penalized "for succeeding in cross-racial domains" (Phelan & Rudman, 2010, p. 278). For some Asians, an ethnic identity could become more important if they experienced negative stereotyping in the workplace related to their ethnicity (Tummala-Narra et al., 2011).

A particularly problematic aspect of both gender and ethnic-Asian stereotyping is that perceivers are likely to categorize such (target) individuals "on [the] basis of physical features" and thus "form category-based impressions" (Rudman & Fairchild, 2004, p. 157). This first impression does not change unless the perceiver has ample opportunity to interact more extensively with the target and is also motivated to change that perception (Rudman & Fairchild, 2004, p. 157). However, there may not be sufficient opportunity for employees to interact more with Asian women, given their low numbers in corporate workplaces. For instance, in the survey conducted by Burris et al. (2013), less than 20% of Caucasian respondents said they had ever had an Asian American supervisor. This is where signals by the organization and a corporate culture of valuing diversity can have an impact on employees' perceptions.

Asian Americans themselves have notions of how these stereotypes affect them in the workplace. Asian women managers felt that they were viewed as reliable and obedient workhorses who did not have the requisite assertiveness or people-skills to be organizational leaders (Nichols, 2017). Many felt that being considered as passive and somewhat submissive made it difficult to be respected for their knowledge and for their authority to be accepted (Mukkamala & Suyemoto, 2018). According to Mukkamala and Suyemoto (2018), Asian women's negative experiences associated with race-related stereotyping included tokenism, mistaken ethnicity, identification as foreigners or outsiders, exclusion, and culture-based labeling. Such resistance to recognizing Asian women's value could keep even an unquestionably qualified and capable Asian woman at the level of (yet another) team player, rather than a leader.

Tokenism and Minority Status

Asian women are likely to be in an extreme minority in many U.S. corporate workplaces. Thus, they might experience "tokenism," which refers to workplaces where there are very few members of a specific group, typically one that is not powerful in that society.

Tokenism was originally studied in the context of gender imbalances. The focus of this research was on women in the workplace and was primarily related to proportional representation. However, tokenism experiences need not only be gender-based. They can also occur based on any (other) characteristics of an individual, such as "race, age, sexuality, etc." (Kanter, 1977, p. 967). Tokenism can happen, for example, with women in a male-dominated professional area or Asians in a non-technical professional field. Kanter (1977, p. 965) argued that tokenism had strong implications for interpersonal, and particularly inter-group, behaviors in the workplace.

Kanter, who was one of the first researchers of tokenism, initially considered the simple proportion of a minority within the group as a significant and sufficient indicator. The cut-off number that signaled tokenism was 15% (Yoder, 1994, p. 150). According to Kanter (1977, p. 965), there were several types of group characteristics linked to proportional representation by a minority group, which included "uniform, only one type of person; skewed, towards one group, numerically dominants control the group, 85:15%; tilted, less extreme proportion, minority becomes differentiated and could be viewed as potential allies, 65:35%; balanced, in culture and interactions, 60:40%." Thus, Kanter believed an increase in numbers of the minority group was sufficient to mitigate the negative effects of tokenism and to improve the workplace experiences of minority members.

Tokenism was considered problematic since it placed the token individual in an unfair situation through no responsibility of their own. The token was viewed as the symbol of a particular group and ascribed to that group characteristics that "carry an assumption of culture, status or behavior (that is) highly salient for the majority" (Kanter, 1977, p. 968). Thus, tokenism referred to the behavior by a dominant, majority, or high-status group directed towards a member of a less powerful, minority, or lower-status group member. It could be argued that token behaviors might occur only when an individual is deliberately placed in such a position, for instance, to satisfy a policy or stakeholder demand. However, that was not the case. These behaviors were observed even when the individual was not deliberately placed in a token situation but simply happened to find themselves in one.

A token becomes highly visible and is considered as different not for any work-related reason but due to a characteristic that the majority perceives as a discrepancy (Kanter, 1977, p. 973). The identification of an individual as a token serves to draw the dominant group members closer together so they become more cohesive (Kanter, 1977, p. 975). Tokenism manifests as behaviors by the dominant group that separate and isolate the token. For example, these behaviors might include formal and informal activities where the token is deliberately not included (Kanter, 1977, p. 978). The isolating behaviors of the dominant group become particularly emphasized when it is "under pressure to share privilege, power, or other desirable commodities" (Laws, 1975, p. 51) with the token's group. Tokens might be offered the promise of inclusion, but only if they pass "loyalty tests (of renouncing their category)," with failure leading to isolation (Kanter, 1977). Some might question a token's decision to put himself or herself in a situation where they are in a clear minority. Laws (1975) commented that both the dominant group and the token might find an advantage in that situation. The dominant group might be required to include minority group members or might want to be perceived as inclusive. The token might have the opportunity to design their job and benefits to a certain degree, since no precedent exists. For some tokens, the job might represent an opportunity to create a perception of themselves since there is nobody to compare them with. For others, the thought of being first and/or different might be attractive in its own right. Yoder (1994) noted that a token gets more attention, although this attention might be tied to performance pressures. Some tokens could view this increased scrutiny as a chance to impress others with their performance achievements.

Tokenism might explain the observed behaviors of certain high-ranking women or ethnic minority members who refuse to identify with their gender or ethnic groups. This refusal might be a response to pressures by the dominant group or an attempt to manage perceptions of themselves. However, despite their efforts, some tokens might never be fully assimilated into the dominant group, continuing as perpetually marginal members for the duration of their organizational stay (Laws, 1975). Kanter (1977) noted that tokenism-like behaviors can occur in many environments but are "heightened when (a) token's category is physically obvious and/or not only rare but new in the situation." This could explain the higher barriers and greater challenges faced by Asian women who are "first" in the workplace.

Tokenism proposed that extremely small numbers of employees of an identified group in an organization had strong implications for the nature of their workplace experience. Devos and Sadler (2019) proposed a similar theory linking workplace experience with the proportional presence of this group and with general diversity in the immediate community outside the workplace. They proposed gauging the extent of ethnic diversity in a society along three dimensions: the number of minority group members, the variety of minorities present, and the extent of integration of minority groups. When the numbers of each minority group are small, variety becomes irrelevant; minorities are grouped as one unit. For instance, Festekjian et al. (2014, p. 105) noted that often "Asian Americans are viewed as a collective group – non-Asians in the US typically do not perceive ethnic differences and thus tend to treat Asian Americans in similar ways and this results in similar outcomes."

Increasing diversity in the outside environment can positively affect how each group is viewed in society and in workplaces and can lead to members being viewed as individuals rather than as group representatives. This reasoning resembles that of Kanter's proportional representation theory. According to Devos and Sadler (2019, p. 191), diverse urban areas where there are greater numbers of many ethnic groups besides Asians and Europeans (variety) are "characterized by a greater implicit inclusion of Asian Americans in the national identity" (Devos & Sadler, 2019, p. 191). In other words, Asians are viewed as another group of Americans, rather than as unknown foreigners. This effect of increased interactions with a greater variety of groups was also noted by Phinney et al. (1997). They found that, for adolescents, "contact among groups can contribute to positive intergroup outcomes, including expressed liking," and somewhat surprisingly they also found that "the stronger the in-group attitudes," the more their attitude towards other groups changed when they had the opportunity to interact with other groups (Phinney et al., 1997, p. 964).

Such findings provide support for diversity strategies and diversity management in organizations. Both increasing numbers and increasing opportunities for interactions of various kinds between members of different groups could lead to better work environments.

Commonly Accepted Values in Asian Cultures

In the effort to understand the experiences of individuals in workplaces and society, researchers attempted to identify cultural characteristics that might be common to Asian cultures. While the classification of Asian "subsumes, under one heading, various cultures, social histories, and experiences of immigration" (Srinivasan, 2001, p. 155), there do appear to be some similarities between these cultures. These similarities might have less to do with obvious markers of culture such as food, clothing, and religion, and are more related to values, attitudes, and behaviors. It is relevant to discuss these aspects to the extent that they inform and influence attitudes and behaviors of non-Asians towards Asians and the attitudes of Asians themselves in workplaces. As noted by Hyun (2005, p. 31), behaviors can be revealing since they are often "based on deeply engraved cultural values." Further, Kawahara et al. (2013) noted that behaviors are "interpreted differently in mainstream US (West) and Asian American (East)" cultural contexts.

It is useful to view Asian cultures in the U.S. not just as stand-alone constructs but also as they relate to the majority culture. One distinguishing feature common to Asian American cultures was the value placed on educational qualifications. Education seemed to be viewed as the means to socio-economic progress, and that strategy seems to have worked until now (Kim & Zhao, 2014). Asian Americans have had "extra-ordinary levels of educational attainment" (Zhou & Lee, 2017) in comparison with other groups. About 50% of Asian Americans above the age of 25 had at least a bachelor's degree, whereas the corresponding numbers for Caucasians, African Americans, and Latino/a Americans were 31%, 18%, and 13%, respectively (Zhou & Lee, 2017, p. 7).

The strong and stereotypical work ethic of Asian Americans is a distinguishing feature of this group in the workplace (Dhingra, 2007, p. 91). Fong (1997) argued that, rather than being uniquely Asian American, values such as the pursuit of education, aiming for achievement, hard work, and frugality are aligned with basic American values. Zhou and Lee (2017) echoed this in stating that framing success as educational and professional achievements is not unique to Asian Americans, although it seemed that Asian Americans accepted this understanding of success wholeheartedly as a means of finding their place in American society. They noted that the 2012 Pew Research Center's report found that Asian Americans "place more value on hard work, career success, marriage, and parenthood than other Americans." The Model Minority theory similarly attributes the socio-economic success of Asian Americans to a combination of values considered as Asian and American—hard work, discipline, family cohesion, and willingness to wait for rewards (Zhou & Lee, 2017, p. 8).

Researchers often commented on collectivism as a distinguishing Asian value. Phinney (1996, p. 921) noted the "broad cultural differences between individualism and collectivism that has been observed to distinguish mainstream American and Western European cultures from the cultures of Asia." Hofstede's model for differentiating cultures, which has been widely used, identified individualism versus collectivism as an important dimension of cultures (Hofstede, 1991, p. 14). According to Oyserman et al. (2002, p. 3), researchers usually view individualism as "the opposite of collectivism, especially when contrasting European, American and East Asian cultural frames," and in present-day America, "being an individualist is not only a good thing, it is a quintessentially American thing."

The implications of individualism or collectivism being a socio-cultural value can be understood in terms of an individual's self-concept as well as their behavior towards others. A core belief of Individualism is that each person is an individual entity and acts in a manner consistent with that status. Consequently, individuals have the responsibility of creating and maintaining a concept of self and working towards their own well-being, and thus relationships are typically contract-based (Oyserman et al., 2002). A core belief of collectivism is that groups function to connect individuals in mutually beneficial relationships. Consequently, individuals are primarily members of groups and their well-being is dependent on that of the group, where social roles are critical and relationships are contextual (Oyserman et al., 2002). Even accounting for differences in individual orientations and characteristics, societies focused on individualism generally function in a different manner from those focused on collectivism. A society's functioning determines default organizational functioning as well, and the individualistic/collectivist orientation of a society in turn affects how employees view their jobs. In individualistic cultures, as the U.S. is understood to be, the main purpose of work is to further one's career. However, in a collectivist outlook, the purpose of work is often "a means of supporting the family" or "raising children well" (Choa et al., 2015, p. 408).

Self-esteem is a part of the self-concept that is related to the regard an individual has of his- or herself as a person (Tsai et al., 2001, p. 285). In individualistic societies, the self is regarded as autonomous. For instance, Caucasian families encourage children to be independent and outwardly directed in their behavior (Rosenthal & Feldman, 1990). In contrast, in collectivist societies, the self is regarded as part of the collective and viewed in connection to others. In these societies importance is placed on maintaining relationships, even if that requires the individual to be self-effacing and present themselves as inferior (Tsai et al., 2001, p. 285). Although American society is identified as individualistic, there are internal variations. For instance, African Americans tend to be highly individualistic, whereas Asians and Hispanics are relatively less so (Oyserman et al., 2002). Interestingly, it appears that Asian Americans might be shifting to more individualistic and autonomous behaviors (Rosenthal & Feldman, 1990). In particular, Asian Indians appeared to identify with Caucasians in the U.S. in terms of adopting the middle-class values of individualism and universality (Tummala-Narra et al., 2011).

Strong socio-cultural values can be assets or liabilities. In their study, Kim and Hong (2004) found that cultural values of importance to Asian Americans included collectivism, conformity to norms, deference to authority figures, emotional restraint, filial piety, hierarchical family structure, and humility. Several researchers have commented on the consequences of adhering to and basing decisions on these values. Fong (1997) commented that certain values considered as common to most Asian cultures, such as "filial piety, obedience to authority, subjugation of the individual to the group, a quiet and passive acceptance of one's situation, self-control, self-abasement and a strong sense of family solidarity" might conflict with values commonly accepted as American, such as "individualism, egalitarianism, independence, future orientation and mastery over one's environment" (Fong, 1997). Additionally, some negative traits related to cultural values are attributed to Asian Americans, such as beliefs that they are introverted, emotionally unexpressive, silent, passive, reserved, and have quiet demeanors (Kawahara et al., 2013, p. 241). Such perceptions might have led to the stereotyping of Asian men as hypermasculine, effeminate, or aggressive and of Asian women as submissive, demure, and obedient.

The behavior of some Asian Americans could be motivated by the "emphasis on maintaining harmony in relationships, the precedence of group interests over individual interests, and the importance of fulfilling obligations to the family" (Phinney, 1996, p. 921). Gee et al. (2015, p. 15) commented that giving too much importance to these values could result in the underdevelopment of skills needed in American workplaces. Thus, Asians might exhibit too much deference to authority, lack effective influencing skills, and be politically naïve. Hyun (2005) cautioned that an emphasis on maintaining harmony could result in a desire to avoid conflict. Further, there can be negative workplace consequences for individuals who do not engage with others or speak up in an effort to avoid conflict.

Researchers have cautioned that Asian American cultures are different from Asian cultures since they are a combination of norms from different cultures (Tsai et al., 2001, p. 286). Sometimes these norms can be oppositional. For instance, individualistic norms that promote the pursuit of career ambitions might require self-enhancement while collectivistic norms that emphasize job performance for the collective good might require self-effacement. Thus, Asian Americans might learn to negotiate a hybrid culture (Durik et al., 2006, p. 437). Similarly, cultural attitudes and role expectations towards men have been changing as well. In Asian American groups, these roles have started to shift from traditional to more egalitarian ones (Fong, 1997).

Asian American Acculturation Processes

Minority groups experience two processes when negotiating their way within a majority society: enculturation and acculturation. Enculturation refers to being socialized in the norms, values, beliefs, and behaviors of an individual's indigenous, minority culture (Kim & Hong, 2004). Acculturation refers to influences on minority individuals due to interactions with others in the (majority) culture and changes taking place in their indigenous cultures (Chang et al., 2005, p. 25). These processes are described in the context of minority groups, but acculturation affects both cultures involved. However, Berry et al. (1986) cautioned that although both the minority (acculturating) and the majority (dominating) cultures are affected in theory, in practice the former often gets subsumed into the latter.

LaFromboise et al. (1993) commented on changes that happened to broader society when members of different cultural groups were present and interacted with each other. They referred to two such types of societal acculturation—multicultural and fusion. In both situations, the group was comprised of individuals belonging to different socio-ethnic cultures who coexisted for economic and professional reasons. A multicultural group was one where these different cultures remained distinct from each other and did not affect each other. In contrast, in fusion groups, cultures affected each other and changed to the extent that the group had a new, resulting culture which was a combination of its constituent cultures.

Ethnic communities have made efforts to help individuals in their enculturation processes. As noted by Barth (1969, p. 15), ethnic cultures and communities need maintenance through "continual expression and validation." Ethnic groups play an important role in this effort and typically exist at multiple levels. For example, Kurien (1999) noted that Indian American groups were present as households, local community centers, and pan-ethnic associations. Such groups can aid in individual identity development (Iwamoto et al., 2013), provide social support, and help uphold cultural traditions.

Acculturation is a process carried out by individuals and initiated by the "conjunction of two or more autonomous cultural systems" (Berry et al., 1986, p. 292). Inman et al. (2001, p. 17) noted that during acculturation an individual "selectively adapts and incorporates behaviors, values and cultural practices, and in turn affects the society." This process manifests as changes in "behavior, identity, values and attitudes" (Chang et al., 2005, p. 26) as individuals and groups attempt to adapt. The effects of acculturation are felt at both the group and individual levels (Berry et al., 1986). Berry (1997) identified the three areas in which adaptive changes occur as psychological (individual), social (group), and economic.

Researchers have modeled acculturation processes in various ways. A one-dimension model (Suinn-Lew, for instance) tracks the process through the different psychological states of an individual (Chang et al., 2005). An individual progresses from one state to another over time based on their experiences. Each stage of the process is characterized by the degree to which the individual retains their original culture (or replaces aspects of it with the other culture).

Berry (1997) proposed a two-dimensional model that identifies four types of individual acculturation. The two dimensions are related to individual choices: whether there is value to maintaining an identity in, and characteristics of, the original culture, and whether there is value in building relationships with the other group (Berry et al., 1986, p. 306). The four states of individual acculturation in this model are assimilation, separation, integration, and marginalization. Integration occurs when the individual maintains significant levels of their original culture and has a lot of contact with the other culture. On the other hand, if the individual does not have contact with the other culture, they are in a state of separation. Assimilation occurs when the individual does not retain the original culture and has a lot of contact with the other culture. Finally, marginalization describes when the individual neither retains their original culture nor has contact with the other culture. Berry (1997) noted that these states encapsulate various ways in which individuals at the intersection of cultures can negotiate their way, but not all individuals "have freedom to choose the kind of acculturation" (Berry, 1997, p. 10). For example, a minority employee who has token status might be marginalized due to being isolated even if they wish to be assimilated.

Hutnick's model is similar to Berry's, and also identifies four types of acculturation: dissociative/traditionalist, assimilative, acculturative/bicultural, and marginal (Dasgupta, 1998). A different perspective was offered by LaFromboise et al. (1993). According to their study, assimilation means absorption into the dominant majority culture, which is often considered as more desirable by the individual. Acculturation happens when individuals learn to function competently in the majority culture, but they always retain minority member status. Alteration occurs when an individual dynamically alters cultural behaviors on occasion to fit in with their needs at that time.

An acculturation process is often not a uniform, one-dimensional, or permanent change. It can be a complex process and individuals within the same group can experience it differently. Berry et al. (1986, p. 297) noted that "individual acculturation does not cohere as a neat package." Many variables can affect the process, including geographical location, degree of cultural diversity or homogeneity in the population, opportunities and necessities for interaction between members of different groups, and the individual's psychological state (Berry et al., 1986). Thus, acculturation is multidimensional and dynamic (Varghese & Jenkins, 2009, p. 237).

Researchers have attempted to study Asian American acculturation behaviors using different models. Chang et al. (2005, p. 26) identified three approaches: the Suinn model (proposed in 1987), the Berry model (proposed in 1989), and the Sue and Sue model (proposed in 2003). The Suinn model is one-dimensional and the Berry model (described above) is two-dimensional. In other respects, their approaches were similar; both models focus on the degree to which an individual retains his or her original culture relative to the dominant one (Chang et al., 2005, p. 26). The Sue and Sue model extends models of Black identity development to the Asian context and identifies five stages of acculturation: conformity, dissonance, resistance/immersion, introspection, and integration (Chang et al., 2005, p. 27).

Chang et al. (2005, p. 35) noted that while general models describe the acculturation behaviors of different subgroups of Asian Americans to a certain degree, adding more dimensions provides greater "insight into content and process of acculturation." They proposed an expanded list of five content areas to consider: language use, cultural identity, social relationships, cultural values, and participation in cultural activities. These areas align with earlier comments made by Barth (1969, p. 15) to the effect that the cultural contents of ethnic differences were primarily visible and overt, such as dress, language, and certain value orientations. Based on these content areas, Chang et al. (2005, p. 36) also proposed two other dimensions of acculturation: overt factors and covert factors. Overt factors include those that are external and apparent to outside observers, such as language, food, clothing, and cultural practices. Covert factors are internal and more related to feelings of identity, values, and attitudes.

According to Chang et al. (2005, p. 37), Asian acculturation was driven by the importance the individual gave to overt, external factors as compared to covert, internal ones. Individuals who gave extreme importance to language and appearance were more likely to identify as American. Individuals who placed a high value on ethnic self-identification and cultural values were more likely to identify as Asian. (The latter might have lived in mono-cultural environments with little exposure to other cultures.) Finally, individuals for whom both overt and covert factors were equally important identified as both Asian and American. Members of this group viewed themselves as Americans in terms of cultural and social behaviors and as Asians in terms of their self-identity and values (Chang et al., 2005, p. 37). For instance, they might retain many aspects of their original culture in some areas, such as in marriage, and aspects of the other culture in other areas, such as parenting (Suinn et al., 1995, p. 140).

Some researchers commented on the dynamic nature of acculturation, both for an individual over a lifetime and for groups over generations. Tsai et al. (2001, p. 286) noted that for Asian Americans navigating two cultures simultaneously and continually, "cultural adaptation and adjustment are persistent and salient parts of their daily experience" (Tsai et al., 2001, p. 286). Immigrants' family structures are likely to be different from those in their countries of origin. As they try to constitute families in the U.S., "the arena of life's closest relationships becomes a place, sometimes battlefield" (Lessinger, 1995, p. 97). Berry (1997, p. 5) noted the difficulty faced by individuals who grow up in one culture when they "attempt to re-establish their lives in another one." These conflicts and dilemmas were reflected in individual acculturation choices, which could be starkly different at generational levels.

Researchers noted differences between first and second generations regarding external as well as internal factors. Many Asian immigrants experienced language challenges. However, younger Asian Americans were not only fluent in English, but were also more likely to speak English even at home (Nielson Reports, 2018). Immigrants typically were concerned with economic and social behaviors and were more ready to adapt for that reason. Individuals who immigrated as adults had already been socialized in another culture and had internalized its cultural values. On the other hand, their children struggled to find a balance between the two value systems (Varghese & Jenkins, 2009) and reported feeling an acute sense of being in-between cultures (Lessinger, 1995, p. 97). Their understanding of Asian culture was often based on explicit education and culturalization (Dhingra, 2007, p. 63). Another generational difference appeared in how Asian immigrants dealt with experiences of racism. Many second-generation members likely encountered forms of racism in school (Lessinger, 1995, p. 135), which adds complexity to their search for identity. In comparison, first-generation immigrants who came in search of a better future often have dual frames of reference and consider the present to be better than their past (Varghese & Jenkins, 2009). They might not internalize racist experiences and such experiences might not affect their core self-identity.

Some immigrants have tried to strike a cultural balance of pursuing upward socio-economic mobility while also being "socially and culturally 'traditional'" (Manohar, 2013b, p. 27). Yet, they are cautioned that such a strategy might not protect them from experiences of cultural and racial discrimination. Strangely enough, such discrimination could be due to, and not occur in spite of, their apparent integration and acceptance into the majority group.

Asian Women and the U.S. Socio-Economic Environment

Root (1995, p. 272) commented that the notion of being Asian American has been interpreted by researchers to mean "hybridization of specific Asian ways of thinking with mainstream American ways." However, this broad approach has ignored nuances in the experiences of Asian women in the U.S., both in their similarities and in their differences. While there is variation within this group, Asian women do have some commonality of experience in the professional sphere due to stereotyping and minority status, and in the personal sphere due to cultural values and gender role expectations. For instance, Yamanaka and McClelland (1994, p. 108) noted that "in spite of heterogeneity, Asian women seem to be alike in one respect—they have achieved their relatively high income only by working longer and harder (than comparable whites)."

The acculturation processes of Asian Americans, both men and women, are heterogeneous and vary across sub-groups as well as individuals. Asian women differ widely both in terms of countries of origin and socio-economic positioning. Their acculturation patterns are also likely to differ based on their personal and professional backgrounds. Asian women are varied in their motivations to migrate to the U.S. Depending on the socio-cultural and economic conditions in countries of origin in Asia, these reasons could range from the purely personal (marriage), to education and the purely professional (jobs). Lessinger (1995, p. 110) noted that until the 1990s, "relatively few Indian women migrated to the US on their own." However, regardless of their reasons for migrating, Asian women found that in the U.S., there was "subtle pressure to get a job" (Lessinger, 1995, p. 111). In responding to these pressures, Asian American women "have demonstrated great resilience in coping with economic obstacles" (Yamanaka & McClelland, 1994, p. 79).

Some researchers have viewed acculturation from a socio-economic lens, rather than only a social perspective. Immigrants adapt socio-economically in various ways, including through assimilation and participation in a dual economy, in ethnic enclaves, and as middlemen (Yamanaka & McClelland, 1994). Using 1980 census data, Yamanaka and McClelland (1994, p. 79) studied "working age immigrant women from Asia." They found that immigrants who perceived hard work as the primary key to economic success attempted to assimilate. In the dual economy view, immigrants' mobility was perceived to be restricted and they were trapped in certain jobs within niche segments. Ethnic enclaves were niche areas dominated by an ethnic group within which certain immigrants found employment. Finally, the middlemen group in Yamanaka and McClelland's study consisted of immigrants who were located between larger, mainstream businesses and immigrant labor. The authors noted that each of these group characterizations applied to certain immigrants and not to others. Not all immigrants, especially those with limited resources, could fit into the assimilation model. However, it was a good fit for "a minority group within Asian American women immigrants who have good education and/or professional skills" (Yamanaka & McClelland, 1994, p. 109).

The many avenues to perform paid work in the U.S. can be broadly classified as core private, core public, periphery public, and core self (Yamanaka & McClelland, 1994). Core private includes for-profit businesses, both large and small, as well as self-owned businesses. As a major part of the economy, these types of businesses are the primary choice for most people seeking work. The core public category includes jobs located within government organizations. It might be more difficult to obtain employment in this area since there could be requirements of citizenship or permanent residency. Affirmative action programs are also active in this sector. Periphery public work includes organizations that are funded by the government, which could be local; schools are an example of this sector. The requirements for periphery public jobs might not be as restrictive as in the core public sector, but there could be a measure of job security in these positions that is not present in the private sector. As mentioned in Chapter 7, the U.S. is different from other countries because of the "at-will-employment" law in place for private-sector jobs. This essentially means that, barring an explicitly stated contract, both the employer and employee can terminate the employment relationship at any time. Finally, core self refers to highly professional jobs, such as in the medical and legal fields, where workers need to clear a high bar for qualification, certification, or licensing. In this book, we focus on a special sub-section of core private work, namely large business corporations.

The participation of Asian women in the U.S. workforce has many unique aspects. Asian women cannot be viewed as a combination of characteristics of women (in general) and Asians (in general). They are distinct from both of these groups and have advantages in some ways and disadvantages in others. Tsai et al. (2001) commented that while general perceptions of Asian women differed from those of Asian men, these perceptions might be more favorable towards the women.

In an economic analysis related to college-educated Asian women, Kim and Zhao (2014, p. 623) noted that the "intersectionality of race and gender shows that racial and ethnic earnings disparities are (actually) smaller for women than men" and that there is a "(positive) net effect of being a well-educated Asian American woman." On the other hand, Kim and Zhao (2014) also noted that Asian American women find it harder to get hired and are more likely to be unemployed, even when they are more highly educated than comparable white women. This would lead to the conclusion that Asian American women, if hired, could perform well in their jobs and succeed professionally. The question would be how they manage to do so despite the structural barriers to their success. While affirmative action approaches addressing minorities might accrue benefits for Asian women in some situations (Yamanaka & McClelland, 1994, p. 87), organizational women's diversity programs often appear to overlook them (Gee et al., 2015, p. 11). Asian women might have had to "work harder than whites in same geographic areas to attain economic parity" (Yamanaka & McClelland, 1994, p. 107). They might also have had to accept slower professional growth than their performance merited. In the workplace, Giscombe and Mattis (2002, p. 104) noted that "Asian-American respondents were significantly less likely than other women of color surveyed to report that their positions involved managing others."

Asian women also appeared to differ from other women in how they negotiate their careers. Yamanaka and McClelland (1994) credited the successes Asian women have experienced to their hard work, marshaling their individual assets, and their reliance on collective resources to fulfill work obligations and demands. They commented that Asian women seemed to work for longer periods (retiring later) and were less likely to leave after marriage, and even the "presence of children" seemed to have "less inhibiting effect on their working" (Yamanaka & McClelland, 1994, p. 98). Echoing these findings, in the context of science and engineering careers, which are typically male-dominated, Kim and Zhao (2014) noted that Asian women were less likely than white women to reduce working hours even as their family demands increased.

Asian cultures are known for the importance given to family structures, roles, and obligations. Asian women, even in the U.S., are subject to these cultural practices and expectations. Dhingra (2007, p. 181) commented that all immigrant women "face stronger familial expectations than do their mainstream peers" and that they "typically must perform, or oversee, most domestic duties regardless of their employment status." Further, in the context of Korean and Indian immigrants in Texas, "even when women and men had specific roles, women clearly had more responsibilities, which caused tensions in balancing work and family" (Dhingra, 2007, p. 184).

Marriage and family have heightened importance and there is a general perception that Asian American women have greater marital stability than women of other groups (Fong, 1997). In many Asian cultures, marriage is viewed not just as an alliance between individuals but as a relationship between families (Varghese & Jenkins, 2009). The responsibility for ensuring the stability of families and marriages rests on women. In many Asian cultures, religion also plays an important social and cultural role; women are held responsible for maintaining associated practices and values in the religious domain as well.

The cultural and social environments Asian women find themselves in affect their perceptions of themselves and others' perceptions of them. When Asian women were a relatively unfamiliar group in the broad U.S. socio-cultural environment, they were stereotyped in different behavioral ways. These included "subservience (bride burning); exotic sexuality (geishas); manipulative, aggressive, diabolical (Dragon Lady); Sexless busy bee worker; innocent, fragile, China Doll" (Root, 1995, pp. 274–275). As the numbers of Asian women in American society and workplaces increased, these perceptions are likely to have changed. However, despite their increasing participation in the workforce, it appears that Asian women continue to be stereotypically perceived as "submissive and lacking career ambition" (Kamenou & Fearfull, 2006, p. 157). This might be due in part to how their cultural and religious backgrounds are understood in broader society.

Asian women might be viewed as "a model minority, with stable families and are represented in prestigious and professional positions" (Fong, 1997, p. 2). However, negotiating their professional and personal lives to achieve this success is not easy. Some Asian women have reported anxiety in performing in their work environments as related to "their upbringing as socially conservative women of color" (Dhingra, 2007, p. 133). As Kamenou and Fearfull (2006, p. 158) noted, "downplaying one's cultural identity to 'fit in' can cause a great deal of stress as individuals try to satisfy demands of both organizations and community." Asian women are undoubtedly challenged in meeting role requirements in their workplaces and in their homes. Their career strategy of maintaining hard work, aiming for competence, and fulfilling domestic responsibilities at the same time might be a heavy lift.

The Role of Family for Asian American Women

The importance of family in Asian American cultures cannot be overestimated. It appears that the role of the family plays out differently in Asian American families than in other groups. According to Lourenço and Cachado (2012, p. 53), in many Asian American groups, "the family is one of the essential elements in maintaining balance and social cohesion" across the diaspora.

Being in, creating, and maintaining families is viewed as a central role for many Asian American women. A significant part of their identity is associated with the family. It is likely expected that they will subsume their desires for the good of the family. Hence, Asian women might struggle to find an effective balance between their individuality and family identity (Root, 1995, pp. 280–281). In a study of "how first and second generation South Asian women across the US think about and are socialized about their gendered experiences within familial and community contexts," Mehrotra (2016, p. 351) commented on the importance and impact of "cultural scripts." A cultural script refers to a "large collective identity" and provides "notions of how a proper person of that kind behaves," along with "loose norms or models" (Mehrotra, 2016, p. 354). For South Asian women, marriage "emerged as central to women's narratives about gender and family relationships" (Mehrotra, 2016, p. 351) and was a key part of the cultural script they received (Mehrotra, 2016, p. 357). Family, and even community, relationships were likely to be strained if such scripted expectations were not met (Mehrotra, 2016, p. 368). In a study of Korean and Indian families, Dhingra (2007, p. 58) noted that this was true for Asian men as well, and a "commitment to marriage and even education" was viewed as a cultural value.

In many, if not all, Asian countries a woman's fundamental duty is still considered to be performing the role of wife and mother (Choa et al., 2015, p. 408). Although that viewpoint changes to a degree in the American context, here too children are considered equally as important as marriage. Thus, parenting is also part of the cultural script for Asian women.

Researchers have noted that Asian American parenting is an interesting blend of Asian and American styles. In the broader American culture, children are brought up to "individuate" and pursue their independent interests (Farver et al., 2007, p. 189). In contrast, Asian cultures emphasize family membership and collective identity. Farver et al. (2007) described the Asian American parenting style as one with parents exercising significant control, a stress on educational attainment, and physical closeness. They noted that when the mother is more comfortable with mainstream American culture and is acculturated as assimilated or integrated, her parenting style becomes closer to that of European Americans. Some of these women might transition from being Asian American to "Multicultural Moms" (Hyun, 2005).

Asian women working in corporate environments and demanding jobs are still expected to perform the roles of wife and mother. Their participation in the workforce and their career success enhance their social status and that of their families. Yet, some cultural traditions, particularly relating to family structures and interactions, pose challenges (Choa et al., 2015, p. 408). For instance, it might not be uncommon for some Asian families to live in multi-generational households, the so-called "joint family system." Nielson Reports (2018, p. 12) found this was the case in several high-income households.

Asian women might have a strategic view of the duality of work-family demands that is different from that of white women (the majority view). Rather than viewing work and family as competing for their time and energy, Asian women view them as enhancing each other. In other words, "professional work is complementary rather than contradictory" to parenting and taking care of the family (Manohar, 2013a, p. 171). This finding was illustrated in an ethnographic study of South Asian moms in Georgia, which is discussed in the following section.

Asian women in the U.S. appear to be strongly affected by Asian cultural values related to family. Cultural expectations of Asian women have them adhering to gender roles, upholding traditions, maintaining family harmony, and fulfilling family responsibilities even if it means placing those responsibilities ahead of professional ones (Varghese & Jenkins, 2009). Asian women working outside the home might feel the pressure of meeting those expectations. However, Asian women might be able to reconcile the two roles by articulating a certain motivation for professional achievement: using their professional and career success as an aid to the upward mobility of their families and children (Manohar, 2013a, p. 168).

(Indian) Tamil Moms of Atlanta: An Ethnographic Study

Manohar (2013a) conducted a year-long ethnographic study of Tamil moms in Atlanta, Georgia. The participants in the study were originally from a southern state in India. They had migrated to the U.S. as "trailing spouses," that is, as family members (Killian & Manohar, 2016, p. 139). Having been educated in India, they were able to eventually overcome the trailing spouse status to pursue careers of their own.

These Tamil women considered education and training as an entryway to highly skilled jobs (Killian & Manohar, 2016). For many, the initial entry into the labor market was "downward occupational mobility" since they were overqualified (Killian & Manohar, 2016, p. 146), although that situation improved over time. Killian and Manohar (2016) identified the four mediating mechanisms of their participation in the workforce as local labor market conditions for immigrants, education and experience, social capital in networks, and racialization.

Entry into the labor force was constrained by their legal status. The spousal visa (linked to H-1B), does not permit work. Thus, the women instead turned to other opportunities to acquire professional skills, such as volunteering, interning, and studying. These pursuits helped in building their education and experience and added to their human capital. Participation in community activities and maintaining cultural traditions was also their responsibility (Manohar, 2013b, p. 26). They utilized these and other social opportunities to build ethnic and cross-cultural professional networks and acquire social capital (Killian & Manohar, 2016).

Motherhood was an important aspect of their lives. It had both personal and cultural meaning but mothering also had to factor in the women's "social location as an immigrant community of color and agency" (Manohar, 2013a, p. 160–161). Since these women were working outside the home, motherhood became a "site of power contestation by which they (Tamil moms) negotiate gender arrangements" (Manohar, 2013a, p. 161). Both they and their spouses had to change their "normative ideas about family, gender and motherhood" to accept that they could "rarely be the exclusive, full-time mother that is idealized" (Manohar, 2013a, p. 161). They often had to rely on the support and help of various family members and friends to fulfill professional and personal responsibilities.

The participants did experience racialization, being categorized as a "model minority" (Killian & Manohar, 2016). To insulate themselves from the effects of racialization, they created tight family bonds that they viewed as protective. Thus, they considered motherhood as a "buffer against marginalization in the U.S." (Manohar, 2013a, p. 166) and positioned themselves as "cultural brokers, mediating between the larger American society and their Indian-American children" (Manohar, 2013a, p. 169). In this way, they created their professional identities as not oppositional to parenting identities but "intrinsic to it," so that being "professionals makes them 'better, stronger, more assertive mothers'" (Manohar, 2013a, p. 171). However, all this effort, more than what is required of non-immigrant women, took its toll. These moms experienced high levels of "emotional stress of being constantly cognizant of the demands on them" (Manohar, 2013a, p. 180).

Notes in Conclusion

Workplaces consist of individuals who differ from each other yet have to put in collective effort towards achieving common goals and objectives. Organizational work is designed to overlap and be linked together. This requires employees to interact and connect with each other. As workplaces become more diverse, interaction can become increasingly difficult.

The tendency of people to form closer bonds with others like themselves has been well documented as the phenomenon of "homophily" (Chapter 4). Diversity is counter to this tendency. This homophily, together with employees' unfamiliarity with certain under-represented groups, can lead to undesirable workplace experiences, such as discrimination of various kinds associated with stereotyping.

As relatively new entrants into corporate workplaces, Asian women could be viewed as an unknown group and thus be subject to the negative effects of stereotyping. Since Asian women are few in number in the general population, they are likely to be in the minority in most workplaces and thus to be vulnerable to tokenism. The most common stereotype of Asian women is that they are competent but not warm (lacking in social skills). Some values commonly attributed to Asian cultures, such as collectivism and obedience, might contribute to such perceptions, and a token status can further accentuate these values. The effects of tokenization can be apparent both in performance evaluations and in the everyday working environment. Due to these perceptions, Asian women might not be viewed as potential leaders either by those above or those below them in the organizational hierarchy.

Career management requires individuals to be aware of how they are perceived in the workplace and to strategically manage their images. Asian women in particular might need to examine their attitudes and behaviors in the process of managing their careers. They have the advantage, and difficulty, of negotiating two distinct cultures, with the attached gender role expectations. Acculturation is reflected in the ways they retain and express different aspects of their Asian identities in the workplace. In doing so, they need to balance the impact and repercussions of their choices with the benefits of being authentic.

The role of the (extended) family in Asian women's professional lives has also been a subject of interest. Some women have smoothed out potential work/life conflicts by viewing paid work as an extension of family responsibilities. In a practical sense, (extended) families have provided support (such as childcare) and stability in personal life so they could commit time and energy to work.

REFERENCES

Akutagawa, L. (2013). Breaking stereotypes: An Asian American's view of leadership development. *Asian American Journal of Psychology*, *4*(4), 277–284. doi:10.1037/a0035390

Barth, F. (1969). Introduction. In F. Barth (Ed.), *Ethnic groups and boundaries: The social organization of culture difference* (pp. 9–38). Little, Brown and Company.

Benson, J., & Yukongdi, V. (2005, June). Asian women managers: Participation, barriers and future prospects. *Asia Pacific Business Review, 11*(2), 283–291. doi:10.1080/1360238042000291135

Berry, J. W. (1997). Immigration, acculturation, and adaptation. *Applied Psychology, 46*(1), 5–68.

Berry, J. W., Trimble, J. E., & Olmedo, E. L. (1986). Assessment of acculturation. In W. J. Lonner & J. W. Berry (Eds.), *Field methods in cross-cultural research* (pp. 291–324). Sage Publications.

Burris, K., Ayman, R., Che, Y., & Min, H. (2013). Asian Americans' and Caucasians' implicit leadership theories: Asian stereotypes, transformational, and authentic leadership. *Asian American Journal of Psychology, 4*(4), 258–266. doi:10.1037/a0035229

Chang, T., Tracey, T. J. G., & Moore, T. L. (2005). The dimensional structure of Asian American acculturation: An examination of prototypes. *Self and Identity, 4*(1), 25–43. doi:10.1080/13576500444000155

Choa, Y., McLean, G. N., Amornpipat, I., Chang, W., Hewapathirana, G. I., Horimoto, M., Lee, M. M., Li, J., Manikoth, N. N., Othman, J., & Hamzah, S. R. (2015). Asian women in top management: Eight country cases. *Human Resource Development International, 18*, 1–22. doi:10.1080/13678868.2015.1020717

Dasgupta, S. D. (1998). Gender roles and cultural continuity in the Asian Indian immigrant community in the U.S. *Sex Roles, 38*(11/12), 953–974. doi:10.1023/A:1018822525427

Devos, T., & Sadler, M. (2019). Context diversity predicts the extent to which the American identity is implicitly associated with Asian Americans and European Americans. *Asian American Journal of Psychology, 10*(2), 182–193. doi:10.1037/aap0000149

Dhingra, P. (2007). *Managing multicultural lives: Asian American professionals and the challenge of multiple identities*. Stanford University Press.

Durik, A. M., Hyde, J. S., Marks, A. C., Roy, A. L., Anaya, D., & Schultz, G. (2006). Ethnicity and gender stereotypes of emotion. *Sex Roles, 54*(7-8), 429–445. doi:10.100711199-006-9020-4

Farver, J. M., Xu, Y., Badha, B., Bhadha, R., Narang, S., & Lieber, E. (2007). Ethnic identity acculturation, parenting beliefs, and adolescent adjustment: A comparison of Asian Indian and European American families. *Merrill-Palmer Quarterly*, *53*(2), 184–215. doi:10.1353/mpq.2007.0010

Festekjian, A., Tram, S., Murray, C. B., Sy, T., & Huynh, H. P. (2014). I see me the way you see me: The influence of race on interpersonal and intrapersonal leadership perceptions. *Journal of Leadership & Organizational Studies*, *21*(1), 102–119. doi:10.1177/1548051813486522

Fiske, S. T., Cuddy, A. J., Glick, P., & Xu, J. (2002). A model of (often mixed) stereotype content: Competence and warmth respectively follow from perceived status and competition. *Journal of Personality and Social Psychology*, *82*(6), 878–902. doi:10.1037/0022-3514.82.6.878 PMID:12051578

Fong, L. Y. S. (1997). Asian- American women: An understudied minority. *Journal of Sociology and Social Welfare*, *24*(1), 91–111.

Gee, B., & Peck, D. (2015). *The illusion of Asian success: Scant progress for minorities in cracking the glass ceiling from 2007-2015*. Ascend Report. http://aapidata.com/wp-content/uploads/2017/10/TheIllusionofAsianSuccess.pdf

Gee, B., Peck, D., & Wong, J. (2015). *Hiding in plain sight: Asian American leaders in Silicon Valley*. Ascend Report. https://cdn.ymaws.com/www.ascendleadership.org/resource/resmgr/Research/HiddenInPlainSight_OnePager_.pdf

Giscombe, K., & Mattis, M. C. (2002). Leveling the playing field for women of color in corporate management: Is the business case enough? *Journal of Business Ethics*, *37*(1), 103–119. doi:10.1023/A:1014786313354

Gündemir, S., Carton, A. M., & Homan, A. C. (2019). The impact of organizational performance on the emergence of Asian American leaders. *The Journal of Applied Psychology*, *104*(1), 107–122. doi:10.1037/apl0000347 PMID:30247048

Hofstede, G. (1991). *Cultures and organizations: Software of the mind*. McGraw Hill.

Hyun, J. (2005). *Breaking the Bamboo Ceiling*. Harper-Collins.

Inman, A. G., Ladany, N., Constantine, M. G., & Morano, C. K. (2001). Development and preliminary validation of the cultural values conflict scale for South Asian women. *Journal of Counseling Psychology*, *48*(1), 17–27. doi:10.1037/0022-0167.48.1.17

Iwamoto, D. K., Negi, N. J., Partiali, R. N., & Creswell, J. W. (2013). The racial and ethnic identity formation process of second-generation Asian Indian Americans: A phenomenological study. *Journal of Multicultural Counseling and Development*, *41*(4), 224–239. doi:10.1002/j.2161-1912.2013.00038.x PMID:25298617

Kamenou, N., & Fearfull, A. (2006). Ethnic minority women: A lost voice in HRM. *Human Resource Management Journal*, *16*(2), 154–172. doi:10.1111/j.1748-8583.2006.00010.x

Kanter, R. M. (1977). Some effects of proportions on group life: Skewed sex ratios and responses to token women. *American Journal of Sociology*, *82*(5), 965–990. doi:10.1086/226425

Kawahara, D. M., Pal, M. S., & Chin, J. L. (2013). The leadership experiences of Asian Americans. *Asian American Journal of Psychology*, *4*(4), 240–248. doi:10.1037/a0035196

Killian, C., & Manohar, N. N. (2016). Highly skilled immigrant women's labor market access: A comparison of Indians in the United States and North Africans in France. *Social Currents*, *3*(2), 138–159. doi:10.1177/2329496515620644

Kim, B. S. K., & Hong, S. (2004). A psychometric revision of the Asian values scale using the Rasch model. *Measurement & Evaluation in Counseling & Development*, *37*(1), 15–27. doi:10.1080/07481756.2004.11909747

Kim, C., & Zhao, Y. (2014). Are Asian American women advantaged? Labor market performance of college educated female workers. *Social Forces*, *93*(2), 623–652. doi:10.1093fou076

Kurien, P. (1999, January). Gendered ethnicity: Creating a Hindu identity in the United States. *The American Behavioral Scientist*, *42*(4), 648–670. doi:10.1177/00027649921954408

LaFromboise, T., Coleman, H. L. K., & Gerton, J. (1993). Psychological impact of biculturalism: Evidence and theory. *Psychological Bulletin*, *114*(3), 395–412. doi:10.1037/0033-2909.114.3.395 PMID:8272463

Lavaysse, L. M., & Probst, T. M. (2019). Stereotype threat: impacts for women at work. In A. Antoniou, C. Cooper, & C. Gatrell (Eds.), *Women, business and leadership: Gender and organisations* (pp. 347–361). Edward Elgar Publishing. doi:10.4337/9781786432711.00029

Laws, J. L. (1975). The psychology of tokenism: An analysis. *Sex Roles, 1*(1), 51–67. doi:10.1007/BF00287213

Lessinger, J. (1995). *From the Ganges to the Hudson: Indian immigrants in New York City*. Allyn & Bacon.

Lin, M., Kwan, V. S. Y., Cheung, A., & Fiske, S. T. (2005, January). Stereotype content model explains prejudice for an envied outgroup: Scale of anti-Asian American stereotypes. *Personality and Social Psychology Bulletin, 31*(1), 34–47. doi:10.1177/0146167204271320 PMID:15574660

Lourenço, I., & Cachado, R. (2012). Hindu transnational families: Transformation and continuity in diaspora families. *Journal of Comparative Family Studies, 43*(1), 53–70.

Manohar, N. N. (2013a). Mothering for class and ethnicity: The case of Indian professional immigrants in the United States. In M. Kohlman, D. Krieg, & B. Dickerson (Eds.), *Notions of family: Intersectional perspectives, advances in gender research* (Vol. 17, pp. 159–185). Emerald Group Publishing Limited. doi:10.1108/S1529-2126(2013)0000017011

Manohar, N. N. (2013b). Support networks, ethnic spaces, and fictive kin: Indian immigrant women constructing Community in the United States. *AAPI Nexus, 11*(1–2), 25–55.

McGarty, C., Yzerbyt, V., & Spears, R. (2002). *Stereotypes as explanations: The formation of meaningful beliefs about social groups*. Cambridge University Press. doi:10.1017/CBO9780511489877

Mehrotra, G. R. (2016). South Asian women and marriage: Experiences of a cultural script. *Gender Issues, 33*(4), 350–371. doi:10.100712147-016-9172-7

Mukkamala, S., & Suyemoto, K. L. (2018). Racialized sexism/sexualized racism: A multimethod study of intersectional experiences of discrimination for Asian American women. *Asian American Journal of Psychology, 9*(1), 32–46. doi:10.1037/aap0000104

Nichols, A. (2017). The influence of ethnicity and gender on the leadership experiences of female Asian-American managers. *Global Journal of Human-Social Science Interdisciplinary*, *17*(4), 1–28.

Nielson Reports. (2018). *Asian Americans digital lives and growing influence*. https://www.nielsen.com/us/en/insights/report/2018/asian-americans-consumers/

Oyserman, D., Coon, H. M., & Kemmelmeier, M. (2002). Rethinking individualism and collectivism: Evaluation of theoretical assumptions and meta-analyses. *Psychological Bulletin*, *128*(1), 3–72. doi:10.1037/0033-2909.128.1.3 PMID:11843547

Phelan, J. E., & Rudman, L. A. (2010). Reactions to ethnic deviance: The role of backlash in racial stereotype maintenance. *Journal of Personality and Social Psychology*, *99*(2), 265–281. doi:10.1037/a0018304 PMID:20658843

Phinney, J. S. (1996). When we talk about American ethnic groups, what do we mean? *The American Psychologist*, *51*(9), 918–927. doi:10.1037/0003-066X.51.9.918

Phinney, J. S., Ferguson, D. L., & Tate, J. D. (1997, October). Intergroup attitudes among ethnic minority adolescents: A causal model. *Child Development*, *68*(5), 955–969. doi:10.2307/1132044 PMID:29106715

Root, M. P. P. (1995). The psychology of Asian American women. In H. Landrine (Ed.), *Bringing cultural diversity to feminist psychology: Theory, research and practice* (pp. 265–301). American Psychological Association. doi:10.1037/10501-012

Rosenthal, D. A., & Feldman, S. S. (1990). The acculturation of Chinese immigrants: Perceived effects on family functioning of length of residence in two cultural contexts. *The Journal of Genetic Psychology*, *151*(4), 495–514. doi:10.1080/00221325.1990.9914635 PMID:2074433

Rudman, L. A., & Fairchild, K. (2004). Reactions to counter-stereotypic behavior: The role of backlash in cultural stereotype maintenance. *Journal of Personality and Social Psychology*, *87*(2), 157–176. doi:10.1037/0022-3514.87.2.157 PMID:15301625

Smith, M. (2013). *Fact sheet: the state of Asian American women in the United States*. Center for American Progress. https://www.americanprogress.org/issues/race/reports/2013/11/07/79182/fact-sheet-the-state-of-asian-american-women-in-the-united-states/

Srinivasan, S. (2001). "Being Indian," "being American": A balancing act or a creative blend? *Journal of Human Behavior in the Social Environment*, *3*(3/4), 135–158.

Suinn, R. M., Khoo, G., & Ahuna, C. (1995, July). The Suinn-Lew Asian self-identity acculturation scale: Cross-cultural information. *Journal of Multicultural Counseling and Development*, *23*(3), 139–148. doi:10.1002/j.2161-1912.1995.tb00269.x

Tsai, J. L., Ying, Y., & Lee, P. A. (2001). Cultural predictors of self-esteem: A study of Chinese American female and male young adults. *Cultural Diversity & Ethnic Minority Psychology*, *7*(3), 284–297. doi:10.1037/1099-9809.7.3.284 PMID:11506074

Tummala-Narra, P., Inman, A. G., & Ettigi, S. P. (2011). Asian Indians' responses to discrimination: A mixed-method examination of identity, coping, and self-esteem. *Asian American Journal of Psychology*, *2*(3), 205–218. doi:10.1037/a0025555

Varghese, A., & Jenkins, S. R. (2009). Parental overprotection, cultural value conflict, and psychological adaptation among Asian Indian women in America. *Sex Roles*, *61*(3-4), 235–251. doi:10.100711199-009-9620-x

Williams, J. C., Phillips, K. W., & Hall, E. V. (2014). *Double jeopardy? Gender bias against women in science*. WorkLife Law, UC Hastings Technical Report.

Yamanaka, K., & McClelland, K. (1994). Earning the Model-Minority image: Diverse strategies of economic adaptation by Asian-American women. *Ethnic and Racial Studies*, *17*(1), 79–114. doi:10.1080/01419870.1994.9993814

Yoder, J. D. (1994, June). Looking beyond numbers: The effects of gender status, job prestige, and occupational gender-typing on Tokenism processes. *Social Psychology Quarterly*, *57*(2), 150–159. doi:10.2307/2786708

Zhou, M., & Lee, J. (2017). Hyper-selectivity and the remaking of culture: Understanding the Asian American achievement paradox. *Asian American Journal of Psychology*, *8*(1), 7–15. doi:10.1037/aap0000069

Chapter 6
Social and Organizational Identities

ABSTRACT

Identity refers to a sense of self. It is a complex notion that influences an individual's values, attitudes, and behaviors and can change over an individual's life span. In organizational settings, identity is a powerful force driving employees' motivations, decisions, and actions. Organizations recognize that employees have identities arising from personal and private parts of their lives. At the same time, organizations encourage their employees to develop a (strong) sense of identity as organizational members. Workplaces are thus intriguing environments in which individuals are required to manage and negotiate various identities, both social (personal) and organizational. In this chapter, the authors discuss theories that explain how individuals develop a sense of identity. They then discuss identities that are relevant to Asian American women in work environments. The social identities pertinent in this context include ethnic and racial identities and the model minority stereotype. Work identities, in contrast, include professional and organizational identities.

INTRODUCTION

The organizational setting for work, including its structures (positions, authority, decision-making, power) and functioning (relationships, networks, culture, stereotypes) was discussed in previous chapters. The core of organizational structures consists of the delineation of roles and the placement of authority.

DOI: 10.4018/978-1-7998-4384-9.ch006

Because organizations exist through individual efforts, the human element has to be factored into discussions about workplaces. Organizational functioning typically addresses both individual and group aspects as well as the work and people aspects of the workplace.

This chapter and the next focus on the individual employee in two different ways—in terms of how employees view themselves and the impact of that self-perception on employees' workplace experiences. These two chapters also include discussions on how employees manage their organizational careers and navigate their way through workplaces.

Identity is commonly understood to refer to how individuals view themselves. The choice of assuming an identity rests with the individual and is manifest only when the individual decides to enact it. Asian women are faced with a multitude of identities—woman, Asian, professional, and mother/daughter, to name a few. They can choose to enact any or all or none of these, and these choices can be dynamic—that is, they can choose when and how to display different identities. However, just because identity is an individual choice does not mean that its impact lies only in its internal meaning. Enacting an identity can bring reactions from others and have an external impact, especially in workplaces. Thus, identity choices might need to be made with awareness and perhaps even strategically (with objectives in mind).

This chapter begins with definitions and descriptions of what is meant by identity, followed by discussions of the various identities relevant to Asian women in professional workplaces—ethnic, gender, family-related, professional, and organizational. Researchers in the area of impression management have studied ways in which employees manage how they are perceived in the workplace. Asian women can pick and choose among impression management techniques in their management of various identities.

Identity and Its Development

The term identity has been extensively studied in different disciplines and is part of the popular lexicon. Identity has sometimes been used to refer essentially to ethnicity and the "culture of a people" (Stryker & Burke, 2000, p. 284). However, a broader view of identity focuses on identification with a social group, which need not be restricted to ethnicity, nationality, or culture.

Dutton et al. (2010, p. 266) cited Gecas as defining identity as "the meaning individuals attach to themselves." Ashforth et al. (2008, p. 327) added situational variables by stating that "identity is a self-referential description that provides contextually appropriate answers to the question 'Who am I?' or 'Who are we?'" A comprehensive description by Stryker and Burke (2000, p. 284) stated that identity refers to "parts of a self, composed of the meanings that persons attach to the multiple roles they typically play in highly differentiated contemporary societies." Brubaker and Cooper (2000) provided a more abstract description of identity as "both a category of practice (lay actors to understand themselves, make sense of their actions, what they share with or differ from, others) and a category of analysis (outside actors, political purposes)."

These varied definitions suggest that while identity is intuitively understood, it is difficult to define. It refers to an understanding that individuals have of themselves, but also to how they want to be understood by others. An individual's identity is "constituted largely of how they see themselves with respect to others" (Brickson, 2005, p. 576). Thus, it contains elements of both individual and social perception. As noted by Ibarra (1999, p. 766), identity is based both on "social roles and group memberships as well as [the] personal and character traits."

DeRue and Ashford (2010, p. 629) identified three levels common to all identities: individual, relational, and collective. The individual level of identity is based on how the individual perceives herself as distinct from others. The personal, individual identity refers to a unique sense of self (Ashforth et al., 2008). The relational level dyadic connection between two people refers to how an individual views herself in relation to another person. Finally, the collective level refers to membership in the larger group and how the individual views herself in connection to many others, perhaps in a role-based rather than a personal way (Brickson, 2005, p. 576).

The personal aspects of identity are based on personality characteristics, roles, categories, and associations (Meister et al., 2014, p. 491). Personality characteristics include attributes, traits (e.g., honest), and competencies (e.g., hard-working). Roles refer to social or interpersonal status such as spouse, parent, and boss, and they are typically attached to expectations of attitudes and behaviors. The individual's choice of role-identity implies a willingness to fulfill those expectations. The individual and relational levels explained above primarily relate to these personal aspects.

The collective level of identity, however, is related to social aspects. Groups may be centered on certain characteristics, such as gender and ethnicity, profession, or interests (such as hobbies). These are primarily groups that the individual is associated with either through her choice or by others. Social identity also contributes to an individual's self-concept. Ashforth et al. (2008, p. 327) noted that the meaning of such identity is derived from "knowledge of his (her) membership in a social group (or groups) together with the values and emotional significance attached to that membership." Individuals gain a sense of who they are as group members and evaluate the implications of this group membership by comparing their group with other groups.

Individuals can, and do, choose to identify with different groups at different points in time. They might experience that each social identity is "activated at certain times and not at others" (Brewer, 1991, p. 477). Activation is the result of an identity choice being available as well as the individual's willingness to accept that identity. According to Tajfel and Turner (1986, p. 16), this dynamic switching of identities is motivated by an individual's desire to maintain an overall positive identity that is "based to a large extent on favorable comparisons" with other groups. If an individual finds a particular social identity to be less valuable than expected, the individual will either leave the group for a more valued one or attempt to make the existing group identity more positive for themselves. In this context, Shih et al. (2006) noted that the value an individual associates with a specific social identity is domain-specific. A characteristic associated with a group identity could be positive in some situations and negative in others. For instance, the characteristic of hard work associated with Asian Americans might be viewed favorably at lower levels of an organization, while at higher levels, it might be interpreted a little less favorably. For example, individuals with this characteristic of hard work might be perceived at higher organizational levels as needing too much direction and overly specified work, or as not being flexible.

Identities do not simply appear in an individual. Rather, they are developed through various processes. Since identity has both personal and social components, Pessar (1984, p. 3) commented that identity development is "not an individual process." Pessar (1984, p. 5) also noted that a crisis is often the trigger for an identity development process to be (re)started. Further, Leung (2008, p. 781) observed that, despite the nature of the trigger, identities change gradually based on "positive feedback." The development process is thus motivated by a desire to construct a more positive identity for oneself. This can be done by viewing oneself as "more virtuous, holding one's identity in high regard, adapting to or progressing toward an ideal state or balancing identity tensions" (Dutton et al., 2010, p. 284). Aligning with these findings,

LaFromboise et al. (1993, p. 402) presented a view of identity development as the "evolution of (an) individual's sense of self-sufficiency and ego strength."

Identity development is not always linear or smooth. In most instances it is a complex and vacillating process, going back and forth as various identity claims put forward by the individual are accepted or denied by others (Dutton et al., 2010, p. 284). Phinney (1990), in a study of ethnic identity development, proposed that there are two phases in the identity development process: search and commitment. These phrases can occur consecutively or concurrently at different times during different periods in an individual's life. Pessar (1984, p. 5) extended this notion to propose a 2x2 model based on the search for, and commitment to, a choice of identity. The four states Pessar identified were diffuse, foreclosed, moratorium, and achieved. An individual who was not motivated to search and did not commit to an identity was in a diffuse state. An individual who unquestioningly committed to an identity, perhaps due to familial influences, and who was not interested in searching, had foreclosed. An individual who was not prepared to commit to an identity despite searching for one was in a moratorium. Finally, an individual who was prepared to commit to an identity after having searched could be said to have achieved that identity.

Pessar (1984, p. 12) described the stages of the development process in the case of ethnic, or minority, identities. In the beginning, the individual accepts and internalizes (majority) identity unquestioningly. However, more often than not, the individual experiences a situation that leads them to question this acceptance of a majority culture and their own place in it. Often that is an experience of racism, where the individual is discriminated against for perceived belonging to a low-status group. This conflict leads the individual to begin exploration in search of clarity and personal edification related to their belonging in the majority and minority groups. This stage is likely to be emotional; the individual could feel angry at various others and believe that they will always be treated unfairly. Such feelings could result in the individual adopting an oppositional identity to the majority group. However, further experiences could alter this process so that the individual again identifies with the majority group (although perhaps to a lesser extent than before). Such a back-and-forth process, triggered by various experiences and influenced by different people and situations, could continue over a period of time. An ideal final stage would be the individual resolving these inter-group contradictions and internal conflicts. In the achieved stage, the individual accepts and then internalizes an ethnic or minority identity that they view positively in the context of the majority culture.

An ethnic identity is, however, only one kind of identity. Individuals can acquire, use, and discard various identities over the course of their lifetimes. Individuals can also acquire new identities without discarding old ones, and so possess multiple identities simultaneously. Dutton et al. (2010, p. 266) noted that individual identities are "multiple, multifaceted and dynamic." Some identities are generated by the roles that individuals occupy (Ashforth et al., 2008, p. 327), while others are acquired by interests or needs. Depending on their levels of social interactions with others, individuals choose self-identities dynamically (Meister et al., 2014, p. 490). Individuals contextually experience different identities as they become accessible and salient, and each identity affects how they perceive and process information. As a result, their affect and behavior evolves "in response to the surrounding social environment" (Meister et al., 2014, pp. 491–492). Thus, each identity can be activated situationally, in response to a different trigger (Shih et al., 2006). In addition to simultaneously possessing a multitude of identities, individuals also move fluidly between various identities. These changes might not always be obvious to others, and so can be confusing to them (Swann et al., 2009). Meister et al. (2014, p. 492) proposed the concept that individuals organize their self-identities and that such organization is a "hierarchy with various identities having a probability of being invoked in a given situation or context." This hierarchical organization implies that an individual can choose and manage various identities both situationally and strategically.

Social Identities

Social identities are those that individuals develop socially and culturally. While these identities are likely to be of significance to the individual at the workplace, they are independent of identities attached to the work they do or their place of work. In the case of Asian women, arguably the main social identities of relevance are those attached to their ethnic group and gender. The former is manifest in two ways: as ethnic and as racial identities. Since they are distinct from other groups of women in the U.S., it would be more relevant to address the gender portion of their identity in the context of being Asian women, rather than as Asians and as women.

Ethnic and Racial Identity

As described above, identity refers to the psychological states of an individual that are affected by both internal and external factors. As we saw in the previous section, individuals typically deal with multiple identities, each of which can become more or less salient at different points in time. It is not unusual for individuals to experience conflict between different identities at certain times and in certain circumstances.

The notion of asymmetry in identities (in the workplace) and the subsequent stress individuals experience as a result of this asymmetry was studied by Meister et al. (2014, p. 488). They defined internal identity asymmetry as occurring when an individual believed there was an incongruence between who they really were and how they were perceived by others. External identity asymmetry occurred when there was incongruence between an individual's self-perception and how others perceived them. Both kinds of asymmetry caused anxiety and stress for the individual: directly in the case of internal asymmetry and indirectly in the case of external asymmetry. In the latter case, there would be a discrepancy between the responses the individual expected from others and the responses they received. Individuals attempted to resolve these asymmetries in various ways. They might try to change other people's perceptions to align those perceptions with their own, or they might choose to believe that others have changed their perceptions in that way. If those methods do not succeed, they might try to change their own self-perception to fit the perceptions of others.

Members of minority or low-status groups are likely to experience high levels of identity-related stress. In workplaces where they are few in numbers (tokens) and are highly visible, they could experience conflict "between positive social identity and distinctiveness" (Brewer, 1991, p. 479). Gushue et al. (2013, p. 346) commented, "in the US, people of color (non-White) may experience internalized racism as a result of constant exposure to blatant (externally defined) societal stereotypes." One reason for the stress that these individuals felt arose from the fact that, in order to accrue career and workplace-related benefits, they were required to suppress essential parts of their minority group identity. Eidheim (1969, p. 45) noted this trend in a study of members of the Lapp community in Norway, a traditionally lower socio-economic group, in their experience of attempting to gain material benefits.

The attempts of members of minority or low-status groups to negotiate their way in a majority or high-status group's culture manifest as acculturation processes. Acculturation can be described as a process by which "individuals change, both by being influenced by contact with another culture and by being participants in the general acculturation changes underway in their own culture" (Chang et al., 2005, p. 25). Ideally, acculturation should be a change that affects all groups; an individual from a minority group "selectively adapts and incorporates behaviors, values and cultural practices" that become more widely accepted and are adopted by different groups (Inman et al., 2001, p. 17). However, not all groups might (be required to) change to the same extent. Berry (1997, p. 8) noted that "in a plural society" where there are groups with different cultures, "not all groups are equal in power." Thus, more change is typically expected of groups with less power than of those that have more power.

Researchers have considered acculturation important in understanding different groups within a society. Suinn et al. (1995) considered acculturation useful to individuals in resolving conflicts, establishing values, and developing personality characteristics. At the same time, different individuals experience acculturation in different ways. Individual preferences for acculturation paths vary depending on the context, such as location and social environment (Berry, 1997, p. 12). Acculturation has been differentiated based on the degree of retention of the original (minority) culture versus the degree of contact/interaction with the other (majority) culture.

Thus, an individual's acculturation depends on the importance the individual places on identity in the minority group (and which parts of it) and how willing the individual is to be a participant in the majority group. Berry noted that such decisions need not necessarily be problematic for all individuals and that "not everyone experiences acculturative stress" (Berry, 1997, p. 12). According to (Farver et al., 2007), the acculturation process has different states: assimilation, marginalization, separation, and integration. In the assimilation stage the individual does not retain the original culture and has extensive contact with the other culture; in separation the individual maintains the original culture and has minimal contact with the other culture; in the marginalization state the individual neither retains the original culture nor has any contact with the other culture; and integration describes a situation in which an individual maintains the original culture and has extensive contact with the other culture. In practice, the integration or "bicultural acculturation" strategy appeared to be a "consistent predictor of more positive outcomes" (Berry, 1997, p. 27). However, integration can occur only when the other (majority) group agrees to it. In other words, integration cannot be the choice of only the minority group member; it requires "mutual accommodation" (Berry, 1997, p. 10).

In contrast with acculturation, enculturation refers to identity development within a group. According to Kim and Hong (2004), it is the process by which an individual is socialized and becomes familiar with the norms and values of their group. Farver et al. (2007, p. 186) noted that enculturation enables individuals to "function as competent individuals in their societies (cultural groups)." This process can play an important role in the formation of an ethnic identity, which can be understood as self-identification with a group that includes a "sense of belonging, attitudes towards group members, [and a] degree of affiliation and involvement" (Farver et al., 2007, p. 186).

Ethnic identity is rooted in a sense of belonging to a group where members have "shared ethnic characteristics" (Ibrahim et al., 1997, p. 36). Enculturation and acculturation can be interpreted as socialization processes through which ethnic identity is formed. Some constituents of ethnic identity include "general knowledge, beliefs, and expectations of the ethnic group; [a] cognitive processing framework to perceive objects, situations, events, people; [a] basis for behavior" (Ibrahim et al., 1997, p. 36). Identification with an ethnic group can vary in the individual's degree of affiliation and involvement with that group (Farver et al., 2007, p. 186). This identification also includes attitudes towards other groups' members.

The ethnic identity development process, as described by Phinney (1990), goes through various stages including an unquestioned acceptance of an identity, questioning, exploring its various facets, and consolidation into an accepted understanding. Acceptance of the group's "values, beliefs, behaviors, conventions, and customs" (Dasgupta, 1998, p. 953) is important. While the degree of acceptance could vary, the individual must be familiar with these features of the culture.

Dhingra (2007, p. 13) differentiated racial identity from ethnic identity. Ethnic identity is related to group membership that is directed inward towards that group. It refers to a sense of self as "a member of an ethnic group, that is, a group that considers itself having and is believed by others to have a shared culture, geographic origin, history and possibly interests." In contrast, racial identity is directed outward and arises as a response to the behaviors of other groups. It is a sense of self as "a member of a racial group, that is, a group of people distinguished from others based on supposedly common physical characteristics and stereotyped culture."

Gushue et al. (2013, p. 345) noted that racial identity includes "beliefs, values, cognitive styles and attitudes" towards those in an individual's own group as well as towards people in other racial groups. Individuals develop a racial identity over time and as a result of changes in their own attitudes, emotions, and behaviors with regard to their ethnic identity.

Racial identity development can also be viewed as a process. Different stages in this process include conformity (when racial stereotypes are accepted); dissonance (when the individual feels conflicted and confused about their racial identity); rejection (of the racial stereotype associated with that identity); and internalization of a positive identity (Gushue et al., 2013, p. 346). In the pluralistic society of the U.S., minority members often reported feeling greater dissonance associated with their racial identities (Gushue et al., 2013, p. 354). Their responses to this dissonance were likely to be emotional. Indeed, some minority members resorted to emotionally cutting-off from their ethnic culture as a way to deal with the conflict regarding their racial identities (Gushue et al., 2013, p. 354).

Asian American Identities

The presence and prominence of Asian Americans in U.S. society has been growing over the years. Projections show that about 10% of the U.S. population will have some Asian ancestry by 2050 (Kim & Hong, 2004, p. 15). Asian Americans' participation in economic (business), political, and other social activities has also been on the upswing. Thus, developing a clearer and deeper understanding of Asian American identities is important.

Barth (1969, p. 10) described an ethnic group as one that is, in a general sense, "largely biologically self-perpetuating; shares fundamental cultural values, realized in overt unity in cultural forms; makes up a field of communication and interaction; has a membership that identifies itself and is identified by others, as constituting a category, distinguishable from other categories." Barth (1969, p. 15) also emphasized that an ethnic group is defined more strongly by its self-determined boundaries, rather than by "the cultural stuff that is in it." This could explain how ethnic identity can be both important and powerful. It can be affirming to the individual, as a "positive self-concept" that "consciously anchors an individual to a particular ethnic group" (Dasgupta,1998, p. 953). For minority and low-status groups, ethnic groups can also provide a space where members do not have to be concerned about how they are viewed by majority group members.

As has been discussed in previous chapters, there is no single Asian American identity. Further, group members have multidimensional identities, including one that is Asian (Ibrahim et al., 1997, p. 34). Complex identities are a shared experience of minorities in American society. Their self-concept necessarily includes both "the way others define them" and "the way they wish to be considered" (Ibrahim et al., 1997, p. 35). Thus, among others, Asian American identities include ethnic, racial, generational, and gender dimensions.

Ethnic identity can be of different types depending on an individual's degree of enculturation and mode of acculturation. Fong (1997) referred to Chow's delineation of four types of Asian American ethnic identities: traditionalist, assimilationist, pluralist, and ambivalent. These types seem aligned to Berry's models for acculturation. As per Chow's model, traditionalists (high Asian, low American) were individuals living within ethnic geographical neighborhoods and subscribing strongly to values of obedience and family honor. Assimilationists (low Asian, high American) were individuals who questioned tradition, defied their parents, and mostly rejected their ethnic culture. This rejection could be the result of triggering events and associated identity crises; their self-worth was tied to their acceptance in general society, particularly by Caucasians. Pluralists (high Asian, high American) were individuals who balanced their Asian and American identities; their sense of self-worth was based on pride in their heritage as well as being part of the American mainstream. Ambivalent individuals (low Asian, low American) did not find comfort in either Asian or mainstream American cultures and appeared to reject both. They could experience socio-cultural isolation, and their sense of self was tied to their individual selves.

Asian immigrants can retain a strong sense of culture from their countries of origin and their customs (Inman et al., 2007). Depending on the degree to which they actively practice these customs, those effects diminish quickly or slowly in succeeding generations. Both the family and the community play a role in this regard. In a study of Indian women in Atlanta, Manohar (2013, p. 26) observed that community building was primarily done by women, especially mothers. Iwamoto et al. (2013) commented that community events and exposure to cultural practices, such as religious rituals, music, and dance, are also important to ethnic identity development. Aligning with these findings, Kurien (1999) noted that ethnic communities can be created at three levels— households, local community centers, and pan-ethnic associations.

Chang et al. (2005, p. 36) noted that ethnic identity included both overt and covert elements. Overt or externally visible aspects included language, food, clothing (physical appearance), and participation in cultural practices. Covert or internal aspects included personal cues, values, norms, and attitudes.

Inman et al. (2007) commented that Asian Indians seem to favor an alternation model where they hold on to what they perceive as core ethnic cultural values but are largely adaptable concerning etiquette and behaviors. This can be interpreted to mean that they placed importance on retaining internal and less visible aspects of ethnic identity while relinquishing external and visible ones. Chang et al. (2005, p. 37) attempted to classify acculturation modes based on the relative importance individuals placed on internal versus external aspects. According to their study, those identifying only as Americans placed great importance on external indicators rather than on internal ones; those identifying primarily as Asian were the reverse, basing their identities almost completely on internal cues and cultural values. Finally, those identifying as both Asian and American gave importance to both external and internal aspects. The authors also note that if community resources are lacking, individuals might not have an opportunity to "use ethnic languages, participate in cultural traditions, or celebrate ethnic holidays" and so would "have no choice but to adopt ethnic cultural elements that are less overt and more internal, such as cultural identity and values" (Chang et al., 2005, p. 37). These individuals might appear less Asian and more American but could have a strong sense of Asian identity.

Iwamoto et al. (2013, p. 225) noted that few studies have examined how Asian Americans respond to racial discrimination, how they internalize racial messages, and what effects these experiences have on their identities. Devos and Sadler (2019, p. 182) noted that "prior research showed Asian Americans seen as implicitly less American than Whites." In the past, Asian Americans have experienced what can be termed as the "perpetual foreigner syndrome" (Hyun, 2005). This is the phenomenon of being perceived as foreigners, regardless of how long they (or their ancestors) have been in the U.S. (Devos & Sadler, 2019). This perception might be erased in the future when demographic changes affect the prevailing understanding of "who is an American." In the meantime, explicit experiences of being challenged to continually prove their American-ness can affect individuals. Chang et al. (2005, p. 37) noted that the more experiences of such kind an individual had, the "less they identified as American."

Researchers have attempted to understand ethnic identities based on how their cultures differ. Hofstede's model (arguably) has been the most influential in this regard. The main dimensions of difference between cultures, as described by Hofstede (and described in Chapter 3), are power distance, individualism/collectivism, masculinity/femininity, and uncertainty avoidance. In Hofstede's modeling, Asian cultures are understood to be more collectivist with higher power distance (Rosenthal & Feldman, 1990). However, Asian Americans are influenced by both American and Asian norms, and their cultures include features of both. Since they are in a minority, Asian Americans need to strategically choose aspects of both cultures to "overcome barriers of race and ethnicity" (Tsai et al., 2001, p. 286). Hence, Asian Americans are bicultural, needing to be aware of, and even well-versed in, the norms, values, and customs of both the mainstream American culture and their own ethnic cultures.

Phinney (1988) noted that Asian Americans typically began a process of searching for identity during adolescence. Dhingra (2007, p. 64) noted that this quest might begin in response to experiences of racism. Asian Americans might actively seek an ethnic identity and even build ties to their parents' countries of origin. Farver et al. (2007, p. 207) noted that both generations maintained "varying degrees of connections with both cultures on their own terms and as it makes sense to them." These varied choices of individuals can result in the creation of new acculturation styles and ethnic identities.

According to Kim and Hong (2004), cultural values important to Asian Americans include collectivism, conformity to norms, deference to authority figures, emotional restraint, filial piety, hierarchical family structure, and humility. American society is commonly described as having an individualistic orientation where members are encouraged to view themselves as "separate from others" and "demonstrate uniqueness through self-enhancement" (Tsai et al., 2001, p. 285). In contrast, members of Asian cultures view themselves as connected to others and are encouraged to "maintain relationships through self-effacement" (Tsai et al., 2001, p. 285). This difference is reflected in cultural attitudes: mainstream American society promotes autonomy and outer-directed behavior whereas Asians tend to be more self-contained (Rosenthal & Feldman, 1990).

Another major difference between mainstream American and Asian cultures is in the sense of self (Ibrahim et al., 1997). In American culture, the orientation of self is autonomous: separate from others and independent. In Asian cultures, the orientation is allocentric: connected to others, mainly family, and interdependent (Farver et al., 2007, p. 189). Due to these differences, autonomous individualist attitudes can clash with allocentric collectivist ones (Varghese & Jenkins, 2009, p. 235). Behaviorally this can manifest in the expression of emotion. While individualist cultures might encourage the expression of emotion as a method of explicit communication, collectivist cultures tend to "discourage the expression of emotion that might undermine group cohesion" (Durik et al., 2006, p. 437). Studies have shown that Asian Americans tend to consider expressions of emotions such as amusement, anger, contempt, disgust, fear, happiness, sadness, and surprise as "less appropriate than do European Americans," especially in the workplace (Durik et al., 2006, p. 438). This finding was borne out in other studies as well. White women were stereotyped as most likely to express emotion in the workplace, and white men as the least likely to do so. Both Asian men and Asian women fell between these two poles (Durik et al., 2006, p. 441).

The importance of family in Asian and Asian American cultures has been noted by many researchers. Family dynamics can impact an individual's sense of identity and self-worth (Gecas, 1982, p. 9). According to Rosenthal and Feldman (1990, p. 497), in Asian cultures, there is an emphasis on maintaining the family through "cohesion among family members, dependence on family, unquestioning acceptance of parental authority, preservation of status and profound loyalty." The view of family could differ between generations, however: immigrants are more comfortable in organized family structures with clear role definitions, whereas their children might view the same structures and roles as restrictive regulations (Rosenthal & Feldman, 1990).

Researchers have proposed the view that "training" is a prototypical Asian American parenting style characterized by physical closeness, a degree of parental control, and emphasis on education (Farver et al., 2007). Within this broad grouping, researchers have found that individual parents had different styles. Some Asian parents were comfortable with a traditional, authoritative style where parents were considered as unquestioned authority figures. Asian parents who were more assimilated or integrated into American norms softened, while not relinquishing control completely.

Research has shown that immigrants develop their ethnic identities in their countries of origin and internalize their cultural values. However, the second generation faces struggles in the effort to balance two cultures and internalize two different value systems (Varghese & Jenkins, 2009). As could be expected, immigrants uphold Asian cultural norms and values more strongly than later generations (Kim & Hong, 2004). However, even immigrants can find it difficult to adhere to a culture based on past experiences. Consequently, they sometimes create a version of their culture that does not exactly resemble the one they left behind or that culture's current circumstances, or this new version might significantly overlap with mainstream American culture (Farver et al., 2007).

Identity work, which is the process of "creating a personal meaning of a social identity that aligns with one's self-concept" (Dhingra, 2007, p. 65), is likely to be a lifelong process for most immigrants, and perhaps for the second generation as well. Ideally, they would be able to realize that Asian American is an important identity, but it is not the only one available to them (Phinney, 1988), and hopefully they will become successful in managing their multidimensional, sometimes hyphenated, identities (Butt et al., 2012).

The Model Minority Stereotype

Stereotypes can have a deep impact on how individuals view themselves. Indeed, the difference between how an individual views herself and how she is stereotypically viewed leads to identity conflict. This conflict is accentuated in the work environment, where such differences can impact both the individual's experience and career progression.

Stereotypes are cognitive understandings about groups (Fiske et al., 2002, p. 878). Two dimensions are understood to broadly describe the content of any stereotype—warmth and competence (Fiske et al., 2002, p. 878)—although these need not be the only dimensions. Abele and Wojciszke (2007, p. 753), referring to these dimensions as "communion" and "agency," stated that groups can be stereotyped as warm or cold (communion) and as competent or incompetent (agency). Similarly, the mixed stereotypes hypothesis of Fiske et al. (2002, p. 880) proposed that stereotypes of low-status groups are one of two types: high warmth but low competence, or low warmth but high competence. The former is applied to compliant subordinates and the latter to successful competitors. The model minority stereotype portrays Asian Americans as "too competent, too ambitious, too hardworking and, simultaneously, not sociable" (Fiske et al., 2002, p. 880). According to Fiske et al. (2002, p. 898), this stereotype should be understood to mean that a strategy of cooperation will not be effective for Asians in altering the stereotype to include warmth. Only the reduction of competence (hence competitiveness) could do that.

Stereotypes have been known to be persistent and difficult to change. They have numerous negative effects on stereotyped individuals, including psychological, emotional, and material impacts. Examples of psychological and emotional issues can range from identity conflicts to stereotype threats. A stereotype threat is reflected in a behavior of an individual that confirms a negative characteristic of the stereotype (Steele & Aronson, 1995, p. 797). While this might appear counter-intuitive, it has been observed in practice in a variety of situations. Any stereotyped person can experience this phenomenon, even if they do not believe in that stereotype (Steele & Aronson, 1995, p. 798).

Asians can experience a model minority stereotype and the attached stereotype threat. The model minority model for Asians includes negative traits of passivity, a lack of social and political skills, and a lack of the aggressiveness required for leadership positions. Nichols (2017) interpreted these negative characterizations as the racialization of the Asian model minority stereotype. Many Asian women themselves emphasized that corporate culture values extraversion and outgoing personalities. Thus, the stereotyping of Asian women as passive places them in a disadvantageous position (Nichols, 2017). Asian American women perceived that they were viewed as "obedient workhorses" but that they "lacked the assertiveness and soft skills to be genuine leaders" (Nichols, 2017). Thus, despite the seemingly complimentary model minority stereotype of possessing the valuable qualities of being hard workers and high achievers, Asian American women are rarely found in leadership positions they would seem to merit. Nichols (2017) commented that the Asian model minority stereotype also appears to serve the purpose of denying discrimination by highlighting the educational and professional achievements of Asian women. Thus, Asian women seemingly appear to require special consideration as high-educated achievers, while at the same time they are denied equal treatment based on the negative traits of the stereotype.

Asian American women need to be aware of the potency of stereotypes in the workplace. They are viewed in ways that differ from how other women are viewed; namely, as more competent but less warm. This image is in opposition to the general stereotype of women as more people-oriented. Asian American women need strategies and tactics to deal with these stereotypes and align their responses to their ethnic identities as well.

The Significance of Ethnic Identity

Ethnic identity can be viewed as part of social identity or as a key component in an individual's sense of belonging. Phinney (1990, p. 501) noted that ethnic identity becomes salient and relevant only when two or more groups interact with each other. The components of ethnic identity are "self-identification, chosen label, sense of belonging, ethnic involvement and participation, and friendships" (Phinney, 1990, p. 503). Thus, ethnic identity can manifest as overt cultural aspects such as language, food, and behaviors or as covert ones, such as shared values and attitudes (Chang et al., 2005).

Developing a sense of belonging is challenging for all minority groups. Sue (2009, p. 409) noted that in the U.S., the "issues that have confronted different ethnic groups are same." According to Phinney (1988), there has been a strong link between ethnic identity and self-esteem for individuals from ethnic or minority groups. Moreover, developing a secure ethnic identity requires the individual to explore and understand the meaning of being a member of a minority or low-status group. Abele and Wojciszke (2007) pointed to the different aspects by which an individual judges herself versus those by which she is judged by others. Identity development in the context of self-judgment relates to ambition, dominance, competence, desire to be part of a larger group, and emotional expression. Responses to judgment by others in the workplace are related to choices of "intellectual vs. social desirability, and competence vs morality." Judgment by others includes stereotyping, which affects stereotyped individuals in a multitude of negative ways. For example, as was discussed above, stereotype threats cause anxiety and can lower performance (Shih et al., 2006).

Ethnic identity refers to the degree of attachment an individual has to their group; it is "important to [the] well-being of individuals" (Nguyen et al., 2015, pp. 273–274). Phinney (1988, p. 5) noted that ethnic identity helps individuals "to develop a sense of well-being and to reduce self-hatred." A strong sense of belonging and positive feelings about one's group can lead to openness and positive feelings towards other groups as well (Phinney et al., 1997). Fostering these positive feelings can help the individual to effectively respond to "the dominant group's often disparaging views" (Phinney, 1990, p. 499). Nguyen et al. (2015, p. 274) commented that individuals who had a "strong ethnic identity and affiliation to their ethnic heritage and community" were better able to negotiate acculturation and less likely to experience culture shock. Thus, a strong ethnic identity has benefits for the individual in their self-concept and in their interactions with members of other groups. However, Phinney (1988) also noted that while ethnic identity development often starts in childhood and adolescence, it can continue into adulthood and can even be a lifelong process.

Identities and Roles of Asian Women in America

Asian women, particularly those working in corporate America, manage a multitude of identities. Their identities are affected by factors such as generational status, socio-economic situation, and countries of origin in their ancestry.

Some factors are common to the experience of Asian women across various cultures and countries of origin. Yoon et al. (2019, p. 122) commented that despite variation in cultures across Asian countries, most have some form of patriarchy at work. The identities of immigrant women are significantly impacted by the countries where they grew up and attended schooling. Thus, most immigrant Asian women might be socialized with gender role expectations that primarily relegate women to the home sphere. Many immigrants maintain strong ties to family and friends in their countries of origin. Thus, Asian women might find themselves being compared with their counterparts in their countries of origin, as well as in the U.S. (Srinivasan, 2001).

As noted previously, many Asian women (immigrants) find that they need to enter the workforce once they are in the U.S. (Yamanaka & McClelland, 1994). This means that their motivation to work outside the home is primarily economic, to support themselves and their families. However, Asian women could enter the workforce for other reasons, such as a desire to supplement family income towards upward socio-economic mobility or individual professional ambitions. Whatever the motivation, once they are in the workforce, their identities will need to include professional ones as well.

Yamanaka and McClelland (1994, p. 87) noted that the type of earned work Asian women took up depended on the (individual and group) resources available to them and their life situations. These researchers added other strategies to the broad categories of economic adaptation for ethnic women (described in Chapter 5): assimilation (working hard to attempt mainstream employment); dual economy (taking jobs with low growth potential primarily done by immigrants); ethnic enclaves (businesses aimed at niche ethnic groups); middlemen (the businesses that connect larger companies with labor pools); affirmative action (job opportunities that had not been available previously); brain drain (professionals who had been educated and trained in another country). The last two categories were added to reflect opportunities and behaviors that affected immigrant Asian women. Their choices among these pathways impact their identity development. Yamanaka and McClelland (1994) noted that educated and professional Asian women fit best into the assimilation mold.

In their home environments, Asian women might have to manage specific roles. A role refers to social expectations regarding the behavior of an individual as related to the individual's specific social position (Callero, 1994, p. 229). For example, traditional female gender roles in almost all societies emphasize acceptance, caring, and taking responsibility for the home while discouraging aggressiveness (Eagly & Steffen, 1986, p. 310). In several Asian countries, gender roles are unambiguously demarcated and separate (Ibrahim et al., 1997, p. 40). This understanding of roles changes over time as Asian women and their families face different realities in the U.S. Despite the changes they might undergo, however, most immigrant cultures continue to display expectations that women (daughters) rather than men (sons) will adhere to traditional cultural ideals and ensure the continuity of cultural practices (Nguyen et al., 2015, p. 275). Asian American women can thus experience varying degrees of "gender role pressure within [the] community" (Dasgupta, 1998, p. 969). This is true of both married and unmarried women. Subramanian (2013, p. 312) noted that a woman who behaves in a manner inconsistent with the desired cultural image is viewed "as a threat not just to her own future, but also the future of a family, community and ethnic or religious group."

Women in Asia are expected to uphold certain cultural values and beliefs, including "strong attachment to, and sense of responsibility to, family; family harmony and interdependence" (Varghese & Jenkins, 2009). In a study of professional women in India, Naqvi (2011) observed that while many women reported that their parents had encouraged them to seek employment, many quit their jobs after marriage and motherhood. Even those who continued to work gave more importance to their husband's job. It appeared that most of the respondents aspired mainly to be good mothers and role models; they seemed not to aspire to obtain work achievements in the same way. One respondent stated, "In my family, I am the only one who will play my role. No one can replace me. At work, if I am not there, someone else will do my job." Similar sentiments and expectations were reported by Chinese women. Fong (1997) noted that Chinese culture "values women as good wives and good mothers as well as valuing their contributions to the well-being of the family, be it working at home or engaging in employment."

However, once in America, immigrant Asian women seem to renegotiate gender roles as their lifestyles become different from those in their countries of origin. Bhalla (2008, pp. 73–74) reported on letters to the editor in a publication called *India Abroad* from the 1980s–90s "on [the] topic of Asian Indian men and housework." The letters indicated that, over the decades, Asian (Indian) women were moving away from "traditional identities as wives and mothers" to "dual identities as wives and workers." Moreover, it appeared that these women intended the inclusion of a professional identity in their larger identities to be permanent. To this end, they encouraged their daughters to be career-oriented and their sons to take on home responsibilities. In other words, they perceived the need "to instill new (gender-egalitarian) values in their children" (Bhalla, 2008, p. 82). Fong (1997) also noted that "the sex role attitudes of Asian women have begun to shift from a traditional stance to a more egalitarian one (equality between sexes)."

While the values of Asian American women in giving importance to education, an ethics of hard work, and achievement can be similar to general American values, marriage remains one area of difference. In general, Asian women have greater marital stability (Fong, 1997), although this might be attributable to their flexibility and desire to uphold cultural expectations. In most Asian cultures, marriage is viewed as a relationship not between two individuals but between two families (Varghese & Jenkins, 2009). Thus, being a wife and mother might have special significance in Asian women's identities.

Identity choices vary across generations, even among Asian women with a shared country of origin. For instance, immigrants can arrive in the U.S. "steeped in gendered values" (Srinivasan, 2001, p. 137), which might persist for some time. However, their daughters, women in the next generation, are socialized in American society and are likely to have a quite different gender identity. Indeed, generation, education level, and socio-economic position can all affect gender identity (Ibrahim et al., 1997, p. 40). Ethnic identity too varies across generations. Srinivasan (2001) commented that being Indian has a different meaning for immigrant women and for their daughters. Immigrants have a clear sense of their ethnic identity, having been socialized in that culture's norms and values. Additionally, they are typically focused on economic and social survival. They might be comfortable viewing themselves as bicultural. On the other hand, second-generation women can experience conflict between the values of Asian and mainstream American cultures (Ibrahim et al., 1997, p. 25). According to Inman et al. (2001, p. 18), conflict surrounding cultural values is "an experience of negative affect (guilt, anxiety, etc.) and cognitive contradictions that result from contending simultaneously with the values and behavioral expectations that are internalized and those that are imposed." Since these cultures differ widely along some dimensions, second-generation women might struggle to choose value systems to form an ethnic identity. Srinivasan (2001, p. 138) noted that "first generation women do not have so much of a problem" with such conflict "since they have dichotomized or compartmentalized the two cultures."

Some researchers offer an optimistic path forward for Asian American women in their quests for identity. Fong (1997, p. 2) hoped that "in the midst of conflicting values, identity crises and consciousness-raising, Asian American women" can build "their Asian American womanhood." From an individual rather than collective perspective, Inman et al. (2001, p. 18) noted that some Asian women negotiate a balance by holding on to "'central values' related to family relationships, while adapting to the pragmatic aspects of survival such as the use of English language." Further, the researchers observed that it is easier to change old behaviors and adopt new ones rather than acquire (new) cultural values (Inman et al., 2001, p. 17). Second-generation women growing up in American society are "more acculturated to a racialized society" (Inman, 2006, p. 309). Sometimes the feeling of being an outsider can lead individuals to seek closer family bonds, which would resonate with traditional Asian values upholding the importance of family (Ibrahim et al., 1997). Finally, and perhaps surprisingly, Inman (2006, p. 308) noted that it appeared that "higher education does not translate to less culture retention or conflict."

Identities Related to the Work Environment

Asian women working in corporate organizations have identities beyond their personal and social ones, such as those related to work. Work-related identities are linked to the activities, tasks, and roles in the work they do, as well as to membership in work-related organizations and occupations (Meister et al., 2014, p. 492).

Work identities change over time, depending on the situations, environments, and individual choices of the employee. Work identities are viewed positively by the individual when they are associated with "virtuous qualities" or "character strengths" (Dutton et al., 2010, p. 269). This was the case in the study of Tamil moms in Atlanta discussed in Chapter 5; women in that group viewed work as important for socio-economic and familial (role-modeling) reasons. Dutton et al. (2010, p. 269) noted that individuals like to feel good about the work they do and often adapt their identities for this reason.

In this section, we discuss professional identity and organizational identity. While professional identity is based on the individual's profession or type of work, it is distinct from organizational identity, which is dependent on the organization where the individual happens to be an employee. An employee's organizational identity is of significance to the organization and to the employee as well because it is related to the sense of belonging the employee feels and contributes to motivation, effort, and organizational citizenship. Organizational identity is anchored to the organization while professional identity moves with the individual.

Professional Identity

In the U.S., work is a "pervasive life domain and a salient source of meaning and self-definition for most individuals" (Dutton et al., 2010, p. 265). As with social identity, professional identity development is also an individual process that occurs over time. Ibarra (1999, p. 765) commented that professional identity is influenced by "varied experiences and meaningful feedback" that allows the individual to "gain insight about their central and enduring preferences, talents and values." However, the same experiences and feedback could affect different individuals in different ways, underlining the variability of professional identity.

Individuals differ in their choices of which identities they consider "central to their self-concept" (Dutton et al., 2010, p. 284). A professional identity may or may not be important to their self-concept. However, Asian women immigrants often realize they have to work and consequently see working as a norm for their daughters as well. In other words, a significant percentage of Asian women in America factor in some kind of work outside of the home as part of their life experiences. Thus, it appears that they accept the importance of a professional identity.

Creed et al. (2010, p. 1339) noted that a positive professional identity can be a "significant driver of action" spurring individuals to put in effort when compared to professional peers across organizational boundaries. A professional identity can lead an individual to challenge directives if their autonomy and self-concept as an expert are threatened. On the other hand, if an individual's professional identity rests on certain ways in which their work is done, a strong identity can cause them to resist change. Professional identities can change over time, depending on the work individuals do and the work roles they are assigned (Ibarra, 1999, p. 765). Individuals can learn to manage their professional identities through their choices of work, the acquisition of human capital related to work, and their attitudes towards work.

Professional identities are significantly affected by workplace perceptions of an individual. Indeed, most people quickly realize that perceptions matter in the workplace (Meister et al., 2014, p. 488) and that they need to be aware of how others view them not just when considering their career security and advancement, but also in getting everyday work done. An inaccurate assessment of how they are perceived can lead to misdirected efforts and erroneous expectations. "Perceived professional image" refers to an individual's belief about how others view them in the workplace (Meister et al., 2014, p. 492).

However, there is room for error in this image; there could be a gap between what an individual believes is a perception of themselves and what the perception actually is (Meister et al., 2014, p. 493). This disjunction can lead to identity asymmetry, both internal and external, with the related stress and negative impact on employee performance (Meister et al., 2014, p. 488).

Organizational Identity

Ashforth et al. (2008) studied the meaning and importance of organizational identification, which they viewed as an individual's attempt to find a place for herself or himself in the organization. They proposed a model for the process of development and manifestation of organizational identity (Ashforth et al., 2008, p. 328) which shows that the core of an individual's identity (including the responses to phrases like, "I am," "I value," "I feel about") feeds into the content of that identity (including: "I care about," "I want," "I believe," "I can do"). In turn, the content of identity feeds into behaviors related to identity (including: "I do"). They noted that the outcomes of this process of developing an organizational identity are "self enhancement, self-knowledge, and coherence" (Ashforth et al., 2008, p. 333).

According to Brickson (2005), organizational identity can be viewed from three perspectives: individualistic, relational, and collectivist. Individuals identify with specific roles and jobs as well as with teams and other contacts, rather than with the abstract notion of an organization (Ashforth et al., 2008, p. 326). Some identity traits related to these perspectives include "top performer as individual; accommodating and loyal to team members as relational; promoting sustainability as collectivist" (Brickson, 2005, p. 577). Organizational identity has been studied more from the individualistic perspective of how an individual views herself or himself as an organizational member rather than their view of themselves as a team member (Ashforth et al., 2018, p. 28). The reason for this emphasis might be that individualistic perspectives have a more direct impact on motivation and performance. Additionally, teams' composition and assigned purpose can change frequently (Ashforth et al., 2008, p. 328). Another aspect of identity that can appear in organizations is when an employee identifies closely with another employee, typically someone at a higher status (Ashforth et al., 2018). This perception of closeness could be helpful or harmful (Ashforth et al., 2018, p. 29), but this identification need not be based on all attributes and need not be relational. Such personal identification could occur in a mentor relationship, for example. Another important identity in organizations is that of a leader. Employees can choose to take on a follower identity by accepting someone else as a leader. In turn, an individual can attempt to create a leader identity by using social interactions to get others to grant them that identity (DeRue & Ashford, 2010, p. 629).

Organizational identities are formed through intentional actions by organizations as well as individuals' experiences. The processes of "sense-breaking and sense-making" serve to "strip away old identities and establish new ones" (Ashforth et al., 2008, p. 341). A strong organizational culture, where there is pressure on employees to think and act in certain ways, can serve this process. Intentional efforts to create an organizational culture might not work, as was discussed in the context of diversity training programs. For example, minority employees might view the under-representation of their group at higher levels as the true picture of how they are viewed, rather than believing what the organization conveys through explicit mission statements (Swann et al., 2009). Similarly, praise without other tangible rewards would not change an employee's sense of how their social or ethnic identity is viewed (Swann et al., 2009).

When individuals work at an organization for a period of time, their self-identity can start to "merge with the company's identity (Ibarra, 2018)." This might be actively encouraged by the organization as a means to enhance performance and create a sense of belonging (which could increase retention). At the same time, individuals often move within the organization, taking on different roles or even different types of jobs. Ibarra (2018) noted that changing jobs can be a major transition for employees with a significant impact on their identity. Swann et al. (2009) noted that individuals' self-identity is chronic and long-lasting; they perform well when they perceive that this identity is supported within the organization.

Management researchers have studied workplace-related employee attitudes such as job satisfaction (positive or negative feelings about the job, its environment, and their co-workers), job involvement (degree of dedication), corporate citizenship (loyalty to the organization), and employee engagement (connection to the organization). These are some of the issues that affect employee job performance and length of job tenure at the organization. The degree to which an individual identifies as a member of the organization is a critical factor determining these outcomes. It is possible for an employee to be satisfied with the work they do and to have a positive professional identity yet also be dissatisfied with the organization. For instance, Herzberg differentiated between key factors that contributed to employee satisfaction, such as achievement and the work itself, and those that caused dissatisfaction, such as company policy and administration (Herzberg, 2003).

Identity Strategies

An identity is not simply a static sense of self; it is dynamic and changes over time. Individuals have multiple identities, each of which evolves in response to external and internal changes. In the organizational environment, identities matter in terms of individual work and performance, relationships with others, and in contribution to the organization. Thus, individuals cannot focus only on the self-perception aspect of their identities; they need to be aware of how other people perceive them as well. A mismatch in these two perceptions can lead to many negative personal and workplace outcomes. In other words, identities need to be managed. Impression management refers to techniques and tactics that individuals can use to influence others' perceptions of themselves.

Managing Multiple Identities

As discussed in the previous section, most individuals have combinations of personal, social, and work identities. Asian women's social identities include ethnic and racial identities, which refer to their status as women and as women of Asian ancestry in the U.S. Further, Asian women in corporate America also have professional and organizational identities.

Ibarra (1999) discussed the notion of provisional selves as they relate to identity. According to Ibarra, individuals go through a process of "building a repertoire of possible selves." They then find out what constitutes a "credible role performance" and allowable variations for a provisional self. Ibarra noted that individuals pick and choose aspects of such provisional selves based on what they observe and according to their sense of self and authenticity. They check if the role is feasible for themselves by comparing the role's expectations and requirements with their values and preferences. If these are aligned, they adopt the provisional self as an identity (Ibarra, 1999, p. 776). Individuals might fashion selves to portray a role while drawing on "styles and tactics that felt familiar and authentic." Sometimes these choices turn out to be "inappropriate for [the] new role" (Ibarra, 1999, p. 779). They would then need to either find another role or adapt their approach. Sometimes they might try out completely new and even uncomfortable approaches in a quest to be accepted in a role. Also, some individuals might try to combine old and familiar tactics with new ones "to form a vague amalgam" (Ibarra, 1999, p. 779). Thus, individuals undergo a process of experimentation, using and discarding approaches, in an attempt to create a proto-identity. They might later choose to develop some of these potential selves into identities.

Swann et al. (2009) discussed the process by which an individual negotiates identities. According to Swann et al., the individual's identity-related personal and social goals are a result of past experiences and relationships. In the work environment, the individual might also have work-related goals, such as competence and autonomy, that are associated with the identity. Identity negotiation is a process between the individual and a perceiver. The perceiver's identity and goals are important in the process. The individual negotiates with the perceiver by communicating (sometimes indirectly through signals and cues) and finding opportunities that allow for expressing identity in a certain way and through certain behaviors. It is important to recognize that the perceiver (who could be the organization) is not merely the recipient but also a participant who communicates in the process. The perceiver could communicate formally, informally, or through signals. Formal responses could include training programs, while informal ones could involve socialization through employee groups, and implicit responses could include psychological contracts with the organization. The resulting identity that the perceiver develops may or may not be desirable in terms of meeting the individual's goals. If it is not, the individual has to choose between changing their approach and pushing for acceptance.

Individuals whose identity in the workplace faces resistance and non-acceptance, but who are unwilling or unable to relinquish that identity, sometimes attempt institutional change. Creed et al. (2010, p. 1337) noted that such individuals "see themselves as agents of institutional change in response to their experiences of institutional contradictions and marginalization." Meyerson (2004) referred to them as "tempered radicals," noting that they are organizational employees who do not seem mainstream. Meyerson (2004) noted that this phenomenon can be found in different industries, roles, and situations. Tempered radicals are unwilling to change or hide certain key aspects of their identities, which they view as non-negotiable, even if those aspects are not accepted or supported in the organization. For example, these might include observing specific religious occasions or sexual orientation. According to Meyerson (2004), tempered radicals succeeded in gaining acceptance and support by broadly following the same methods. Effective strategies included clarifying the issue from other personal, performance, or organizational matters; galvanizing support and action by framing the issue broadly; focusing on internal organizational culture; and actively soliciting and forming a support collective that includes different groups. These strategies are supported by recommendations by Creed et al. (2010, p. 1337) for employees in this position to reconcile identities, lay claim to a role, and use the role.

Quite often individuals who experience challenges to their identities are at the border between two cultures. Some researchers have referred to them as marginal individuals who need to have (at least) what DuBois called "double consciousness" (LaFromboise et al., 1993). Even though they face great challenges in the workplace in terms of reconciling their identities, marginal employees also have potential advantages. Being members of different groups, they can choose the group (or groups) in which they want to be an active member. Thus, they can reduce frustrations when being in one group does not meet their expectations by simply moving to another group (LaFromboise et al., 1993, p. 395). Thus, some women could deal with workplace challenges by making their parent identity salient (Mainiero & Sullivan, 2005). On the other hand, such flexibility might not help them in attaining certain personal or work-related goals, especially if one or more of their identities is associated with a low-status group.

Individuals can also pursue identity management strategies that lead them to disavow certain identities. Typically, these are identities associated with low-status or minority groups. They might try to leave their group and pass as a member of a high-status one (Phinney, 1990). However, in the case of certain ethnic identities where physical appearance is a determining factor of membership, this might not an option. Rejection by the majority group can then lead the individual to identify more strongly with their ethnic group, develop pride in it, and stress its distinctiveness. Dhingra (2007, p. 119) noted that Asian Americans sometimes "adopted a complementary strategy of highlighting both their acculturation and their cultural distinctiveness" in an attempt to combat racial stereotyping that cast them as foreigners. Thus, rather than "rejecting a 'spoiled' identity," the individual can develop "tactics to buffer against negative situations and take advantage of positive ones" (Shih et al., 2006).

In some cases individuals can also move nimbly between identities in pursuit of an overarching goal. Asian Indian women in America, according to Srinivasan (2001), viewed themselves as culturally pluralistic. They appeared to differentiate between different situations in which they were comfortable with a different identity. Thus, the contexts in which they considered themselves Indian were different from those in which they considered themselves American

(Srinivasan, 2001, p. 150). It appeared that in each case they stressed their sameness with members of the group on core aspects of their self-concept (Brubaker & Cooper, 2000). These findings illustrate that individuals can use their multiple identities strategically.

Impression Management

Most individuals in most workplaces "manage their behavior and person characteristics in the presence of others" in an attempt to "create a specific impression" (Guadagno & Cialdini, 2007, p. 484). Impression management is specifically related to self-presentation and consists of the process by which an individual attempts to control the perception that others have of them (Kumra, 2014, p. 273; Leary & Kowalski, 1990, p. 34). This process is complex since individuals choose different, and even contradictory, ways to "create different impressions on different audiences" based on their specific goals for the interaction (Guadagno & Cialdini, 2007, p. 484). Since individuals have multiple selves, they can choose to show different aspects of those selves depending on the situation (Kumra, 2014, p. 274). Organizations also perform impression management, as they are interested in ensuring that their employees and other stakeholders view them in certain (desirable) ways. Thus, according to Rosenfield et al. (1994, p. 601), impression management provides an understanding of the motivations and concerns of individuals (people) and organizations for making positive impressions on others.

Impression management is not a one-time effort but a continuing process, both "dynamic and recursive," as the individual constantly assesses whether the tactics they have employed have accomplished the desired goals (Leary & Kowalski, 1990, p. 43). If desired results are not achieved in terms of the image and perception created, the individual can respond in different ways. They might continue with the same tactics, hoping they will eventually work in attaining the desired results. Alternatively, they might conclude that their current tactics will never lead to the desired results and thus switch tactics. Leary & Kowalski (1990) noted that some individuals might also conclude that the desired results will never be attained and give up trying.

Leary and Kowalski (1990) identified two distinct parts of impression management: impression motivation and impression construction. The motivation for an individual to perform impression management is important; the individual would need to have a strong sense of self, clarity of goals, and determination to follow through with the process. Impression construction includes the development of a self-concept, resolving incongruity between private and public selves, and determining a desirable identity. Impression management thus includes several behavioral techniques and tactics.

Kumra (2014, p. 277) noted that the two most common impression management behaviors are self-promotion and ingratiation. This combination addresses both internal and external, or agency and communal, aspects. Self-promotion can be viewed as communicating to others the details of one's achievements. Ingratiation concerns relationships with important persons in the workplace. Cialdini and Richardson (1980) identified what they called "basking" and "blasting" as two commonly used impression management techniques. They defined basking as an indirect way in which the individual attempts to improve their image not by focusing on their own positive qualities but "by making observers aware of their (often meaningless) connections with some others who possess positive qualities" (Cialdini & Richardson, 1980, p. 407). Blasting is a way of making public something to which the individual has a negative link, with the aim of lowering the value of their link to that entity, or with the aim of publicizing the connection of a rival to that thing and thus negatively impacting the rival's image (Cialdini & Richardson, 1980, p. 408).

Guadagno and Cialdini (2007) focused on the relationship between impression management and gender in organizational environments. According to their study, the "psychological goals driving Impression Management" include being liked and appearing competent (Guadagno & Cialdini, 2007, p. 485). Tactics that help attain the goal of likeability include flattery, ingratiation, emphasizing similarity, physical attractiveness, and seeming modest (Guadagno & Cialdini, 2007). Tactics that indicate competence and disclaim incompetence include self-promotion, staging a show of performance, making excuses for failure, and claiming obstacles to success. Guadagno and Cialdini (2007) also identified a third goal of impression management as conveying the appearance of having status and power. Tactics that aid in this goal include attire and accessories/looks, conspicuous consumption, association with powerful others, and communicating dominance nonverbally. They noted that individuals choose their tactics based on personal preferences and desired goals, as well as on the organizational context (Guadagno & Cialdini, 2007, p. 486).

Guadagno and Cialdini (2007) further characterized individuals based on impression management goals as "acquisitive" or "protective." Acquisitive individuals wanted to be seen in a positive light and protective ones wanted to avoid being viewed negatively. Further, Guadagno and Cialdini (2007) categorized impression management tactics as direct and indirect. Direct methods were used by the individual herself whereas indirect ones were effected by other people. Based on these categorizations, the authors described four groups of impression management tactics. Direct methods aimed at creating a positive image included tactics such as emphasizing similarity, using charm, praising, being self-deprecating, and taking responsibility for positive outcomes. Tactics such as basking (enhancing positivity), altering physical appearance, boosting (reducing unfavorable features), burnishing (enhancing favorable features), blurring (disclaiming negative links), and belittling (reducing the effects of a negative link) were indirect methods that were also aimed at creating a positive image. Direct methods intending to limit negative effects included tactics such as downplaying ability, setting up obstacles, excusing (admitting wrong but denying responsibility), apologizing (admitting blame and responsibility), justifying (admitting responsibility but denying wrong), and disclaiming (giving excuses before the incident). Finally, tactics such as blasting (denigrating negatives in others), dissociating (distancing oneself from others after a negative result), blaring (stating a negative link to unfavorable entities), and burying (disclaiming positive links to unfavorable entities) are indirect methods used to limit negative impressions. Guadagno and Cialdini (2007, p. 489) noted that most of the tactics used by women were "not only feminine typed but are also submissive/passive." These included appearing modest, flattery, apologizing, appearing uncertain, emphasizing similarity, and conforming to opinions. Male-typed tactics, on the other hand, included self-enhancement, taking responsibility for positive outcomes, saying nice things through others, basking, and blasting. According to Guadagno and Cialdini (2007), women who were successful in ascending organizational hierarchies used a combination of feminine-typed and male-typed methods.

Researchers noted that Asian Americans might be reluctant to use certain impression management tactics. At the same time, certain techniques are likely to be more effective than others for certain career goals. Guadagno and Cialdini (2007, p. 484) noted that gender and impression management were linked to "outcomes such as salary and performance evaluations." In other words, individuals might have to overcome their discomfort with using certain effective tactics. In doing so, Asian Americans need to take into consideration both stereotypes and imperatives of their own ethnic identities.

Effective impression management might require Asian American women to temper their adherence to some cultural values. For instance, modesty is stressed as a virtue in many Asian cultures. However, this value is incongruent with the common workplace experience of employees being told to "speak up" and take ownership. According to Wosinska et al. (1996), modesty is often linked to the impression management tactic of ingratiation. They found that modesty was effective depending on the context, although it was generally perceived more positively than being boastful. When women were relating to their co-workers, presenting themselves very modestly was perceived favorably. Being moderately modest was also effective when the individual was being evaluated by a superior.

Even individuals who are reluctant to use impression management methods and who would like to simply focus on letting their work speak for itself can be spurred to action by events in the workplace (Leary & Kowalski, 1990). For example, this might include not getting recognition for achievements, perceived inequity in others being rewarded for similar work, or experiencing a lack of acceptance by the group. Individuals might then act instinctively rather than strategically, simply to ensure that some image of them is intact. They need not necessarily aim to create a different one. However, Rosenfield et al. (1994, p. 602) commented that understanding how one's behavior might be viewed by others in an attempt at impression management "can also serve as a basis for smoother interactions and a means for resolving some of the most insidious communication problems among individuals of different racial, ethnic and gender backgrounds."

Notes in Conclusion

Employees are sometimes told to bring their whole selves to the workplace, implying that they should be able to express all facets of their personalities and all aspects of their identities. However, they need to feel it is safe to do so without backlash. Employees also need to have self-awareness and a sense of their own identities.

Identity is both a sense of self and a sense of belonging. Asian women in organizations have multiple identities, each of which might be salient at different times and in different situations. Their personal identities are influenced by their gender, ethnicity, and (possibly) life status (as a mother, for example). Their workplace identities are influenced by their area of specialization (profession) and their organizational membership. Asian women can pick and choose how and when they portray aspects of each of these identities. Sometimes, however, they might not have a choice, for example when are they are confronted with a racial identity.

Identities are visible to others through an individual's presentation and behaviors. The choice of displaying identity is part of overall impression management in the workplace. Many employees attempt to influence the impressions others have of them in the workplace. For example, one common technique, basking, involves highlighting and enhancing one's successes; displaying modesty and downplaying one's accomplishments is another. Asian women need to strategically choose impression management approaches that align with their identities to help them achieve career goals.

REFERENCES

Abele, A. E., & Wojciszke, B. (2007). Agency and communion from the perspective of self versus others. *Journal of Personality and Social Psychology*, *93*(5), 751–763. doi:10.1037/0022-3514.93.5.751 PMID:17983298

Ashforth, B. E., Harrison, S. H., & Corley, K. G. (2008). Identification in organizations: An examination of four fundamental questions. *Journal of Management*, *34*(3), 325–373. doi:10.1177/0149206308316059

Ashforth, B. E., Schinoff, B. S., & Rogers, K. M. (2018). "I identify with her," "I identify with him": Unpacking the dynamics of personal identification in organizations. *Academy of Management Review*, *41*(1), 28–60. doi:10.5465/amr.2014.0033

Barth, F. (1969). Introduction. In F. Barth (Ed.), *Ethnic groups and boundaries: The social organization of culture difference* (pp. 9–38). Little, Brown and Company.

Berry, J. W. (1997). Immigration, acculturation, and adaptation. *Applied Psychology*, *46*(1), 5–68.

Bhalla, V. (2008, Summer). "Couch potatoes and Super-women": Gender, migration, and the emerging discourse on housework among Asian Indian immigrants. *Journal of American Ethnic History*, *27*(4), 71–99.

Brewer, M. B. (1991). The social self: On being the same and different at the same time. *Personality and Psychology Bulletin*, *17*(5), 475–482. doi:10.1177/0146167291175001

Brickson, S. L. (2005). Organizational identity orientation, Forging a link between organizational identity and organizations' relations with stakeholders. *Administrative Science Quarterly*, *50*(4), 576–609. doi:10.2189/asqu.50.4.576

Brubaker, R., & Cooper, F. (2000, February). Beyond "identity." *Theory and Society*, *29*(1), 1–47. doi:10.1023/A:1007068714468

Butt, G., MacKenzie, L., & Manning, R. (2012). The career development of recently qualified British South Asian women teachers: "Everybody's the same. I don't feel my ethnicity is an issue at all. *Educational Review*, *64*(2), 181–194. doi:10.1080/00131911.2011.598915

Callero, P. L. (1994, September). From role-playing to understanding role as resource. *Social Psychology Quarterly*, *57*(3), 228–243. doi:10.2307/2786878

Chang, T., Tracey, T. J. G., & Moore, T. L. (2005). The dimensional structure of Asian American acculturation: An examination of prototypes. *Self and Identity*, *4*(1), 25–43. doi:10.1080/13576500444000155

Cialdini, R. B., & Richardson, K. D. (1980). Two indirect tactics of image management: Basking and blasting. *Journal of Personality and Social Psychology*, *39*(3), 406–415. doi:10.1037/0022-3514.39.3.406

Creed, D. W. E., DeJordy, R., & Lok, J. (2010). Being the change: Resolving institutional contradiction through identity work. *Academy of Management Journal*, *53*(6), 1336–1364. doi:10.5465/amj.2010.57318357

Dasgupta, S. D. (1998). Gender roles and cultural continuity in the Asian Indian immigrant community in the U.S. *Sex Roles*, *38*(11/12), 953–974. doi:10.1023/A:1018822525427

DeRue, S. D., & Ashford, S. J. (2010). Who will lead and who will follow? A social process of leadership identity construction in organizations. *Academy of Management Review*, *35*(4), 627–647.

Devos, T., & Sadler, M. (2019). Context diversity predicts the extent to which the American identity is implicitly associated with Asian Americans and European Americans. *Asian American Journal of Psychology*, *10*(2), 182–193. doi:10.1037/aap0000149

Dhingra, P. (2007). *Managing multicultural lives: Asian American professionals and the challenge of multiple identities*. Stanford University Press.

Durik, A. M., Hyde, J. S., Marks, A. C., Roy, A. L., Anaya, D., & Schultz, G. (2006). Ethnicity and gender stereotypes of emotion. *Sex Roles*, *54*(7-8), 429–445. doi:10.100711199-006-9020-4

Dutton, J. E., Roberts, L. M., & Bednar, J. (2010). Pathways for positive identity construction at work: Four types of positive identity and the building of social resources. *Academy of Management Review*, *35*(2), 265–293.

Eagly, A. H., & Steffen, V. J. (1986). Gender and aggressive behavior: A meta-analytic review of the social psychological literature. *Psychological Bulletin*, *100*(3), 309–330. doi:10.1037/0033-2909.100.3.309 PMID:3797558

Eidheim, H. (1969). When ethnic identity is a stigma. In F. Barth (Ed.), *Ethnic groups and boundaries: The social organization of culture difference* (pp. 39–57). Little, Brown and Company.

Farver, J. M., Xu, Y., Badha, B., Bhadha, R., Narang, S., & Lieber, E. (2007). Ethnic identity acculturation, parenting beliefs, and adolescent adjustment: A comparison of Asian Indian and European American families. *Merrill-Palmer Quarterly*, *53*(2), 184–215. doi:10.1353/mpq.2007.0010

Fiske, S. T., Cuddy, A. J., Glick, P., & Xu, J. (2002). A model of (often mixed) stereotype content: Competence and warmth respectively follow from perceived status and competition. *Journal of Personality and Social Psychology*, *82*(6), 878–902. doi:10.1037/0022-3514.82.6.878 PMID:12051578

Fong, L. Y. S. (1997). Asian-American women: An understudied minority. *Journal of Sociology and Social Welfare*, *24*(1), 91–111.

Gecas, V. (1982). The self-concept. *Annual Review of Sociology*, *1*(1), 1–33. doi:10.1146/annurev.so.08.080182.000245

Guadagno, R. E., & Cialdini, R. B. (2007). Gender differences in impression management in organizations: A qualitative review. *Sex Roles*, *56*(7-8), 483–494. doi:10.100711199-007-9187-3

Gushue, G. V., Mejia-Smith, B. X., Fisher, L. D., Cogger, A., Gonzalez-Matthews, M., Lee, Y., Mancusi, L., McCullough, R., Connell, M. T., Weng, W. C., Cheng, M., & Johnson, V. (2013). Differentiation of self and racial identity. *Counselling Psychology Quarterly*, *26*(3–4), 343–361. doi:10.1080/09515070.2013.816839

Herzberg, F. (2003). One more time: How do you motivate employees? *Harvard Business Review*. Accessed on June 15, 2020. https://hbr.org/2003/01/one-more-time-how-do-you-motivate-employees

Hyun, J. (2005). *Breaking the Bamboo Ceiling*. Harper-Collins.

Ibarra, H. (1999). Provisional selves: Experimenting with image and identity in professional adaptation. *Administrative Science Quarterly*, *44*(4), 764–791. doi:10.2307/2667055

Ibarra, H. (2018, November 20). How your identity changes when you change jobs. *Harvard Business Review*. https://hbr.org/podcast/2018/11/how-your-identity-changes-when-you-change-jobs

Ibrahim, F., Ohnishi, H., & Sandhu, D. S. (1997, January). Asian American identity development: A culture specific model for South Asian Americans. *Journal of Multicultural Counseling and Development*, *25*(1), 34–50. doi:10.1002/j.2161-1912.1997.tb00314.x

Inman, A. G. (2006). South Asian women: Identities and conflicts. *Cultural Diversity & Ethnic Minority Psychology*, *12*(2), 306–319. doi:10.1037/1099-9809.12.2.306 PMID:16719579

Inman, A. G., Howard, E. E., Beaumont, R. L., & Walker, J. A. (2007). Cultural transmission: Influence of contextual factors in Asian Indian immigrant parents' experiences. *Journal of Counseling Psychology*, *54*(1), 93–100. doi:10.1037/0022-0167.54.1.93

Inman, A. G., Ladany, N., Constantine, M. G., & Morano, C. K. (2001). Development and preliminary validation of the cultural values conflict scale for South Asian women. *Journal of Counseling Psychology*, *48*(1), 17–27. doi:10.1037/0022-0167.48.1.17

Iwamoto, D. K., Negi, N. J., Partiali, R. N., & Creswell, J. W. (2013). The racial and ethnic identity formation process of second-generation Asian Indian Americans: A phenomenological study. *Journal of Multicultural Counseling and Development*, *41*(4), 224–239. doi:10.1002/j.2161-1912.2013.00038.x PMID:25298617

Kim, B. S. K., & Hong, S. (2004). A psychometric revision of the Asian values scale using the Rasch model. *Measurement & Evaluation in Counseling & Development*, *37*(1), 15–27. doi:10.1080/07481756.2004.11909747

Kumra, S. (2014). Gendered constructions of merit and impression management within professional service firms. In S. Kumra, R. Simpson, & R. J. Burke (Eds.), *The Oxford handbook of gender in organizations* (pp. 269–290). Oxford University Press.

Kurien, P. (1999, January). Gendered ethnicity: Creating a Hindu identity in the United States. *The American Behavioral Scientist, 42*(4), 648–670. doi:10.1177/00027649921954408

LaFromboise, T., Coleman, H. L. K., & Gerton, J. (1993). Psychological impact of biculturalism: Evidence and theory. *Psychological Bulletin, 114*(3), 395–412. doi:10.1037/0033-2909.114.3.395 PMID:8272463

Leary, M. R., & Kowalski, R. M. (1990). Impression management: A literature review and two-component model. *Psychological Bulletin, 107*(1), 34–47. doi:10.1037/0033-2909.107.1.34

Leung, A. S. (2008). The big five career theories. In J. A. Athanasou & R. Van Esbroeck (Eds.), International handbook of career guidance (pp. 115–132). Springer Science + Business Media B.V.

Mainiero, L. A., & Sullivan, S. E. (2005). Kaleidoscope careers: An alternate explanation for the "opt-out" revolution. *The Academy of Management Executive, 19*(1), 106–123. doi:10.5465/ame.2005.15841962

Manohar, N. N. (2013). Support networks, ethnic spaces, and fictive kin: Indian immigrant women constructing community in the United States. *AAPI Nexus, 11*(1–2), 25–55.

Meister, A., Jehn, K. A., & Thatcher, S. M. B. (2014). Feeling misidentified: The consequences of internal identity asymmetries at work. *Academy of Management Review, 39*(4), 488–512. doi:10.5465/amr.2013.0102

Meyerson, D. E. (2004). The tempered radicals: How employees push their companies—little by little—to be more socially responsible. *Stanford Social Innovation Review*, 14–23.

Naqvi, F. (2011). Perspectives of Indian women managers in the public sector. *Indian Journal of Gender Studies, 18*(3), 279–309. doi:10.1177/097152151101800301

Nguyen, C. P., Wong, Y. J., Juang, L. P., & Park, I. J. K. (2015). Pathways among Asian Americans' family ethnic socialization, ethnic identity, and psychological well-being: A multigroup mediation model. *Asian American Journal of Psychology*, *6*(3), 273–280. doi:10.1037/aap0000026

Nichols, A. (2017). The influence of ethnicity and gender on the leadership experiences of female Asian-American managers. *Global Journal of Human-Social Science Interdisciplinary*, *17*(4), 1–28.

Pessar, P. R. (1984, Winter). The linkage between the household and workplace of Dominican women in the U.S. *The International Migration Review*, *18*(4), 1188–1211. PMID:12340234

Phinney, J. S. (1988, June). *The development of ethnic identity in adolescents* [National Institutes of Health Paper.] Utah State University Workshop on Identity Formation: Theoretical and Empirical Issues, Logan, UT. https://files.eric.ed.gov/fulltext/ED298224.pdf

Phinney, J. S. (1990). Ethnic identity in adolescents and adults: Review of research. *Psychological Bulletin*, *108*(3), 499–514. doi:10.1037/0033-2909.108.3.499 PMID:2270238

Phinney, J. S., Ferguson, D. L., & Tate, J. D. (1997, October). Intergroup attitudes among ethnic minority adolescents: A causal model. *Child Development*, *68*(5), 955–969. doi:10.2307/1132044 PMID:29106715

Rosenfield, P., Giacalone, R. A., & Riordan, C. A. (1994). Impression management theory and diversity: Lessons for organizational behavior. *The American Behavioral Scientist*, *37*(5), 601–604. doi:10.1177/0002764294037005002

Rosenthal, D. A., & Feldman, S. S. (1990). The acculturation of Chinese immigrants: Perceived effects on family functioning of length of residence in two cultural contexts. *The Journal of Genetic Psychology*, *151*(4), 495–514. doi:10.1080/00221325.1990.9914635 PMID:2074433

Shih, M., Pittinsky, T. L., & Trahan, A. (2006). Domain-specific effects of stereotypes on performance. *Self and Identity*, *5*(1), 1–15. doi:10.1080/15298860500338534

Srinivasan, S. (2001). "Being Indian," "Being American": A balancing act or a creative blend? *Journal of Human Behavior in the Social Environment*, *3*(3/4), 135–158.

Steele, C. M., & Aronson, J. (1995). Stereotype threat and the intellectual test performance of African Americans. *Journal of Personality and Social Psychology*, *69*(5), 797–811. doi:10.1037/0022-3514.69.5.797 PMID:7473032

Stryker, S., & Burke, P. J. (2000). The past, present, and future of an identity theory. *Social Psychology Quarterly*, *63*(4), 284–297. doi:10.2307/2695840

Subramanian, M. (2013). Gossip, drama, and technology: How South Asian American young women negotiate gender on and offline. *Gender and Education*, *25*(3), 311–324. doi:10.1080/09540253.2012.746647

Sue, S. (2009). Ethnic minority psychology: Struggles and triumphs. *Cultural Diversity & Ethnic Minority Psychology*, *15*(4), 409–415. doi:10.1037/a0017559 PMID:19916675

Suinn, R. M., Khoo, G., & Ahuna, C. (1995, July). The Suinn-Lew Asian self-identity acculturation scale: Cross-cultural information. *Journal of Multicultural Counseling and Development*, *23*(3), 139–148. doi:10.1002/j.2161-1912.1995.tb00269.x

Swann, W. B. Jr, Johnson, R. E., & Bosson, J. K. (2009). Identity negotiation at work. *Research in Organizational Behavior*, *29*, 81–109. doi:10.1016/j.riob.2009.06.005

Tajfel, H., & Turner, J. C. (1986). The social identity of intergroup behavior. In S. Worchel & W. G. Austin (Eds.), *Psychology of intergroup relations* (pp. 7–24). Nelson-Hall Publishers.

Tsai, J. L., Ying, Y., & Lee, P. A. (2001). Cultural predictors of self-esteem- A study of Chinese American female and male young adults. *Cultural Diversity & Ethnic Minority Psychology*, *7*(3), 284–297. doi:10.1037/1099-9809.7.3.284 PMID:11506074

Varghese, A., & Jenkins, S. R. (2009). Parental overprotection, cultural value conflict, and psychological adaptation among Asian Indian women in America. *Sex Roles*, *61*(3-4), 235–251. doi:10.100711199-009-9620-x

Wosinska, W., Dabul, A. J., Whetstone-Dion, R., & Cialdini, R. B. (1996). Self-presentational responses to success in the organization: The costs and benefits of modesty. *Basic and Applied Social Psychology*, *18*(2), 229–242. doi:10.120715324834basp1802_8

Yamanaka, K., & McClelland, K. (1994). Earning the Model-Minority image: Diverse strategies of economic adaptation by Asian-American women. *Ethnic and Racial Studies*, *17*(1), 79–114. doi:10.1080/01419870.1994.9993814

Yoon, E., Cabirou, L., Bhang, C., & Galvin, S. (2019). Acculturation and patriarchal beliefs among Asian American young adults: A preliminary investigation. *Asian American Journal of Psychology*, *10*(2), 122–130. doi:10.1037/aap0000130

Chapter 7
Organizational Careers

ABSTRACT

An organizational career is located within an organization and consists of the positions held by an employee within its structure. The management of organizational careers has been well studied. Career management strategies and approaches had originally assumed that employees wanted not only to remain in their organization but to progress upward in its hierarchy. However, more recent research has noted that this was not true for all individuals; some people were content to remain at a certain level and others were open to moving between organizations. Thus, a view of careers needs to allow for a variety of career motivations and include the possibility of frequent movement across organizations. In this chapter, the authors discuss different patterns and orientations of organizational careers. They also discuss the choice of professions and work experiences of Asian women in the past and the career environments they are likely to experience in the future.

INTRODUCTION

Common understandings of what a career is change over time depending on evolving environments and circumstances. Researchers have used several working definitions in discussions about career forms and management. For instance, Greenhaus and Kossek (2014) provided a general definition of a career as a "pattern or sequence of work experiences that evolve over time, that is, over [the] life course."

DOI: 10.4018/978-1-7998-4384-9.ch007

Career management differs depending on the organizational context. Most careers in the U.S. are located within organizations. These entities might be for-profits, nonprofits, or governmental. Even the founders of many small businesses or entrepreneurial ventures, if these are successful, transition into working for an organization, albeit one which they lead. Careers that are untethered to organizations include (sub)contracting and freelancing.

Successful organizational careers are closely related to the value perceived by the organization in what the individual employee has to offer. This valuation is usually linked to organizational goals and strategies and varies across organizations. There is some similarity in the perception of value across private, for-profit organizations since their overarching goals are short-term revenue generation and long-term organizational sustainability. Value is viewed differently by nonprofit and governmental organizations, where work contributing to the achievement of social purposes (rather than generating revenue) is likely to be considered critical (Moore, 2000). Further, nonprofit organizations and governmental agencies obtain revenue in different ways than for-profits. Nonprofits need to convince donors of the value they create and deliver. Governmental agencies need to garner "sources of legitimacy and support, and operational capacity to deliver the value sources of legitimacy" and build "operational capacity to deliver the value" (Moore, 2000, p. 183). These distinctions imply that employee performance and value are viewed differently across these sectors.

Organizational careers in the private sector have been researched extensively from both the organizational and individual perspectives. Organizational issues that have been studied include employee retention, employee development, organizational commitment, and performance evaluation. Individual employee areas of interest are career choices, career patterns, effects of biases in the workplace, and multi-organizational careers.

This chapter focuses on careers in for-profit, private (non-governmental) organizations. In previous chapters, we have discussed organizational aspects of relevance to Asian women such as authority and power, performance evaluations, and employee resource groups. In this chapter, we discuss careers, beginning with a brief overview of research on individual careers, followed by a discussion of how women's careers differ from the prototypical organizational careers of men. Finally, it appears that organizations are undergoing an across-the-board shift due to changes related to globalization and organizational function, which in turn is giving rise to new career orientations and forms. We present these developments as important factors for Asian women to consider in their career planning and management.

Careers: Terms and Theories

In the U.S., career choice has often been influenced at schools, and even colleges, by career counselors. School career counselors attempt to match student abilities and interests with appropriate career and study choices. This approach led to the development of career and vocational development models that used like vocation, occupation, and career orientation.

A vocational identity reflects an individual's "preference for behaviors, situations, contexts in which activities occur and/or the outcomes associated with preferred actions" (Nye et al., 2012, p. 385). In other words, it refers to the kind of work an individual likes (or dislikes) and the kind of rewards they value. An individual who is clear about her vocational preferences, and who is not likely to change them, will be able to articulate a clear and "relatively stable picture of self-goals, interests, skills and suitable occupations" (Holland, 1996, p. 403). A caveat is that, while this certainty might be ideal when external conditions are stable, individuals need to be more flexible in dynamically changing work environments.

An occupation can be differentiated from a career. Super et al. (1961, p. 11) defined an occupation as "a group of jobs and positions, and hence essentially a group of tasks performed by one person" and a career as a series of "occupations, jobs and positions in the life of an individual."

Every individual was viewed to have the potential to be successful in a variety of jobs. Since individuals are different in "aptitude, interests, and values" (Super, 1953, p. 187), their career choices differ as well. Career counselors attempted to guide individuals regarding what to expect in different careers and career predictions. Some models were proposed to help individuals in making career choices. Holland's approach described six types of vocational personalities based on skills and values (Leung, 2008). These categories were: realistic, investigative, artistic, social, enterprising, and conventional (Nye et al., 2012). This model's expectation was that an individual who identified with a vocational type would seek work that aligned with that type's characteristics. However, individuals needed to understand that, regardless of their preference, actual jobs could be a mix of different vocational types, depending on the industry and organization in which they were located.

Bandura's social cognitive theory considered an individual's self-efficacy as the driving force behind their education and career choices (Leung, 2008). According to this viewpoint, individuals would choose jobs they felt they had the ability and competency to do. Gottfredson's theory of circumscription and compromise, on the other hand, proposed that individuals made career decisions based on their understanding of what each career was about by following a process of eliminating careers that did not align with their self-concept (Leung, 2008). In contrast, Super's theory viewed a career as an ongoing process of developing one's self-concept (Leung, 2008).

The theory of work adjustment placed careers in an organizational context by viewing a career as a process of seeking a match between the individual and an organization. This was a process of continual adjustment since both the individual and the organization were likely to change over time. For instance, individuals typically face various issues related to different life stages, such as flexibility in time to meet childcare needs when they are parents of young children. Additionally, their ideas of self, certain values, vocational preferences, and competencies also change over time (Super, 1953).

Career development models have typically been anchored in organizations. The idea of an organizational career "was implicit in (Weber's) conceptualization of an ideal bureaucracy with its well-defined hierarchy of authority and selected and promotion based on technical competence" (Clarke, 2013, p. 685). A career was viewed as a process that passed through well-defined stages of growth, exploration, establishment, maintenance, and decline (Super, 1953). Kanter referred to the "logic of advancement" as the movement of career-minded employees "up the ladder through a sequence of well-defined positions in the organizational hierarchy" (Clarke, 2013, p. 685). Implicit in this understanding of career development was the idea of continuity, which referred to "staying in the same job or moving jobs that belong to the same occupational category" (Holland, 1996, p. 397). In 1996, Holland noted that "the average career has substantial continuity" (Holland, 1996, p. 397), a statement that might not be true for a significant number of organizational employees at the present time.

With the advent of women in workplaces, researchers began to examine women's career choices and experiences. They noted that women's careers often have forms and trajectories that are different from a prototypical organizational career, presumably based on the experiences of men. Some ways to view women's careers as linked to career goals and outlooks were proposed.

Some recent career models have proposed the concept of career orientation. An individual's career orientation, which reflects his or her preferences, is based on a mix of idealistic preferences and pragmatic options. It is established at an early age and is considered to be stable over a lifetime. According to Rodrigues et al. (2019), career orientations are influenced by the individual's disposition and career preferences, as well as social background and labor market conditions. This is aligned with the findings of Hodkinson and Sparkes (1997, p. 33), who noted that individuals follow a pragmatically rational method in making career decisions rather than a purely rational approach of weighing pros and cons.

Traditional Career Planning Approaches

Since most individuals experience work in an organizational context, careers have largely been studied "in terms of an individual's relationship to an employing organization" (Sullivan & Baruch, 2009, p. 1542), with the underlying assumption of stability in the organizational structure. Several theories (for example, those of Hall, Super, and Holland) viewed career movement as being driven by a motivation to find a good match between an individual and an organization (Nieva & Gutek, 1981). In this view, both entities are motivated towards this goal. A lateral move within an organization, for instance, fits in with this understanding. The upward movement of careers could also be viewed in this manner—the employee's motivation could be their ambition or their desire to make a certain kind of impact through their work. The organization needs leaders, and (in theory) the employee who fits the need of a managerial or leadership position would be chosen. In any case, this points to the importance of an employee to be informed about, and involved in, decisions affecting their career.

Career movements can be initiated by the organization or the employee. However, other than termination, a movement takes place only if the individual employee accepts it (perhaps unwillingly). It is not unusual for organizational decisions affecting an employee's career movement to be contrary to the employee's wishes. If that is the case, the employee's only choices might be to accept the decision or to quit. This situation underscores the importance for employees to be engaged in their own careers and to manage them.

Early career theories (such as vocational matching) assumed that individuals made career decisions in a rational manner. However, the reality is that career decisions are often made based on partial information, such as past experiences (maybe as interns or trainees), or they are based on "advice/ information from [a] trusted contact" and "factoring in family and culture" (Hodkinson & Sparkes, 1997, p. 33). In this context, the authors commented that "prime factors determining choice remain within [the] influence of the individual" (Hodkinson & Sparkes, 1997, p. 32). However, that might not be entirely true, given environmental situations and a potential imbalance in power between organizations offering jobs and individuals needing them. Despite this potential disadvantage, individuals can affect their career outcomes in significant ways through appropriate planning and management.

Career management can be defined as the process by which "individuals develop insights into themselves and their environments, formulate career goals and strategies, and acquire feedback regarding career progress" (De Vos & Cambre, 2017, p. 504). Greco and Kraimer (2019, p. 1) noted that various career management models have attempted to respond to the need for career management.

An important aspect of career planning, as with planning in general, is goal setting. Greenhaus's 1987 model emphasized that goal-setting facilitates career planning and helps in the implementation of a career strategy (Greco & Kraimer, 2019). London's 1983 model of career motivation also stressed the importance of individuals being clear about their career goals, and also emphasized that trying to meet goals contributed to their motivation (Greco & Kraimer, 2019). At the same time, not all individuals uniformly accrue positive outcomes from career planning. Gould (1979) found that the employees who realized the most benefits from career planning were those who fit the high growth and achievement needs profile. Gould further noted that good career planning might be linked to personal planning skills of a general kind. Other factors that could play a role included certain psychological characteristics, experience with career planning, and knowledge of the work environment. It might be to an individual's advantage to acquire such knowledge and skills.

Career motivation has been considered an important factor in career mobility. Hirschi (2012, p. 372) provided a broad description of career motivation as a "set of individual characteristics and associated career decisions and behaviors that reflect the person's career identity, insight into factors affecting career and resilience in face of unfavorable career conditions." Individual characteristics or personality traits are important to career resiliency as well as to success. Seibert and Kraimer (2001) found that among the big-five personality traits, only extraversion was of significance to promotions and extrinsic success. Interestingly, some traits, while appearing desirable in an employee, could lower the probability of success. Two such traits were being nice and being cooperative, both of which women are socialized to be.

Career resiliency is likely to become increasingly important and relevant in the future. In general, resiliency refers to a willingness to "let go of the outdated and learn the new, bounce back from disappointment, to live with high levels of uncertainty, find security from within rather than from outside"

(Arthur & Rousseau, 1996, p. 36). Career resilience can be described as the "ability to thrive, mature, and increase competence in the face of adverse circumstances" (Fourie & Van Vuuren, 1998, p. 53). Resilience was also identified as one of the domains contributing to motivation, along with career identity and career insight. Although (the big five) personality traits were not linked to career resilience, Fourie and Van Vuuren (1998, pp. 54–56) identified four factors that might affect it resilience: belief in oneself, disregard for traditional sources of career success, self-reliance, and receptivity to change.

In pragmatic terms, individuals can affect their career movement by building competencies and by using capital. Career competencies are important at all levels of the organization and in all kinds of jobs (Hirschi, 2012). They include the basics of performing an assigned job such as simply being able to do it and having requisite skills and related knowledge. Beyond this, competencies include a sense of internal motivation and identification with the job, as well as external knowledge of building and maintaining networks and contacts (Hirschi, 2012).

Equally important as competencies that individuals (can) build for themselves are the resources that they can acquire for themselves. Hirschi (2012) identified four critical career resources: human, social, psychological, and career identity. Human capital refers to aspects related to job performance such as knowledge, skills, and ability, which can be accumulated through experience and education. Social capital is the goodwill generated through social relationships; it is dependent on the individual's networks (Rodrigues et al., 2019). A network translates to capital depending on the characteristics of contacts in the network, the types of relationships the individual has with them, and their willingness to exert effort on behalf of that individual. (Different types of relationships were discussed as strong links and weak links in Chapter 4.) Psychological resources refer to traits and cognitions, such as self-evaluations and self-efficacy (Hirschi, 2012). Finally, career identity refers to an individual's job-related awareness, interests, and values, as well as their willingness to identify as a member of the profession (Hirschi, 2012). The value of any resource is contextual. Hirschi (2012) noted that any resource could be an asset in some situations and a liability in others. For instance, an advanced degree in a field unrelated to the job might be considered as "over education" and decrease the value of an employee. Additionally, a resource could have indirect, yet critical, effects on career success. For instance, Asian women acknowledged and gave importance to spousal support as extremely valuable (Ocampo et al., 2018).

Career success means different things to different people. It could include extrinsic markers like salary, promotions, and status as well as intrinsic factors such as satisfaction and personal meaning (Seibert & Kraimer, 2001). A broad definition that covers both aspects defines career success as "accumulated positive work and psychological outcomes resulting from one's work experiences" (Ng et al., 2005, p. 368). Human capital, organizational sponsorship, socio-demographic status, and stable individual differences (Big Five) were found to be predictors of career success (Ng et al., 2005, p. 370). Both individuals and organizations attempt to influence career success. For instance, individuals can build their human capital through education and work experience, and organizations can enable sponsorship through mentoring programs.

Careers progress in different ways through organizations, and their progressions are affected by organizational policies and practices as well as by individual employee choices. Some progression models for promotion in organizations include the seniority-based model, individuals sorted via education tracks (common in Japan), tournaments, early decisions as to who is a future star, and contests (Ishida et al., 2002). Many U.S. corporate environments had a contest style of career progression. Ishida et al. (2002) commented that in many U.S. companies, early promotions did not indicate a clear advantage for later career progression, although delayed promotions at every stage indicated a disadvantage. International assignments were sometimes considered as indicators for later career success. Yan et al. (2002, p. 373) explained that this could be because "critical corporate stakes may ride upon the success of these assignments." Individuals need to be aware of how careers are designed to progress in their specific organization.

Alpha and Beta Careers

A different perspective on career success was provided by the "Alpha and Beta" typology. The traditional view of organizational career success, while it included intrinsic factors, mostly focused on hierarchical progress and status within the organization, including material benefits and compensation. However, recognition that individuals could have other motivations in pursuing organizational careers and could value outcomes differently broadened the prevailing understanding of success.

This approach proposed three key parameters important to individuals in planning careers: authenticity, balance, and challenge (Mainiero & Sullivan,

2005). Authenticity refers to the sense of being true to oneself while managing personal and career development. Balance is related to managing work and personal life so that they form a coherent whole for the individual. Challenge, possibly the closest parameter to traditional ideas of career success, refers to engaging in activities that provide an opportunity for learning and the demonstration of "responsibility, control, autonomy" (Sullivan & Mainiero, 2007, p. 253).

According to this perspective, at different stages of their work-life and different points in time, individuals give overwhelming importance to *one* of these parameters over the others. This emphasis drives their career and work-related decisions at that time. An Alpha career pattern is one in which the individual changes focus over time, progressing from challenge to authenticity and finally to balance (Sullivan & Mainiero, 2007, p. 238). Typically, individuals following this pattern are strongly focused on a career for quite some time before shifting to other non-work aspects of their lives. Individuals following an Alpha career path "show devotion to family by being the breadwinner and by spending time (with them) later in a career" (Sullivan & Mainiero, 2007, p. 254). In the past, this would have been considered a prototypical (male) organizational career. It has been viewed as a simpler pattern compared to the more complex paths followed by most women's careers. In contrast, a Beta career pattern shifts focus over time, shifting from challenge to balance to authenticity (Sullivan & Mainiero, 2007, p. 238). Typically, individuals following this pattern perceive the necessity of making adjustments earlier in their careers to satisfy other, non-work demands on their time and resources. According to Sullivan and Mainiero (2007, p. 254), the career paths of many women could fit into this model. Individuals following the Beta pattern typically start their careers in a manner similar to an Alpha pattern. However, issues of balance become increasingly important mid-career. Interestingly, the authors found that marriage and children did not have particularly significant impacts on the progressions of individuals following a Beta pattern. Sullivan and Mainiero (2007) also noted that both men and women appeared to start careers with a focus on challenge. However, there is a divergence during mid-career between those focusing on balance and those continuing to focus on challenge or perhaps authenticity. In contrast to those following (traditional) Alpha careers, individuals following Beta careers may have more job security and be valued more by their organizations. Companies might want to have Beta careerists who look for balance because "having a culture that promotes balance often positively affects the bottom line" (Sullivan & Mainiero, 2007, p. 268).

Alpha and Beta careers are not necessarily strictly divided along gender lines. Women have followed Alpha career paths as well as Beta paths; arguably, the former are women who have ascended to the top of corporate hierarchies. However, there are possibly more instances of men following Beta career paths than of women following Alpha patterns, particularly in the recent past where the role of men has changed to include more home and family responsibilities.

Women's Career Paths

Despite challenges in the workplace, some women have made their way to the top of corporate ladders. As discussed in previous chapters, the challenges faced by women are structural and interpersonal in workplaces and involve family demands at home.

The structural organizational challenges that limit women's hierarchical progress and career success have been labeled as the "Glass Ceiling" (Antoniou & Aggelou, 2019), the "Glass Cliff" (Ryan & Haslam, 2007), and, in the case of Asian women, the "Bamboo Ceiling" (Hyun, 2005). Although workplaces have changed to a certain extent, researchers have argued that the numbers show that parity has not been completely achieved in the workplace, especially at higher organizational levels. This is true despite the development of parity in the pipeline levels, namely, college education and lower management.

Women's career progress to executive and board levels in some large corporations makes for an interesting study, as it raises the question of whether there is a particular strategy that is effective for women. Nieva and Gutek (1981, p. 14) referred to women who are the only ones in their profession, that is, who selected "sex-atypical occupations," as "career pioneers." They noted that women pioneers were not necessarily more academically advanced or different in terms of likeability or hobbies. These women appeared to choose careers based on immediate factors such as grades and school performance as well as alignment to personality traits, and they also made pragmatic decisions. Their choices of careers appeared to rely on the encouragement they received: "support of people in school and college, and actual support for pursuing careers mattered" (Nieva & Gutek, 1981).

Women who experienced exceptional career success appear to have followed variations of the commonly accepted strategies for organizational success. They adapted such careers to suit needs specific to them as women. For instance, researchers have found that such women use impression management strategies that mix gender-typed approaches (Guadagno & Cialdini, 2007, p. 490). A study of technology companies found that such women had a greater number of women in their career and personal networks compared to those who were not as focused on career growth. They also had extensive and wide-ranging networks as compared to men. In response to the stereotypical view that "feminine communication is more indirect, elaborate, and emotional, whereas masculine communication is more direct, succinct and instrumental" (von Hippel et al., 2011, p. 1313), these women adopted a hybrid style. This mixed communication style would help with addressing both the competence and warmth components of stereotypes about women.

Researchers have noted that the career paths of most women are different from a traditional (male) organizational one. Cabrera (2009, p. 2) commented that "there is a profound disconnect between the traditional career model and the needs of women workers." According to Mainiero and Sullivan (2005, p. 108), there was a need for new models that better fit women's careers. Hewlett and Luce (2005, p. 47) noted that "a majority of highly qualified women describe their career as nonlinear" and that these careers have not followed a "progression through the hierarchy of an industry." Fitzgerald and Crites (1980, p. 44) added that traditional career theories explaining career decisions as driven by exploration and choice "may not describe or apply to women." They concluded that this is because "potential marriage and homemaking affect choices and stages" of women's careers. Currently, marriage, children, and other responsibilities such as elder care are included in the term "home (family) responsibilities."

Arguably, the two aspects in which the careers of men and women have differed are workplace fairness/equity and work continuity. Issues related to fairness and discrimination have been discussed elsewhere (for example, the effects of stereotyping, performance evaluation, and leadership opportunities). Work continuity has been studied from the perspective of women's interrupted careers, which differ from the norm of (men's) continuous employment. Different perspectives presented women's career choices as voluntary, imposed, or a mix of the two. Researchers noted that even if women remained in the same organization or industry, they might switch jobs or roles. Even if they remained at the same job, their degree of time commitment to it might vary in different periods.

A controversial statistic regarding women's career choices was the number of women obtaining college educations and even advanced professional degrees but leaving the workforce after some years. This was identified as a phenomenon and even labeled a "revolution," with the added label of "opt out" (Belkin, 2000). Hewlett and Luce (2005, p. 44) commented that "opting-out," either temporarily or permanently, was quite common, and that "nearly 4 in 10 qualified women report they have left work voluntarily at some point in [their] career."

Based on an extensive survey of media portrayals of women who opt out, Kuperberg and Stone (2008) identified three major themes: family first/child-centric, mommy elite, and choice. According to the authors, the "family first" theme focused "almost exclusively on women as mothers" and argued that their decision to opt out was based on considerations of family rather than the challenges they had faced in work situations (Kuperberg & Stone, 2008, p. 503). The "mommy elite" view presented women who opted out as being highly educated individuals who worked in high-status jobs and had husbands with high-paying and high-status jobs as well (Kuperberg & Stone, 2008, p. 505). The "choice" theme focused on women acting in line with their preferences, without mention of "barriers, constraints, or lack of options" (Kuperberg & Stone, 2008, p. 506). The authors noted that women's career paths were complex and often women felt conflicted regardless of which direction they went. They also noted that, contrary to a "revolution" as implied in the article by Belkin (2000), the percentage of women leaving the workplace had hovered between 25–35% during 1988–2003. Finally, they noted that, rather than opting out of the workforce altogether (type 2 adaptation noted previously), the reality was that women stayed in the workforce in different ways (type 3 adaptation), including by starting their own businesses. Mainiero and Sullivan (2005) noted that opt-out is a loss for the organization since it is a drain of trained talent.

Nieva and Gutek (1981) put opting out in the context of general career strategies followed by women. They suggested that women's adaptations to family responsibilities can take several forms, which can be broadly categorized as: 1) continuous employment with adjustment for family and home; 2) continuous employment until marriage or children, then quitting the workforce altogether; 3) stepping in and out of the labor force, taking on different long-term or short-term jobs. As described by Belkin (2000), women were increasingly likely to choose the second option. Belkin (2000, p. 736) explained their behavior thus: "Women today have the equal right to make the same bargain that men have made for centuries—to take time from their family in pursuit of success. Instead, women are redefining success. And in doing so, they are redefining work." Belkin (2000, p. 737) commented that the money or power associated with career success came with an attached price tag that these women did not consider worthwhile. In talking about success, women used words like "satisfaction, balance and sanity."

The significance of career interruptions was addressed in several publications. It appeared, over a work lifetime, that career outcomes for men and women were different. The cause of this difference was attributed to career interruptions. As noted by Cabrera (2009, p. 2), men and women both start careers with similar preferences and expectations, but these "diverge over time due to different experiences." Cabrera (2009) qualified this by noting that "younger women started out with more (gender) egalitarian ideas and major career expectations but life situations (often children) moved them away." Fitzgerald and Crites (1980, p. 45) explained this shift by stating that women's careers are made complex "due to that combination of attitudes, role expectations, behaviors and sanctions known as the socialization process." All of these factors appeared to suggest that while women might feel as much ambition and need for work as men, they feel an equal need to fulfill certain other responsibilities. Mainiero and Sullivan (2005, p. 110) stated that in their study, "women indicated they were far more likely to have non-traditional careers, characterized by various interruptions that required attention to non-work needs." This implied that were it not for non-work demands, these women would likely have continued in uninterrupted careers. Sullivan and Baruch (2009, p. 1551) made the difference even clearer by stating that "women experienced career interruptions due to family demands," while for men it was "more due to job loss." It must be noted, however, that women do pay a price for these interruptions. Even if they re-enter the workforce, they do so at lower levels of pay than previously and might never catch up. Some women, after leaving full-time employment, might never find a full-time job again (Hewlett & Luce, 2005, p. 46).

Even though men might equally value family and job flexibility, their "timing is different" (Mainiero & Sullivan, 2005, p. 114) in that they might be able to choose when to focus on family rather than their careers. Women, on the other hand, might not have the choice of timing. Under pressure to fulfill family responsibilities, women might step away from demanding careers and lower their time commitment to their jobs (Nieva & Gutek, 1981). For instance, they might move from a physician job to that of an administrator. Some women might make an initial career choice of a traditional job, such as a teacher, since that type of position might be viewed in society as compatible with family life. Thus, women's career decisions often involve combinations of marriage, childbearing, career preparation (which may include education or training), and work (Nieva & Gutek, 1981). According to Mainiero and

Sullivan (2005, p. 111), women often make career decisions for relational reasons, and these are "part of a larger and intricate web of interconnected issues, people and aspects" (Mainiero and Sullivan, 2005, p. 111). Thus, women presented work motivations other than individual ambition, achievement, or curiosity alone. In addition to these aspects, women factor in the needs and demands of other people in their lives. Women's career priorities shift based on "family as well as work factors" (Sullivan & Mainiero, 2007, p. 240).

Researchers have cautioned against explaining family and home as the main (or only) reason women leave employment, however. Mainiero and Sullivan (2005, p. 107) stated that women leave "not only or primarily for family" but that "lack of advancement opportunities may be [the] foremost reason." Kuperberg and Stone (2008) noted that media and popular portrayals of women leaving their jobs primarily to fulfill their desires (to be a mother) underplayed the conflicts they felt and the difficulties they had faced in the workplace. Workplace challenges and lack of advancement despite achievement and effort could, and did, incite some women to change jobs, organizations, or sectors (perhaps to move to nonprofits). Hewlett and Luce (2005, p. 44) proposed that "under-stimulation and lack of opportunity" were the major problems women faced and that surveys suggested that in the for-profit, business sector, "push factors are particularly powerful."

Different models have been proposed to explain women's careers. We present three of them here: Kaleidoscope, Labyrinth, and Alpha/Beta. The Alpha/Beta model (Sullivan & Mainiero, 2007) was discussed in the previous section. Although it is presented as a general model, where the two career types are not gender-specific, Sullivan and Mainiero do mention that a Beta career pattern fits many women's career paths and goals.

A kaleidoscope "produces changing patterns." Mainiero and Sullivan (2005, p. 111) presented this tool as an apt analogy for career approaches where women "shift the pattern of their career by rotating different aspects of their lives." Their study revealed that while both men and women might have experienced "career interruptions, employment gaps, top-outs, opt-outs," the ways that women described their careers differed from how men did so (Mainiero & Sullivan, 2005, p. 108). For women, the non-work needs that affected their careers went beyond family, particularly since a family had been narrowly defined in the study as meaning spouse and children. The difference between women and men was that "women made career decisions through a lens of relationalism—factoring in needs of many people," whereas men made decisions "from a goal attainment view" (Mainiero & Sullivan, 2005, p. 111). Thus, women might need to shift work commitments continually in response to different relational responsibilities. Mainiero and Sullivan (2005, p. 110) commented that the resulting collection of "a series of job opportunities, some part-time, some full-time" should be considered a career just as much as a "linear career."

Eagly and Carli (2007) described a labyrinth as a "complex journey to a goal worth striving for." They proposed the "Labyrinth" as a metaphor for women's career paths to organizational leadership positions. They noted that women faced more difficulty than men in this pursuit because of the weight of family responsibilities they bore (no differences were observed between men's and women's career paths until the birth of the first child) and a lack of social capital. Belkin (2000, p. 736) noted that many women "never get near" that glass ceiling because "they are stopped long before by the maternal wall." Despite difficulties along this path, women might be well-positioned to be effective leaders. According to Eagly and Carli (2007), this is due to women's preference for, and practice in, using a transformational leadership style. In their view, a transformational style is a better fit for both current organizations and business environments.

New Career Forms

Management scholars have been stressing for some time now that organizations have changed in unalterable ways and that the concept of an organizational career has "lost traditional features" (Sidiropoulou-Dimakakou et al., 2015, p. 40). Both the general business environment as well as workplace environments have become "increasingly competitive and turbulent" (Greenhaus & Kossek, 2014, p. 364).

A traditional career begins with an orientation to the organization at the entry point and a progression, often linear, from position to position until the termination of employment. However, current careers are likely to be less linear and predictable (Hirschi, 2012). Rather than an implicit understanding of tenure at an organization and professional advancement within it, careers are now understood to be "the unfolding sequence of an individual's work experiences over time" (Clarke, 2013, p. 685). The forms and natures of careers have altered considerably. In particular, the shifting of responsibility for professional development from the employing organization to the individual employee has had a significant impact on careers (Hirschi, 2012).

Organizations have been signaling that they were changing permanently over the last few decades by putting into practice strategies such as outsourcing and downsizing (Peirpel & Baruch, 1997, p. 14). Hall (2004, p. 5) noted that the "1980's saw the beginning of massive restructuring of the US and world economies." Mass layoffs were one consequence of new organizational practices of frequent strategic changes. This practice led to many employees taking up "forced entrepreneurship" (Sullivan & Baruch, 2009, p. 1542) within or beyond organizational boundaries.

These deep organizational changes disrupted the assumptions on which individuals structured their professional lives, such as job security and an increase in income over time. They often took away "secure, predictable and rewarding career paths from many employees" (Lips-Wiersma & Hall, 2007, p. 774). In previous times, an implicit psychological contract between an individual employee and the organization promised reciprocal obligations (Yang & Konrad, 2011). In other words, if employees put in the effort, performed their jobs as needed, and otherwise were productive organizational members, they would gain a measure of job (economic) security and benefits. Researchers claimed that this was no longer the case, thereby leading employees to approach their careers in new ways. Researchers thus studied new career forms that arose in response to organizational changes. Thus, the area of career management shifted focus to studying careers beyond purely organization-centered ones to include those that were "flexible and (had an) individual approach such as Boundaryless and Protean, and post corporate" (Lips-Wiersma & Hall, 2007, p. 771).

Another consequence of these changes was that organizations no longer formed a collection of full-time employees with a mutual understanding of long-term continuity. Rather, they were more likely a collection of three kinds of workers—core (full-time), continuous part-time, and temporary. Hall (2004, p. 5) labeled these as "Shamrock" organizational structures. Career development, previously addressed by organizations in the interest of having skilled, long-term employees, increasingly became the responsibility of individual employees as organizations moved away from maintaining a permanent workforce. Rather than a long-term and vertical career growth pattern, employees experienced a combination of medium-term roles with lateral, vertical, and even backward moves (Clarke, 2013, p. 697). Employees had to rely on professional groups for career guidance rather than on organizations providing structures for career advancement (Greco & Kraimer, 2019). In order to succeed—and even survive—in such an environment, Clarke (2013, p. 697) noted, individuals need the "capacity to adapt and change, to be flexible and cope with uncertainty."

Alternative models to the traditional organizational approach thus viewed careers as "physically and psychologically independent of organizations" (Rodrigues et al., 2019, p. 1). Factors determining career patterns include the individual's career orientation, personality characteristics, and social capital, as well as the labor market situation as reflected in the individual's employability (Rodrigues et al., 2019). Personality traits that mattered were the individual's ability to cope with uncertainty, instability, and ambiguity. Researchers also identified two main career mindsets: "protean" and "boundaryless." Initially, these were described as being different simply in the context of the (new) employer-employee relationship (Sullivan & Baruch, 2009, p. 1545). Later, they were differentiated as distinct career orientations.

A protean career model, as conceptualized by Hall in 1996 (Sullivan & Baruch, 2009), was one in which the individual rearranged and repackaged knowledge, skills, and abilities to meet the challenges of changing workplaces. In 2006, Briscoe and Hall reconceptualized this model by adding two dimensions of motivation, namely "value-driven and self-directed" (Sullivan & Baruch, 2009, p. 1545). Thus, a protean careerist views herself, and not the organization, as being in charge. An important aspect of such careers is that the individual's core values determine their career decisions and the main criteria for success are subjective and psychological (Hall, 2004, p. 1). The individual takes responsibility for her career and makes career decisions based on "personal values rather than organizational demands or merely to obtain material rewards" (Wiernik & Kostal, 2019, p. 281). A protean careerist is a continual learner (Hall, 2004, p. 6) and is associated with social networking and information seeking (Rodrigues et al., 2019) Thus, a protean careerist has an attitude of independence and freedom and is self-directed and value-driven (Rodrigues et al., 2019; Wiernik & Kostal, 2019). The protean orientation can lead to positive outcomes because these individuals are proactive in managing their careers. Additionally, they are adaptable to situations since they are driven by values, are focused on psychological well-being, and aim for both job and life satisfaction (Rodrigues et al., 2019).

A boundaryless career model, in contrast, is conceptualized as one that moves across the boundaries of separate employers, draws validation from extra-organizational sources, and is sustained by external networks or breaks traditional assumptions about organizational hierarchy and career advancement (Sullivan & Arthur, 2006, p. 20). A boundaryless career often emerges in response to a drastic reduction in organizational resources and support. Individuals then "seek resources or opportunities from outside their current employer," such as by changing organizations and relying on external professional networks (Wiernik & Kostal, 2019, p. 280). Thus, boundaryless careers are characterized by loosening ties of dependence on the employees' organizations and associated career arrangements (Sullivan & Arthur, 2006). Although this model is most apparent in terms of employees simply moving from one organization to another or to self-employment, researchers identified two types of separation and movement relevant in this context: psychological mobility and physical mobility (Wiernik & Kostal, 2019). The original and most studied type of movement is physical mobility, where the individual separates from an organization and is no longer part of the structure. This departure reflects the individual's willingness to change employing organizations. However, such individuals often continue doing the same kind of work and even work in similar roles in other organizations. Psychological mobility refers to the individual's willingness to change the type of work they do. This could be driven by a desire for variety in work or accepting different work as a necessity, such as for staying in a certain geographical region. A boundaryless career thus represents career mobility between organizations, either physical or psychological. Sullivan and Arthur (2006) noted that typically there is a combination of such physical/structural and psychological/mental/skill mobility, each being characterized as high or low. For a boundaryless careerist, career success could be both extrinsic (needing to earn a livelihood) and intrinsic (resonating with internal needs and values). Rodrigues et al. (2019) noted that such careers often have mixed results in terms of career outcomes. This might be because such careers could have resulted as the individual's response to organizational changes. Absent such changes, the individual might have preferred a traditional career. However, Arthur and Rousseau (1996, p. 37) cautioned that "we may wish that both chaos and boundaryless careers would go away, but we know in our better judgment they will not."

Protean and boundaryless careers seem similar to the extent that in both of these models, individuals display a lack of dependence on one organization for a career. However, these models represent distinct orientations. A willingness for physical mobility (changing organizations) in a boundaryless career is not strongly linked to either psychological mobility or protean orientation (Wiernik & Kostal, 2019, p. 289). On the other hand, a psychologically mobile boundaryless career resembles a protean one. Interestingly, a protean careerist might be satisfied with, or even seek, a traditional organizational career if that career fits with her core values.

There is no expectation that organizations will return to the old format of providing lifelong, or even long-term, employment. In fact, the way that organizations have been functioning in recent periods has left employees with few opportunities for vertical mobility and has resulted in high levels of voluntary and involuntary inter-organizational mobility (Greenhaus & Kossek, 2014). These trends point to a need for self-management of careers along with a willingness to be flexible and adaptable (Hirschi, 2012, p. 369). Social changes have affected career patterns as well. Employees are less willing to sacrifice home and personal life for the sake of the job. Career and home experiences also become inextricably interlinked in many careers (Greenhaus & Kossek, 2014). This is accentuated by the rise of work-from-home status in many workplaces.

Contemporary careers are likely to be a hybrid of traditional and non-traditional career concepts. For instance, individuals seek some traditional career outcomes, such as job security and upward mobility. At the same time, they also desire non-traditional outcomes, such as training both in and outside the organization. Increasingly, individuals might also exhibit aspects of a protean outlook in seeking work environments conducive to their well-being (Sullivan & Baruch, 2009, p. 1557).

A Note on At-Will Employment in U.S. Corporations

Asian women who might not be familiar with American organizations need to be aware of employment being "at-will." This is a unique aspect of employment in private U.S. companies. As per this principle, both the employer and employee can terminate the employment relationship with or without notice and with or without providing a reason (Bienstock, 2019). This doctrine, which is specific to U.S. employment practices, serves equality interests (in theory) since the "rights of an employer and an employee to terminate the relationship at will are formally symmetrical" (Bagenstos, 2013, pp. 244–245). There are exceptions to the rule, however; in particular, employers are forbidden to terminate employees for certain reasons, such as discrimination or as punishment for whistleblowing. However, a significant source of power in the workplace is the organization's authority to fire an employee. In practice, it is difficult for an employee to contest the reasons for their termination because the at-will rule "facilitates employers' assertion of pretextual reasons for termination" (Bienstock, 2019) and employees often lack resources to pursue legal avenues. The prevalence of at-will employment in the American workplace means that Asian women need to be aware that doing their jobs (even exceptionally well) might be a necessary but not sufficient condition for maintaining employment.

Asian Women in America: Careers and Environments

Asian women in America participate in the labor force in larger percentages than women in most Asian countries. Paid work outside the home might be necessitated by economic circumstances (Grahame, 2003, p. 74), or it might be pursued to enhance the family's socio-economic status through a second income, or, as was the case with many professionally qualified women, to fulfill career aspirations (Grahame, 2003, p. 73). In general, in comparison to the nonprofit or public sectors, Asian participation in the private sector is high, as indicated by the U.S. Department of Labor's 2011 data (Lim, 2017, p. 2). It appeared that many Asian women either work in their families' enterprises or start their own businesses. In the latter case, their businesses are predominantly micro-enterprises with fewer than five employees (Tuminez, 2012, p. 42). Some Asian women have had significant success, however; Tuminez (2012, p. 37) noted that the Forbes World's 100 Most Powerful Women from 2012 included 12 Asian women, with 6 in business and the other 6 in politics and multilateral organizations.

Most research on Asian women in American corporate organizations is subsumed within research on women in general or with research on minority women. Few studies, such as Lim (2017) and Na (2017), focused only on Asian women. In Lim's study of white males evaluating job applications, data did not support a hypothesis of racial backlash affecting hiring decisions. It appeared that, at least in that situation, hiring was not impacted by applicants being Asian American women. However, Lim (2017, pp. 7–8) cautioned that, after the hiring stage, "some Asian Americans may express lower levels of leadership motivation, either due to stereotype threats and challenges or due to repeated failure."

Na (2017) reported on the experiences of eight Asian immigrant women, representing a range of Asian countries, who came to the U.S. as children and later "rose to [the] highest corporate levels." Using a narrative inquiry framework, Na (2017, p. 37) collected information on their life experiences and commented that they often presented Asian cultural values in only positive tones. The most commonly identified Asian values across different ethnicities were "conformity to norms; family recognition through achievement; emotional self-control; collectivism; humility and filial piety" (Na, 2017, p.

41). The participants identified the approaches that had been effective for them, including not focusing only on fast and independent work but ensuring that others are included, even if it made work less efficient; the necessity of taking risks; pride in their identity as Asian women at work; using both masculine and feminine styles as the situation demanded; being authentic and having integrity; being explicit in communication; and including collegiality as well as Asian values of collectivism, deference, and respect for authority in leadership style. Na (2017) noted that the participants did not mention either money or physical appearance as affecting their careers. Rather, they appeared to have accepted the framework of pursuit of the "American Dream," namely that they would encounter career opportunities and success "based on skills and professional advancement" (Na, 2017, p. 146).

While some inferences about Asian women can be made from broader research where they are one of the groups considered, Mukkamala and Suyemoto (2018, p. 32) cautioned that viewing them as "sharing [the] experience of Asian Americans and White women" is inaccurate. As has been documented extensively, men and women have different experiences in the workplace. Asian women are perceived very differently from Asian men, and Asian women also differ from women in general due to their (perceived) racial/ethnical identity. The impact is particularly stark on the first generation, but it is evident to an extent in second-generation women, too. Asian cultures differ from mainstream American culture along some dimensions of Hofstede's model, such as individuality, power distance, and long-term orientation (Adya, 2008, p. 606). In an individualistic culture, like American society is considered to be, people are held responsible for their own progress and outcomes, whereas in collectivist Asian cultures, family and institutions are expected to take care of individuals in exchange for loyalty. A long-term orientation leads to individuals trading short-term gains for long-term benefits. These cultural attitudes have an impact on career decisions; for instance, they might lead an individual to give up a promotion and higher pay to remain in a more secure lower-level job. The difference in power distance orientation is linked to the individual's willingness to accept authority.

It has been well documented that stereotypes are persistent in workplaces, especially those associated with visible features. The stereotype content model characterized two dimensions on which stereotypical perceptions are based in the workplace—competence and warmth (Lim, 2017). Competence is related to one's ability to get the work done and is linked to the perceiver's respect. Warmth is related to the management of interpersonal relationships and is linked to an individual being liked by the perceiver. The common gender stereotype of women, in general, viewed them as deficient in the competency/agency dimension while scoring them high on warmth. In contrast, Asian women were perceived as "intelligent and mild-tempered, reserved and socially aloof" (Lim, 2017). According to Nichols (2017), they were depicted in the media as being "technically competent, hardworking, self-disciplined, serious and well-assimilated." At the same time, the stereotype viewed them as "passive, non-assertive, subservient" (Kawahara et al., 2013). The influence of the Asian model minority stereotype was clear, since the negative aspects of that stereotype characterize individuals as "passive, lacking social skills, apolitical, submissive and lacking in [the] aggressiveness required for high ranking managerial positions" (Nichols, 2017). Asian women appeared aware of the discrepancy between valued behaviors in Asian cultures as compared to the behaviors valued in workplaces. Nichols (2017) noted that Asian American women middle managers in Fortune 1000 companies emphasized that corporate cultures encouraged and rewarded outgoing personality traits. Hence, the perception (or reality) of social aloofness and passivity in an individual was a disadvantage.

Asian American women managers themselves felt that they were perceived as "obedient workhorses who lack the assertiveness and soft skills to be genuine leaders" (Nichols, 2017). Tinkler et al. (2019, p. 7) noted that Asian American women likely "rated low in leadership ability related to communal condition" since they were often "deferential and polite." These perceptions might be due to cultural factors or stereotypes. In their attempt to counter such workplace stereotypes, Asian women might be unknowingly feeding into them. For instance, it was noted by Nichols (2017) that Asian women worked longer hours than white women, and Yamanaka and McClelland (1994, p. 108) similarly added that these women have "achieved their relatively high income only by working longer and harder (than comparable whites)." Asian women might also be unaware of how certain behaviors are interpreted in the workplace. For instance, Asian cultures generally discourage the expression of emotion, especially in the workplace (Durik et al., 2006, pp. 437–438). Workplace gender stereotypes related to emotion include "individuals' beliefs about the extent to which women and men express and experience specific emotions" (Durik et al., 2006, p. 429). In this regard, Asian women were stereotyped as less comfortable in expressing emotion compared to white women (Durik et al., 2006, p. 441). Thus, Asian women have an ambivalent descriptive stereotype in workplaces—high on competence, low on warmth (Lim, 2017). The ambivalence stems from this stereotype's contrast with the general female stereotype of lower competence and higher warmth.

As noted above, Asian women enter the labor force for varied reasons. Ocampo et al. (2018) commented that family-related factors were a unique and independent aspect distinguishing the work motivations of Asian employees. It is possible that Asians also follow a pragmatic approach to making career decisions (Hodkinson & Sparkes, 1997, p. 33), relying on information and guidance from trusted contacts and placing a career in the context of family and culture. The community might also have a role in this process; Manohar (2013b) noted that immigrant communities can facilitate the assimilation and upward mobility of their members. Asian women have exhibited a commitment to education and have the largest percentage of college graduates among groups of women. It appears that they have followed a strategy of amassing human capital by establishing unquestioned professional credentials, mainly through education. This is not limited to undergraduate education. For instance, Killian and Manohar's (2016) study of Tamil (Indian) immigrants showed that these college-educated women experienced "downward occupational mobility" when they attempted to enter the U.S. labor market on arrival in the country. According to Manohar (2013b), "the devaluation of Indian credentials and glass ceilings limited their professional mobility." They were also initially restricted from paid work due to their legal status (as H-1B spouses). Thus, they turned to various strategies to gain human capital and skills, such as by volunteering and, although they were already qualified, some turned to further education as the means to obtain highly skilled jobs. Zhou and Lee (2017) noted that the success frame which views educational achievement as a means to acquire a good job and livelihood is not unique to Asian Americans, but that they appear to accept and implement it to a greater degree than other groups. Grahame (2003, p. 66) discussed a "larger field study examining Asian immigrant women's entry into the labor market via job training programs" which indicated that despite the complexity and difficulty of managing work, family, and training, the women were optimistic and believed that this would improve their lives. Indeed, most participants planned to pursue more education, and their plans were related "to a desire to support their families" (Grahame, 2003, p. 81).

Asian women differ from women in general both in the kinds of jobs they seek and in their approaches to careers. It appeared that Asian women were more oriented toward STEM careers, even though those fields were male-dominated. In a study of women in IT careers, Adya (2008, p. 602) commented that it appeared that, for Asian women, "computer science and IT are considered to be feminine careers." This categorization contrasts with the broader view in American society, which considered these careers as masculine and as male-dominated settings. A distinctive workplace attitude of Asian women (noted by several researchers) is their awareness and perceptions of—and their responses to—experiences of workplace discrimination. Adya (2008, p. 614) noted that in the study of women in IT, "discrimination and stereotyping were more frequently cited by American than South Asian women." Remedios et al. (2011, p. 283) concluded that their study of Asian women in Canadian workplaces revealed that the Asian women were "more likely to attribute racism than sexism to internal factors" even though they perceived "more racism than sexism in their environment." The study by Dhingra (2007, p. 139) of Asians in the U.S. had slightly different findings: "Many women complained of possible barriers based less on race and more on gender." However, all researchers noted that Asian women appeared either unaware of discrimination occurring or were accepting of such an environment: "passive responses such as acceptance as part of work culture and social expectations were often observed among these women" (Adya, 2008, p. 617), and "overall, respondents downplayed the effects of racism and planned on gradually attaining economic and social equality with the support of their own communities" (Dhingra, 2007, p. 112). Thus, "Asian women internalize the causes of racism more than sexism" (Remedios et al., 2011, p. 283). Adya (2008, p. 624) explained the (non)response of Asian women to potentially discriminatory workplace experiences as rooted in a long-term orientation: they might choose to overlook such experiences, even when they were aware of them, as a trade-off of "short-term challenges in return for long-term career advancement." Dhingra (2007, p. 11) proposed the explanation that their lack of response to discrimination was an acculturation strategy to appear as "desirable workers."

For Asian women, career management thus includes the need to manage cultural expectations and negotiate gender roles. Asian cultures emphasize traditional gender roles (Srinivasan, 2001, p. 137), and immigrant women are likely to adhere to them. Based on a study of marriage in South Asian communities, Mehrotra (2016, p. 357) noted that even in the U.S., women were given the message that "to be a good, middle-class South Asian woman means to be married." Researchers have noted the importance of ethnic communities in acculturation and identity formation. In particular, ethnicity can become salient to Asian women if they experience stereotyping in the workplace. Gee et al. (2015) cautioned that skewing close to traditional upbringing and cultural norms could be a hindrance, however, if those cultural attitudes differ widely from workplace norms and values. Fong (1997) noted that some Asian values, such as achievement and hard work, were similar to American values but others, such as filial piety, obedience to authority, and passive acceptance of one's situation, contradicted American society's emphasis on individualism and independence.

Working outside the home and contributing to the economic status of the family could alter traditional household power relationships, however (Manohar, 2013a, p. 161). The immigrant women in the study of Tamil moms attempted to craft a hybrid of Asian and American normative behaviors. As working mothers, "with no (role) models in the US, they reference the American 'mythical construct' of supermoms and become highly efficient mothers" (Manohar, 2013a, p. 172).

In contrast to women in general, Asian women appear "less likely to drop out of the labor force as they get older, or when they get married and the presence of children appears to have less inhibiting effect on their working" (Yamanaka & McClelland, 1994, p. 98). Some women managed this balance by relying on a variety of "kith and kin arrangements to manage both work and family" (Manohar, 2013a, p. 161). An interesting finding by Kang and Cohen (2018, p. 128) based on pooled data from the American Community Survey (2009–2011), was that "married, first-generation Asian immigrant women's employment rates are higher when they live with their parents or parents-in-law" (Kang & Cohen, 2018, p. 128). The authors noted that this was ironic since an "ostensibly 'traditional' practice—extended family living arrangements—encouraged the 'modern' practice of women's labor force participation" (Kang & Cohen, 2018, p. 149). It appeared that Asian women viewed work and family not as opposing, distinct choices or as a "duality of experience" (Grahame, 2003, p. 66) but as "extensions of their familial responsibilities" (Grahame, 2003, p. 68).

Both by choice and circumstance, then, Asian women are often presented in the workplace as bicultural. Familiarity with two cultures that vary strongly along multiple dimensions positions these women favorably in diverse workplaces of global businesses. Inman et al. (2001, p. 18) commented that Asian (Indian) women have a strong tendency to hold on to "central values related to family relationships while adapting to the pragmatic aspects of survival such as the use of English language." Srinivasan (2001, p. 150) commented that the contexts in which women consider and portray themselves as either Asian or (mainstream) American are different. It appeared the women made these choices strategically. Na (2017, p. 142) noted that some women described their choice of which self to apply in a given situation as related to a desired outcome. Na (2017, p. 143) described several elements of such bicultural competence, such as "caring for others in the company, community, family; collectivist perspective; use expertise for influence and also built networks; strong work ethic—a high expectation of themselves and others; learned topics beyond work roles and acquired skills unrelated to work; had deep curiosity; effective and strategic communicators."

Asian women approach their careers by incorporating their individual preferences and aspirations while moderating them with family and long-term career concerns. They acquire human capital primarily through education, which they are willing to continue throughout their work-life. They consider their careers and personal responsibilities as intertwined and view their jobs as extensions of their family responsibilities. Although they face more complex challenges in the workplace, especially the dual stereotypes of gender and race, they can leverage this dual challenge as bicultural competence.

Notes in Conclusion

Traditional models of organizational careers gave importance to entry into the organization and subsequent vertical (up the levels) and horizontal (across departments and divisions) movement. Continuity within the organization was the implicit assumption. The importance given to development and retention in management literature rests on a similar assumption. Negotiating a career within the same organization thus requires familiarity with the organization, being cognizant of organizational politics, and building internal networks.

Researchers noted that women did not have such organizational careers, specifically due to a lack of continuity in one organization and interruptions (breaks) over the span of a career. Such careers were likely to be housed in different organizations at different points in time. Clearly, managing such careers was different from managing those that persisted within one organization. These careers were labeled variously as Kaleidoscopic, Labyrinth, and Alpha/Beta.

An interesting development in recent years has been that careers in general, for both men and women, began to change as organizations themselves changed fundamentally in their functioning and constant restructuring and as outsourcing became the norm. The general organizational career has started to resemble what some once referred to as "women's" careers. These new organizational career forms have been labeled as "boundaryless" and "protean."

Not much is known about the career paths of Asian women in American workplaces, including whether their careers resemble the interrupted patterns of women in general. However, it is certain that in the future they will encounter workplaces where permanence in one organization is unlikely. Asian women must be prepared for careers that span several organizations and even different professions. To navigate this path, they will need to acquire human and social capital beyond organizational boundaries.

REFERENCES

Adya, M. P. (2008). Women at work: Differences in IT career experiences and perceptions between South Asian and American women. *Human Resource Management*, *47*(3), 601–635. doi:10.1002/hrm.20234

Antoniou, A., & Aggelou, V. (2019). Female managers with male-type behavior. In A. Antoniou, C. Cooper, & C. Gatrell (Eds.), *Women, business and leadership: Gender and organisations* (pp. 199–215). Edward Elgar Publishing. doi:10.4337/9781786432711.00019

Arthur, M. B., & Rousseau, D. M. (1996). A career lexicon for the 21st century. *The Academy of Management Executive*, *10*(4), 28–39. doi:10.5465/ame.1996.3145317

Bagenstos, S. R. (2013, November). Employment law and social equality. *Michigan Law Review*, *112*(2), 225–273.

Belkin, L. (2000). The opt-out revolution. *Social Stratification, Class, Race & Gender in Social Perspective*, 735–738.

Bienstock, J. E. (2019). The future of employment at-will in New York: Rough seas or smooth sailing? *Journal of Business and Behavioral Sciences*, *31*(2), 39–59.

Cabrera, E. F. (2009). Protean organizations: Reshaping work and careers to retain female talent. *Career Development International*, *14*(2), 186–201. doi:10.1108/13620430910950773

Clarke, M. (2013, February). The organizational career: Not dead but in need of redefinition. *International Journal of Human Resource Management*, *24*(4), 684–703. doi:10.1080/09585192.2012.697475

De Vos, A., & Cambre, B. (2017, May-June). Career management in high-performing organizations: A set-theoretic approach. *Human Resource Management*, *56*(3), 501–518. doi:10.1002/hrm.21786

Dhingra, P. (2007). *Managing multicultural lives: Asian American professionals and the challenge of multiple identities*. Stanford University Press.

Durik, A. M., Hyde, J. S., Marks, A. C., Roy, A. L., Anaya, D., & Schultz, G. (2006). Ethnicity and gender stereotypes of emotion. *Sex Roles*, *54*(7-8), 429–445. doi:10.100711199-006-9020-4

Eagly, A. H., & Carli, L. L. (2007). Women and the labyrinth of leadership. *Harvard Business Review*. https://hbr.org/2007/09/women-and-the-labyrinth-of-leadership

Fitzgerald, L. F., & Crites, J. O. (1980). Toward a career psychology of women: What do we know? What do we need to know? *Journal of Counseling Psychology*, *27*(1), 44–62. doi:10.1037/0022-0167.27.1.44

Fong, L. Y. S. (1997). Asian-American women: An understudied minority. *Journal of Sociology and Social Welfare*, *24*(1), 91–111.

Fourie, C., & Van Vuuren, L. J. (1998). Defining and measuring career resilience. *SA Journal of Industrial Psychology*, *24*(3), 52–59. doi:10.4102ajip.v24i3.662

Gee, B., Peck, D., & Wong, J. (2015). *Hiding in plain sight: Asian American leaders in Silicon Valley*. Ascend Report.

Gould, S. (1979). Characteristics of career planners in upwardly mobile occupations. *Academy of Management Journal*, *22*(3), 539–550.

Grahame, K. M. (2003). "For the family": Asian immigrant women's triple day. *Journal of Sociology and Social Welfare*, *30*(1), 65–90.

Greco, L. M., & Kraimer, M. L. (2020). Goal-setting in the career management process: An identity theory perspective. *The Journal of Applied Psychology*, *105*(1), 40–57. doi:10.1037/apl0000424 PMID:31169377

Greenhaus, J. H., & Kossek, E. E. (2014). The contemporary career: A work-home perspective. *Annual Review of Organizational Psychology and Organizational Behavior*, *1*(1), 361–388. doi:10.1146/annurev-orgpsych-031413-091324

Guadagno, R. E., & Cialdini, R. B. (2007). Gender differences in impression management in organizations: A qualitative review. *Sex Roles*, *56*(7-8), 483–494. doi:10.100711199-007-9187-3

Hall, D. T. (2004). The Protean career: A quarter-century journey. *Journal of Vocational Behavior*, *65*(1), 1–13. doi:10.1016/j.jvb.2003.10.006

Hewlett, S. A., & Luce, C. B. (2005, March). Off-ramps and on-ramps: Keeping talented women on the road to success. *Harvard Business Review*, 43–54. PMID:15768675

Hirschi, A. (2012, August). The career resources model: An integrative framework for career counsellors. *British Journal of Guidance & Counselling*, *40*(4), 369–383. doi:10.1080/03069885.2012.700506

Hodkinson, P., & Sparkes, A. C. (1997). Careership: A sociological theory of career decision making. *British Journal of Sociology of Education*, *18*(1), 29–44. doi:10.1080/0142569970180102

Holland, J. L. (1996). Exploring careers with a typology: What we have learned and some new directions. *The American Psychologist*, *51*(4), 397–406. doi:10.1037/0003-066X.51.4.397

Hyun, J. (2005). *Breaking the Bamboo Ceiling*. Harper-Collins.

Inman, A. G., Ladany, N., Constantine, M. G., & Morano, C. K. (2001). Development and preliminary validation of the cultural values conflict scale for South Asian women. *Journal of Counseling Psychology*, *48*(1), 17–27. doi:10.1037/0022-0167.48.1.17

Ishida, H. (2002). Models of career advancement in organizations. *European Sociological Review*, *18*(2), 179–198. doi:10.1093/esr/18.2.179

Kang, J., & Cohen, P. N. (2018). Household extension and employment among Asian Immigrant: Women in the United States. *Journal of Family Issues*, *39*(1), 128–154. doi:10.1177/0192513X15606489

Kawahara, D. M., Pal, M. S., & Chin, J. L. (2013). The leadership experiences of Asian Americans. *Asian American Journal of Psychology*, *4*(4), 240–248. doi:10.1037/a0035196

Killian, C., & Manohar, N. N. (2016). Highly skilled immigrant women's labor market access: A comparison of Indians in the United States and North Africans in France. *Social Currents*, *3*(2), 138–159. doi:10.1177/2329496515620644

Kuperberg, A., & Stone, P. (2008). The media depiction of women who opt out. *Gender & Society*, *22*(4), 497–517. doi:10.1177/0891243208319767

Leung, A. S. (2008). Chapter 6: The big five career theories. In J. A. Athanasou & R. Van Esbroeck (Eds.), International handbook of career guidance (pp. 115–132). Springer Science + Business Media B.V.

Lim, J. I. (2017). *Perceptions of Asian American and female leadership candidates: The impact of descriptive and prescriptive stereotyping* [Doctoral dissertation, City University of New York]. CUNY Academic Works: Dissertations, Theses and Capstone Projects: Graduate Center.

Lips-Wiersma, M., & Hall, D. T. (2007). Organizational career development is not dead: A case study on managing the new career during organizational change. *Journal of Organizational Behavior*, *28*(6), 771–792. doi:10.1002/job.446

Mainiero, L. A., & Sullivan, S. E. (2005). Kaleidoscope careers: An alternate explanation for the "opt-out" revolution. *The Academy of Management Executive*, *19*(1), 106–123. doi:10.5465/ame.2005.15841962

Manohar, N. N. (2013a). Mothering for class and ethnicity: The case of Indian professional immigrants in the United States. In M. Kohlman, D. Krieg, & B. Dickerson (Eds.), *Notions of family: Intersectional perspectives, advances in gender research* (Vol. 17, pp. 159–185). Emerald Group Publishing Limited. doi:10.1108/S1529-2126(2013)0000017011

Manohar, N. N. (2013b). Support networks, ethnic spaces, and fictive kin: Indian immigrant women constructing community in the United States. *AAPI Nexus*, *11*(1–2), 25–55.

Mehrotra, G. R. (2016). South Asian women and marriage: Experiences of a cultural script. *Gender Issues*, *33*(4), 350–371. doi:10.100712147-016-9172-7

Moore, M. H. (2000). Managing for value: Organizational strategy in for-profit, nonprofit, and governmental organizations. *Nonprofit and Voluntary Sector Quarterly*, *29*(1), 183–204. doi:10.1177/089976400773746391

Mukkamala, S., & Suyemoto, K. L. (2018). Racialized sexism/sexualized racism: A multimethod study of intersectional experiences of discrimination for Asian American women. *Asian American Journal of Psychology*, *9*(1), 32–46. doi:10.1037/aap0000104

Na, Y. (2017). *The Experiences of Asian Immigrant women: Journeys into corporate leadership* [Doctoral Dissertation, Alliant International University, San Francisco]. ProQuest LLC.

Ng, T. W. H., Eby, L. T., Sorensen, K. L., & Feldman, D. C. (2005). Predictors of objective and subjective career success: A meta-analysis. *Personnel Psychology*, *58*(2), 367–408. doi:10.1111/j.1744-6570.2005.00515.x

Nichols, A. (2017). The influence of ethnicity and gender on the leadership experiences of female Asian-American managers. *Global Journal of Human-Social Science Interdisciplinary*, *17*(4), 1–28.

Nieva, V. F., & Gutek, B. A. (1981). *Women and work: A psychological perspective*. Praeger.

Nye, C. D., Su, R., Rounds, J., & Drasgow, F. (2012, July). Vocational interests and performance: A quantitative summary of over 60 years of research. *Perspectives on Psychological Science*, *7*(4), 384–403. doi:10.1177/1745691612449021 PMID:26168474

Ocampo, A. C. G., Restubog, S. L. D., Liwag, M. E., Wang, L., & Petelczyc, C. (2018). My spouse is my strength: Interactive effects of perceived organizational and spousal support in predicting career adaptability and career outcomes. *Journal of Vocational Behavior*, *108*, 165–177. doi:10.1016/j.jvb.2018.08.001

Peirpel, M., & Baruch, Y. (1997, Spring). Back to square zero: The post-corporate career. *Organizational Dynamics*, 7–22.

Remedios, J. D., Chasteen, A. L., & Paek, J. D. (2011). Not all prejudices are experienced equally: Comparing experiences of racism and sexism in female minorities. *Group Processes & Intergroup Relations*, *15*(2), 273–287. doi:10.1177/1368430211411594

Rodrigues, R., Butler, C. L., & Guest, D. (2019). Antecedents of Protean and Boundaryless career orientations: The role of core self-evaluations, perceived employability and social capital. *Journal of Vocational Behavior*, *110*, 1–11. doi:10.1016/j.jvb.2018.11.003

Ryan, M. K., & Haslam, A. S. (2007). The Glass Cliff: Exploring the dynamics surrounding the appointment of women to precarious leadership positions. *Academy of Management Review*, *32*(2), 549–572. doi:10.5465/amr.2007.24351856

Seibert, S. E., & Kraimer, M. L. (2001). The five-factor model of personality and career success. *Journal of Vocational Behavior*, *58*(1), 1–21. doi:10.1006/jvbe.2000.1757

Sidiropoulou-Dimakakou, D., Mylonas, K., & Argyropoulou, K. (2015, May). Self-efficacy in career planning: A new approach to career exploration. *International Journal of Learning. Teaching and Educational Research, 11*(2), 40–54.

Srinivasan, S. (2001). "Being Indian," "Being American": A balancing act or a creative blend? *Journal of Human Behavior in the Social Environment, 3*(3/4), 135–158.

Sullivan, S. E., & Arthur, M. B. (2006). The evolution of the boundaryless career concept: Examining physical and psychological mobility. *Journal of Vocational Behavior, 69*(1), 19–29. doi:10.1016/j.jvb.2005.09.001

Sullivan, S. E., & Baruch, Y. (2009). Advances in career theory and research: A critical review and agenda for future exploration. *Journal of Management, 36*(6), 1542–1571. doi:10.1177/0149206309350082

Sullivan, S. E., & Mainiero, L. A. (2007). The changing nature of gender roles, Alpha/Beta careers and work-life issues: Theory-driven implications for human resource management. *Career Development International, 12*(3), 238–263. doi:10.1108/13620430710745881

Super, D. E. (1953). A theory of vocational development. *The American Psychologist, 8*(5), 185–190. doi:10.1037/h0056046

Super, D. E., Tiedeman, D. V., & Borow, H. (1961, September). Vocational development: A symposium. *The Personnel and Guidance Journal, 40*(1), 11–15. doi:10.1002/j.2164-4918.1961.tb02077.x

Tinkler, J., Zhao, J. J., Li, Y., & Ridgeway, C. L. (2019). Honorary Whites? Asian American women and the dominance penalty. *Socius: Sociological Research for a Dynamic World, 5*, 1–13. doi:10.1177/2378023119836000

Tuminez, A. S. (2012). *Rising to the top? A report on women's leadership in Asia.* Asia Society. http://sites.asiasociety.org/womenleaders/wp-content/uploads/2012/04/Rising-to-the-Top.pdf

von Hippel, C., Wiryakusuma, C., Bowden, J., & Shochet, M. (2011). Stereotype threat and female communication styles. *Personality and Social Psychology Bulletin, 37*(10), 1312–1324. doi:10.1177/0146167211410439 PMID:21646549

Wiernik, B. M., & Kostal, J. W. (2019). Protean and Boundaryless career orientations: A critical review and meta-analysis. *Journal of Counseling Psychology*, *66*(3), 280–307. doi:10.1037/cou0000324 PMID:30777774

Yamanaka, K., & McClelland, K. (1994). Earning the Model-Minority image: Diverse strategies of economic adaptation by Asian-American women. *Ethnic and Racial Studies*, *17*(1), 79–114. doi:10.1080/01419870.1994.9993814

Yan, A., Zhu, G., & Hall, D. T. (2002). International assignments for career building: A model of agency relationships and psychological contracts. *Academy of Management Review*, *27*(3), 373–391. doi:10.5465/amr.2002.7389910

Yang, Y., & Konrad, A. M. (2011). Understanding diversity management practices: Implications of Institutional theory and Resource-based theory. *Group & Organization Management*, *36*(1), 6–38. doi:10.1177/1059601110390997

Zhou, M., & Lee, J. (2017). Hyper-selectivity and the remaking of culture: Understanding the Asian American achievement paradox. *Asian American Journal of Psychology*, *8*(1), 7–15. doi:10.1037/aap0000069

Chapter 8
Conclusions, Forecasts, and Recommendations

ABSTRACT

In the concluding chapter, the authors present a sketch of what Asian women can expect in generic organizational workplaces. Their work experience is informed by the work environment as well as by outside factors, including family, community, and society. They present a view of organizational careers, past and present, and (likely) forecasts for the workplace of the future with specific recommendations for this group of women. Finally, based on the material presented in the preceding chapters, they identify paths for future research in this subject area.

INTRODUCTION

Asian women are relatively recent entrants to corporate American workplaces, as has been discussed in previous chapters. Asian immigration to the U.S. has a long history, with significant participation by Asians in the business sector. Asians, both men and women, have a strong record of owning small businesses. However, their presence as employees of (large) corporations has gained significance only in the last few decades. Specifically, changes in immigration laws resulted in increased immigration of both trained professionals and students from Asian countries. Immigrant Asian women entered the workforce in different ways—directly, upon graduating with higher

DOI: 10.4018/978-1-7998-4384-9.ch008

education degrees in the U.S., or indirectly after re-education/re-training following their entry to the country as (trailing) spouses.

Immigrants are not the only Asian women in the corporate workforce, however. Sufficient time has passed since the entry of the first wave of immigrants, and changes in immigration law have also affected the circumstances in which their daughters (and perhaps grand-daughters) have entered the workforce. Thus, it is possible to have multiple generations of Asian women in these workplaces. However, the acculturation processes of Asians indicate that the most significant differences are between the first and second generations. At present, these generations are likely the largest groups of Asian women in corporate workplaces.

Asian women have also been active in the U.S. economy in areas other than corporate workplaces. For instance, they work in healthcare, education, law, government, nonprofits, retail, and food services, among many other domains. They are small business owners and entrepreneurs in different sectors and industries of the U.S. economy. For instance, the 2012 Census revealed that there were more than 50,000 female-owned real-estate and rental businesses and 100,000 professional and scientific companies (Census, 2016). Overall, there were more than 600,000 women owned business and around 6.5% of these were owned by Asian American women (Smith, 2013).

The careers of organizational employees are different from those of businessowners or professionals (in areas such as education, law, and medicine). Employees' work in organizations is determined to a large extent by their positions and is directed by their supervisors. In contrast to businessowners who do not report to anyone in their organization, employees are bound by the constraints of their position. The work of professionals also differs from that of typical organizational employees in that it is specialized to the extent of requiring certification or licensing and is subject to regulation. In contrast, the work of most employees in corporations is determined by the organization and is not subject to external regulations or requirements.

Finally, the corporate board members of an organization are (typically) not employees of that organization, aside from the CEO and certain other C-suite personnel (on occasion). However, the representation of Asian women at the corporate board level is an important statistic to track since board positions can be highly influential. (There is data available regarding the board composition of Fortune 500 companies, in contrast to the lack of data on Asian women's representation at industry or company levels.) Over the period 2012–2018, the number of Asian women board members in Fortune 500 companies increased from 13 to 17 (Harvard Law Forum, 2018). In 2018, there were seventeen Asian/Pacific Islander women board members in Fortune 100 companies (Deloitte, 2018). However, in this book we have not concentrated on board membership, as these figures represent Asian women who have already had successful careers. Rather, our focus has been on women in entry and middle organizational levels.

Organizational Workplaces

Organizational workspaces are characterized by two structures that impact decision-making and functioning: positions (with their attached job descriptions) and reporting relationships (between positions, which indicate hierarchy). Positions reflect the division of work and hierarchy is related to the coordination of work across the organization. The job description related to a given position outlines the scope of work to be done by any employee occupying that position. How the responsibilities attached to a position are fulfilled depends on factors like the organizational level of that position, organizational culture, and the supervisor's management style. The work in positions lower in the hierarchy tends to have a greater amount of specificity than the work associated with other positions (typically higher in the hierarchy) that might involve more uncertainty. However, every position requires some degree of decision making and has scope for employees to exercise initiative. Thus, skills in creative thinking and decision making, in addition to efficiency (organization, planning, and time-management), are assets to organizational careers.

Organizational work is subject to periodic assessment and evaluation. Performance evaluations (discussed in Chapter 2) form the basis for career movement (or lack thereof). These evaluations are subject to certain legal criteria, such as common measures intended to reduce bias. Yet, it is difficult to standardize evaluation across all types of jobs, thus leaving room for variation (Prendergast & Topel, 1993). Some variation is due to the unavoidably subjective nature of evaluation (such as judgment on skills or qualities like "willingness to work in a team"). The lack of uniform performance standards and clarity on how evaluation decisions are reached has been critiqued as providing means to cover bias by labeling it as opinions. Researchers have posited that descriptive and prescriptive gender stereotypes are at the root of evaluation bias (both intentional and unintentional) against women. Such bias has been identified as systemic in the context of women's organizational careers; there is every likelihood it exists in other contexts as well.

The functioning of organizations depends on their structure (in which reporting relationships ensure that each employee performs assigned work) and on the operational aids they use, such as policies, processes, and procedures. An important aspect of organizational functioning that pertains to interpersonal interactions is culture. Organizational culture is popularly understood as referring to stories, values, beliefs, and attitudes. Although it is difficult to define precisely, culture is a powerful determinant in employees' workplace experiences, and it has a deep impact on organizational environments. Schein proposed that culture is present at several levels, some explicit and others implicit. The outward presentation of culture is visible in symbols and organizational legends, with values at a deeper level and a set of widely accepted beliefs at the core (Hatch, 1993). Hofstede et al. (1990) suggested that the core of organizational culture is concrete rather than abstract, as has been commonly accepted. They also argue that organizational culture consists of the everyday behaviors and practices employees understand to be acceptable (and rewardable) in the context of the organization.

The ability to do assigned work and the ability to manage relationships successfully are the two dimensions of employee effectiveness through which performance is typically evaluated. These dimensions are sometimes referred to as "task-oriented" and "relationship-oriented" (in management and leadership literature), or as "agency" and "communal/warmth" (in sociology). While the ability to complete assigned work is important, as is the quality of such work, workplace relationships are equally important because every employee's work is linked to that of others. An employee's internal network consists of all his or her contacts within the organization and includes the understanding of the kind of relationship and interactions the employee has with each of them. Organizational culture affects the kinds of internal networks within a business and how they function. Some relationships are designed into the organizational structure, such as reporting and supervisory links. However, there is scope for every employee to initiate other contacts and build relationships beyond those embedded in the organization's structure. Thus, internal networks can include mentors and team members from cross-functional teams as well as members of informal groups (for example, a company sports team). The importance of these internal networks is related to the characteristics of the contacts within them and the utility of each link for the employee. An internal network can thus be the differentiating factor in an employee's career experience.

Finally, while many organizations continue to maintain traditional structures and related ways of functioning, organizational workplaces are constantly changing. One such change is the composition of the workforce, which is itself driven by broader social and cultural changes. One interesting external change affecting organizations is a (possible) shift in the accepted indicators of business success. As U.S. society experiences various changes in demographic composition and culture, there appears to be an increasing focus on balancing the values of individualism with those of collectivism. Individualism focuses on independence, achievement, goal-orientation, and assertiveness. Collectivism, on the other hand, emphasizes interdependence and commitment to group goals and benefits (Oyserman & Sakamoto, 1997). This shift has been reflected in business decisions such as the one announced recently by Blackrock to consider social impact as one measure of business performance (Sorkin, 2018). All these changes have had a ricocheting effect on what is expected of business leaders' behaviors and decisions. Now, more than ever, in addition to agency (exhibited as assertiveness and competence), business leaders will need to give greater weight to people, both within and outside the organization, in words and action.

Organizational Careers: General Characteristics

Organizational careers have been the subject of extensive study. Continuity in an organization was an underlying assumption in the traditional view of organizational careers. There was thought to be an implicit social contract between employees and the organization, where employees put in their best efforts and showed loyalty to the organization, and in return the organization would provide for their needs during their organizational tenure (in the form of compensation and benefits) and even after (as retirement funds). Thus, career management focused on the choice of work, becoming familiar with the workplace and developing skills in negotiating it, building networks and visibility, and acquiring power. Career movements were typically upward (promotions) or sideways (transfers to another area). Researchers also noted the importance of career (and life) goals that individuals sought to fulfill through work. Based on these assumptions, career guidance aimed to help individuals identify the kind of work they wanted or liked to do and to choose jobs accordingly. For instance, Herzberg (2003) found that achievement and the nature of the work itself were the key contributors to employee satisfaction. It was presumed that employees considered these factors when they accepted organizational positions. Thus, it was to the benefit of both the employee and the organization for there be a good fit between the individual and the position the individual occupied (which could change over time). Organizations put in effort towards this outcome through development programs such as training and mentoring. In this understanding of organizational careers, it was also important that employees at all levels and in all positions felt a sense of belonging, since this impacted organizations in terms of employees' motivation, productivity, and turnover. Thus, cultivating a feeling of organizational identity among employees was beneficial to the organization, and it also benefited the employees by contributing to a sense of belonging.

At the same time, organizational functioning had a lot of room for fuzziness and subjectivity. The career paths of individuals who appeared to be comparable in most aspects could evolve in strikingly different ways. These divergences could be due to variability in individual characteristics, but they could also be caused by systemic factors. The most common factor with systemic impact on careers was bias related to gender and race/ethnicity. Extensive research done on women's careers and workplace experiences has highlighted these systemic forces at work. Diversity initiatives were offered as ways in which business sought to reduce (if not eliminate) bias not only against women but against other groups as well. A concurrent stream of research proposed that career interruptions were a distinct feature of many women's careers (across organizations and even industries). It appeared that these women's careers included tenures in (possibly different) organizations separated by breaks in between. The breaks were usually associated with occasions when women felt the need to step out of organizations so they could fulfill certain other responsibilities. (A common reason was taking care of young children.) These interrupted careers contrasted with traditional organizational careers located consistently within one organization.

More recently, researchers have been emphasizing that organizational careers of all kinds have changed, and for everybody, due to changes in the ways business organizations have been choosing to function (such as continual restructuring). For the foreseeable future, it appears that a career entirely within just one organization is a rarity. The more likely career path today is one that moves from one organization to the next, perhaps spending extended periods in each (identified as a "boundaryless" career in Sullivan & Arthur, 2006). In addition, some individuals' career motivations have changed from making a pragmatic choice to earn a living, to doing work that aligns with their core values (called a "protean" career in Hall, 2004). Sullivan and Mainiero (2007) proposed that career forms change depending on the changing nature of individuals' career motivations (known as "Alpha"/"Beta" careers). However, all these new career forms retain vestiges of traditional careers.

Organizational Careers: Asian Women

Much has been made of the high value placed on education in Asian American communities. Data shows that Asian women have the highest rates of college-educated graduates in comparison to other groups of women (Smith, 2013). Further, it appears that they view education and training as a continuing process over their careers (Adya, 2008). They were willing to make time for training, even while being employed and fulfilling family responsibilities (Grahame, 2003). When unable to enter the labor market, perhaps due to legal (work permit) barriers, they turned to education as one way to strengthen their status in preparation for when they would eventually be able to apply for jobs (Killian & Manohar, 2016). All these findings point to the significance that Asian women attach to education as a means to acquire human capital, as well as their willingness to commit to pursuing education as needed.

Management researchers have noted the importance of mentoring to career success. The scant published data on Asian women in U.S. workplaces points to their nuanced responses to mentoring. As discussed in Chapter 4, mentoring has been conceptualized as having two components—career-related advice and psychological support. It appears that Asian women tend to seek the former to improve their professional skills and achieve work goals. They did not necessarily seek out senior women either as role models or for psychological support (Adya, 2008; Na, 2017). Since there are few senior Asian women in corporate workplaces, it is not clear if their responses would change if presented with a choice of an Asian woman mentor.

Asian women have largely been perceived as competent in their jobs. In the workplace context competence refers to focus on work and achievement of objectives. The scant research on successful corporate Asian women noted that they view excellence at work as a minimum requirement. The literature on women's work experiences in general has noted similar comments by women from other groups, particularly among minority group members. However, for Asian women the situation could be more difficult due to their extremely low numbers in the workplace and organizational unfamiliarity with (and possible misunderstandings of) Asian cultures.

The stereotype most commonly associated with Asian women includes family stability (Fong, 1997), and the role of family is likely a distinguishing feature of this group (Ocampo et al., 2018). Typically, home and family have been understood to mean spouse and children (Mainiero & Sullivan, 2005). Work-life conflict is predicated on the notion that employees need to fulfill certain family commitments even as they carry out work commitments, and that these different obligations present competing demands on their (limited) time (Greenhaus & Kossek, 2014). Traditionally, women have assumed most family responsibilities in most Asian and western cultures; they have also taken the initiative in asking for workplaces to be accommodating and to ease such pressure on employees. Organizations have responded in different ways, for example, by offering on-site daycare or flexible work. Rather than a work-family conflict perspective, Asian women might ascribe to a work-family enrichment view which emphasizes how experiences in one of these roles can improve performance in the other (McNall et al., 2010). In this way, they might view working outside the home as an integral part of fulfilling family responsibilities and consider their professional achievements as key to ensuring socio-economic mobility for their children (Manohar, 2013). Their view of family could also include members beyond a spouse and children, such as parents, grandparents, uncles, aunts, and cousins (Dhingra, 2007). Some Asian women have used (extended) family as a resource—for instance, to provide childcare—in their pursuit of professional advancement.

Future Organizational Careers: Challenges for Asian Women

As workplaces and careers change, mobility is likely to be the norm. An organizational career might no longer mean staying in one organization nor career success an upward progress through organizational hierarchy (Mallon & Cohen, 2001). Asian women need to be prepared to navigate their careers through multiple organizations. Given the importance placed on family in Asian communities and cultural pressures to maintain familial stability, they might need to remain in certain geographical regions. Thus, it is more likely that they will change the type of work they do, rather than changing organizations while doing the same kind of work. That is, Asian women need to be prepared for the psychological rather than physical mobility of a boundaryless career (Wiernik & Kostal, 2019).

Even as careers change, they retain many aspects of the traditional organizational model. Important factors affecting organizational careers include understanding workplace dynamics, communicating effectively, building useful connections, and acquiring power. Competence in doing the work, as well as having the ability to manage relationships, will be imperative. In this context, Asian women might need to shift from a predominantly work and achievement focus to one that incorporates group goals, trades inefficiencies for trust, and exchanges expert power for connectivity power.

Human and social capital are also critical components of career success. Human capital is related to the ability to perform well at a given job (occupation) and includes knowledge, skills, and abilities (Hirschi, 2012). Social capital refers to the goodwill of others and is captured in the structure of social relations. Past research indicates that Asian women are adept at building human capital through education and training while their social capital might reside more in family and community relationships. Asian women thus might need to begin acquiring more social capital through their workplaces and professional organizations. Additionally, Asian communities might have to be prepared for Asian women to utilize them as resources to further their professional advancement in more direct ways.

Like members of other minority groups, Asian women need to negotiate (at least) two cultures. The mainstream American and Asian cultures could conflict on certain values and practices. Asian women need to balance their acculturation with pragmatic and personal needs. They can choose to combine displays of extrinsic features of Asian identity (such as language, clothing, or food) with intrinsic aspects (such as values and attitudes) in the workplace. Asians who identified as both Asian and American held external language/culture and internal identity/values as important (Chang et al., 2005). They chose to practice American cultural behaviors while holding on to, or internalizing, certain Asian values. Every Asian woman needs to negotiate the differences between the multiple cultures in which they circulate.

Arguably, one of the most difficult challenges for Asian women is combatting the stereotypes attributed to them. Even Asian women who do not overtly (or implicitly) display an ethnic and gender identity can be subject to racial stereotyping in the workplace. This type of discrimination occurs when a group of people are differentiated based on a supposed common culture and certain physical characteristics (Dhingra, 2007). Such stereotyping can happen even if one's coworkers do not exhibit overt discrimination, which points to the persistent nature of stereotypes. Even when people reject or do not ascribe to prevalent stereotypes, minoritized groups are aware of and affected by these biases (Cuddy et al., 2007).

Stereotypes commonly attributed to Asian women appear related to the "model minority" label. The Asian model minority stereotype originally portrayed Asian Americans as hard-working, achievement-oriented, and not seeking help from others in pursuit of their goals (Fong, 1997). Over time, this image acquired negative associations such as the implication of Asian employees putting in the effort but not possessing communication skills and thereby being socially awkward, overly accommodating (never saying no), unassertive, and deferential to authority rather than having confidence in themselves (Akutagawa, 2013; Dhingra, 2007). Some Asian women speculated whether being perceived as passive and somewhat submissive led to their workplace authority and expertise being questioned (Mukkamala & Suyemoto, 2018). The Asian model minority stereotype for Asian women has also included the image of being family-oriented and having stability in their personal lives (Fong, 1997). This pervasive stereotype could explain why corporate Asian women were likely to receive feedback that they were technically skilled (competent) but were not viewed as possessing leadership abilities (Hyun, 2005).

Interestingly, the stereotypes associated with Asian women differ from general female stereotypes. As noted above, the two dimensions that form the basis of workplace impressions are related to getting the work accomplished and reaching goals (agency, task-related) and being attuned to others and building and maintaining relationships (communal, people-oriented). Typical gender stereotypes held men to be "agentic" and women to be "communal" (Abele & Wojciszke, 2007). Agentic constructs reflect self-oriented efforts, an importance placed on attaining goals, and interest in efficiency (Wojciszke et al., 2009). Further, agency is understood to have two components—competence and assertiveness. The stereotype for Asian American women is one of competence (hard work, achievement focus) rather than warmth. Since this stereotypical view does not include assertiveness, it has led many supervisors to assess Asian women as lacking leadership potential. An interesting point to note in these analyses is that competence can be associated with feelings of respect whereas warmth is likely to be linked to feelings of liking (Lim, 2017).

Future Organizational Careers: Responses by Asian Women

To negotiate changing organizational workplaces, Asian women will need to articulate what career success means to them. Given their unique position in American corporate workplaces, this might be the opportune time for Asian women to recalibrate their careers. The meaning and markers of success for one group need not be the same as those of another group (Rath et al., 2019). The meaning of career success for Asian women will be informed by their expectations of their societal roles, in both American society in general as well as in Asian communities.

In many respects, Asian women are extremely well-positioned for organizational careers of the future, which are likely to be fragmented and characterized by employees moving between several organizations over time. For instance, Asian women's attitudes towards learning as an investment in their careers is a great asset in this regard. This emphasis on education implies a willingness to change workplaces and, if required, the kind of work being performed, and to assume self-direction of their career. Their willingness to commit to work-related education and training will stand them in good stead. However, Asian women will also need to expand their learning repertoires. In societies that are considered to have a more individualist orientation than a collectivist one, such as the U.S., showing independence and assertiveness is considered a pre-requisite for being (considered) successful (Wojciszke et al., 2009). Asian women have shown they can be competent; the challenge will be to round out their skill sets by strengthening their interpersonal skills and acquiring assertive behaviors, if they have not done so already (Tinkler et al., 2019). It might be helpful for them to view assertiveness as a way of standing up for their rights (Twenge, 2001), such as their right to positional authority. A caveat of these recommendations is that assertiveness must be used carefully: too much can damage relationships and too little limits one's ability to achieve goals (Eagly et al., 2014). Interpersonal relationships form the basis of social capital. A critical and distinguishing feature of women who have ascended to higher corporate levels is the ability to build and maintain (professional and social) relationships (Weis & Lay, 2019). Building social connections and gaining knowledge from external sources, particularly from Asian communities, could be a significant asset.

As discussed above, the presence and impact of stereotyping is an important aspect of organizational environments, and Asian women are subject to both gender and racial stereotypes. Dhingra (2007) commented that Asians in his study generally downplayed any experiences of racism, preferring to focus on their attempts at achievement through effort and relying on community support. Remedios et al. (2011) noted that although Asian women reported that they perceived more racism than sexism in their environments, they attributed racism to internal and sexism to external factors. In other words, it appeared that Asian women held themselves responsible for resolving or changing the situation and preferred to associate possible racist experiences with individuals rather than the system. When there are very few Asian women in the workplace (in other words, when they have "token status"), an individual response might be the only possibility. However, as their numbers increase, Asian women might need to find ways to address these systemic and (organizational) cultural issues. An increase in numbers would not necessarily result in a reduction of discriminatory behaviors directed towards tokens. Organizational action can be implemented through structural forms (such as Employee Resource Groups or Diversity Officers) and relationships (mentors, sponsors, and co-workers). Some methods individuals might deploy to attempt to mitigate the possible negative effects of stereotyping include using the stereotype's positive aspects to their advantage and building a strong sense of self. Dhingra (2007) noted that some Asian Americans have attempted to situationally use aspects of the stereotypes associated with them (such as an ethic of hard work) to gain advantages such as being perceived as dependable. The caveat to this approach, however, is that a characteristic that works as an advantage in some situations can become a disadvantage in others.

A strong sense of self-definition also has a significant impact on career and professional success. A sense of organizational identity can be a powerful workplace motivator (Ashforth & Mael, 1996). To function effectively in the workplace and outside it, Asian women, like other employees, need a clear sense of who they are in the organizational context (Ashforth & Schinoff, 2016). This identity is affected by who (they think) they are perceived to be. In considering self-definition, it is important to distinguish ethnic identity as the choice of an individual to identify as a member of an ethnic group. An ethnic group can be understood as one where members have a shared culture, geographic origin, and historical experiences (Dhingra, 2007). An ethnic identity is a complex, psychologically meaningful, multilayered sense of self (rather than a label) and includes attitudes and feelings (Phinney, 1996). Interestingly, an individual can have a strong sense of ethnic identity even when they seemingly have little direct cultural involvement with that group. This is because individuals choose to express aspects of the identity they want to assume either implicitly or explicitly. Asian women appeared to be comfortable in assuming a mainstream, American identity at work (e.g., behaviors and attitudes) while expressing an Asian identity outside of work.

Having multiple identities can be a significant asset. Internally, this helps an individual to maintain a sense of balance and positivity; for example, when one identity is threatened or has negative associations, they can shift to another identity. Externally, having multiple identities can sharpen the individual's ability to reach out across groups and strengthen cultural competence. Thus,

Asian women have a significant asset in their ethnic identity and can utilize it to build bicultural competencies.

An Idealized Forecast of the Future

Organizational life has always been, and will continue to be, confusing and messy. This makes managing an organizational career a difficult skill.

Over the last few decades, businesses have followed an approach of continual reorganization and restructuring, leading to shorter tenure for many employees. Careers consisting of both organizational and non-organizational work might be the norm of the future. Managing such a career will require willingness and ability to be self-directed in the midst of dynamically changing workplaces. Demographic, cultural, and legal changes in American society will continue to affect organizational workplaces. One effect of increasing diversity is the expectation of workplaces to be inclusive rather than simply accepting of various minority groups. Another change is a shift in societal expectations of businesses' impacts. Rather than operating with a focus only on financial results, businesses might (have no choice but to) shift to broader goals that include the impacts of their actions on society and the environment. All these developments will affect the skills and behaviors that are valued by organizations as well as the characteristics expected of business leaders.

As business environments, societies, and organizations change, leadership positions will increasingly require both competence and people-skills (Lim, 2017). Multicultural competencies are likely to be highly valued as businesses will need to nimbly negotiate different cultural and societal environments. Asian women have shown they have the potential for such competencies. For example, they have shown skill in exhibiting different behaviors on different occasions such that their choices matched the cultural demands of a specific situation (Chang et al., 2005). Such competencies will be an important asset at all organizational levels and environments. Asian women who aspire to ascend their organizations' hierarchies might need to emphasize additional aspects of organizational behavior, such as exhibiting assertion. They will need to intentionally develop their professional image: the way their competence, personality characteristics, and potential are perceived by others in the workplace (Little et al., 2015). This will require both an understanding of how they are perceived and a willingness to influence that perception through impression management tactics (Rosenfield et al., 1994).

The internal aspects of a career (Sturges, 1999) are related to individual motivations and goals, including a clear sense of organizational, professional, and personal identity. Identities contribute to a sense of self; for Asian women, their identities include gender and ethnicity. A strong sense of self is useful in combating and handling threats; it can also provide the confidence needed to take advantage of opportunities. Research has found that clarity of expectations for one's career contributes to motivation and can help define goals. Asian women have articulated different career motivations, such as fulfilling family responsibilities, being role models to their children, and improving their family's socio-economic status. These goals and motivations may change over time; in particular, they might evolve to include more personal career ambitions and aspirations. Indeed, that might be the case for second- and third-generation Asian women for whom working outside the home is the norm. Career objectives are attached to the meaning of career success for the individual and can have a powerful impact on career trajectory. For instance, not all individuals want to pursue career movement up the organizational hierarchy; some define success as work satisfaction or job security (these are classified as "Alpha"/"Beta" and "protean" careers in Chapter 7).

The external aspects of a career broadly refer to the work environment. Politics, ambiguity, uncertainty, and complexity are enduring characteristics of organizational workplaces (Ashforth & Schinoff, 2016). Asian women need to be cognizant that an organizational job does not only entail the completion of individually assigned work; it requires interaction and coordination with others. They will need to build networks inside and outside the organization. An internal network, including co-workers and mentors (sponsors), is useful for career progression within that organization. However, as careers increasingly become boundaryless, external networks—professional associations, extended family and friends, and communities—will become critical.

Organizational cultures can (and do) change, too. As discussed in Chapter 3, organizational culture can be understood to mean the core values, commonly accepted assumptions about how to perceive and respond to the environment, or common practices within an organization. Changes to organizational culture, like those in society, can be slow, but they do happen. They are often influenced by stakeholders within and outside the organization, especially employees. For instance, Eagly and Carli (2003) noted that the increasing presence of women in powerful, high-level positions influenced both theories and practices of leadership. Changes in workplaces have been mirrored by findings in the research. For instance, Brass (1985) commented that there was increasing support in research for the view that men and women did not significantly differ in terms of behavior in the workplace. While there might not be gender parity at all organizational levels yet, there has been a change in that direction.

The general understanding of gender stereotypes was that men were associated with being agentic and women with being communal. Over time, there has been a shift in this understanding. As some women ascended to leadership positions, the stereotype, while not changing completely, enlarged to accommodate exceptions. Heilman et al. (1989, p. 939) noted that "not all women are perceived [the] same as women in general—successful women managers are perceived the same as men." Self-concept can change in sync with others' perceptions; with the increasing presence of women in the workplace, "they have started to view themselves, and be viewed by others, as more Agentic" (Rudman & Glick, 2001). Some of these changes can be explained by certain paradoxes described by researchers, notably regarding individuals who behave in counter-stereotypical ways. While people are reluctant to change stereotypes about groups, in practical terms they are often reluctant to apply stereotypes to individuals (Darley & Gross, 1983); thus, managers might deny that they were biased in evaluating their reports. At the same time, people are willing to view certain individuals as exceptions to their social group's stereotypes when there is sufficient supporting information (Glick et al., 1988). A cautionary note is that these attitudes can leave the general stereotype unchanged.

The experience of women in general can be illuminating for Asian women. For instance, the question of whether there is a difference between men and women as employees had been the subject of speculation for many years, with anecdotal evidence supporting both sides. This question has been partially answered: based on surveys and analyses, researchers have found that there is little difference between the characteristics of male and female executives above certain levels. These executives appeared to differ little in terms of motivation, work commitment, and even human capital (Bertrand & Hallock, 2001). This homogeneity can be explained by the theory that organizations expect and reward certain decisions and behaviors, especially in positions where those decisions and behaviors have great organizational impact. Hence it is to be expected that all individuals in those positions would tend to act in the same manner. It is not clear whether this result is the same at all organizational levels. Some researchers have proposed that there is a category of women (in organizations) who are different from men and also different from other women in their values and behaviors (Adams & Funk, 2012). For instance, these women might use both male- and female-typed impression management tactics and have extensive networks including both women and men. The lesser resistance to their authority and experience that these women faced and the similarity of their success to men's was explained by the reasoning that "successful female managers are perceived differently from women in general or from female managers (who may not be as successful)" (Lyness & Thompson, 1997). Such research could explain the exceptional success of a few Asian women in American corporations. Their success need not imply that the perception of (other) Asian women has changed. However, these cases could suggest the existence of a sub-stereotype of successful (high-potential) Asian women. It will be interesting to study whether this stereotype develops in the future and how the characteristics of such a group could be modeled.

The careers and work experiences of second-generation women, and of those in subsequent generations, are likely to be different from those of immigrants. These women might be subject to bias in the form of "powerful but subtle and often invisible barriers that arise from cultural assumptions and organizational structures, practices, and patterns of interaction" (Ibarra et al., 2013, p. 64). Because there is a lack of Asian women in senior corporate positions, few role models of the same gender and ethnicity are available. In contrast to immigrants, who might be willing to put up with hardship (and who tend to view their current situation as better than the past), second-generation women might interpret their experiences differently, especially if they encountered racism during their developmental years (Varghese & Jenkins, 2009). Thus, it is likely that an ethnic identity will have different meaning for them. There is an almost complete lack of research on second-generation Asian women and their work-lives. However, it is likely that a bicultural identity will be advantageous for them. Ethnic identity is known to be salient and powerful for the individual and in developing abilities to deal with a multiplicity of cultures. In this context, some Asian women have shown special capability: they decided when to express an Asian identity and when to identify as mainstream American (Srinivasan, 2001).

Asian women who aspire to leadership positions must note that capital and even power are useful only to the extent that they are utilized. A leader needs to be accepted as such by others; typically an individual who can exert influence and achieve results is perceived as a leader (Conger & Kanungo, 1987). Power is a precursor to leadership. To accumulate power, one must have the desire (motive) and the ability (resources) to do so (Burns, 1978). Being placed in a leadership position is only a start; leadership requires acquiring new skills and adapting to role requirements, even if they fall outside the individual's comfort zone (Ibarra et al., 2013). Apart from these competencies, skills, and abilities, leadership requires strong motivation and sustained interest in an upward movement in the organization. Without such driving ambition, it would be difficult to put in the effort required to succeed and to maintain the strength to deal with potential setbacks.

Asian women are well-positioned to negotiate and rise in the corporate workplaces of the future. Their strategic attitudes towards building human capital through (continual) education and training, their bicultural competencies, and their (possibly) strong family and community support are likely to sustain them through any, and all, changes in organizational environments. However, challenges remain at all levels. Asian women need familiarity with how organizations function, and they need to use that knowledge to inform their career decisions such as the choice of work, decision making, building networks, and choosing leadership styles. They also need to be aware of gender and race/ethnicity-related issues that have an impact on workplace decisions. Most diversity strategies developed in the past were intended for women, in general, or for minorities. As such, these strategies are not necessarily the best or even effective techniques for Asian women professionals (Hyun, 2005). On the personal front, the cultural norms requiring Asian women to fulfill certain familial roles regardless of their employment situation puts extra pressure on them both at home and in the workplace. Even as workplaces and societies change, there is every reason to believe that Asian women are not going to remain passively in preexisting roles and norms but will be active in creating new and effective versions of them (Manohar, 2013). Finally, having gained expertise in negotiating organizational careers, Asian women will need to be prepared to pivot and be comfortable in becoming more self-directed in their career approaches and decisions (Hirschi, 2012).

There is tremendous potential for Asian women to succeed in corporate organizations in the U.S. However, their success will require the collective effort of multiple stakeholders—Asian women at various organizational levels and stages of their careers, Asian women who have successfully negotiated corporate workplaces (and who might have board positions now), Asian men with corporate experience and connections, (non-Asian) supporters in and outside the workplace, researchers and commentators who can track data and highlight issues, families, and finally, Asian communities.

Avenues for Future Research

The paucity of research on Asian women in professional workplaces is at odds with the strides they have been making in these spheres. Asian women are represented in the fields of medicine and healthcare, law, education, government, and most certainly in business. They own businesses, work in them, and even fund them. However, there is a dearth of research and broadly applicable information about how they navigate professional workspaces. Published interviews with a few high-profile corporate Asian women in the U.S. reveal some of the strategies they have developed and utilized, but it is not clear to what extent these methods can be extrapolated to the broader group.

In this section we identify avenues for future research that will help develop a more comprehensive understanding of Asian women in corporate environments in the U.S. These suggestions relate to topics addressed in preceding chapters.

First, it would be informative to have date on the distribution of Asian women in corporate positions across industries, geographies, organizational levels, and departments. The presence of women in Fortune 500 boards has been tracked over many years; the same needs to be done for Asian women on corporate boards and in C-suites.

Businesses, large and small, have been formally addressing diversity for at least two decades. Corporate workplaces have cycled through a variety of diversity initiatives, from inhouse programs to extensive use of consultants, from offering voluntary participation to mandating training, and from general-purpose initiatives to ones geared to specific groups. However, there is little information on whether Asian women find any such programs effective or whether they feel these programs are addressed to their unique needs. One program that currently appears to have traction and general appeal is the development of Employee Resource Groups (ERGs). It would be beneficial to know whether Asian women's ERGs are prevalent and if they have impacted the workplace experiences of their members. At the managerial level, it would also be informative to know the degree of representation of Asian women in key positions such as diversity officers and human resources managers.

The scant data available regarding Asian women in corporate America indicates that some of them have navigated their careers very successfully. However, little is known of the general experience of Asian women in these workplaces. Some areas to explore in this regard include their career aspirations and expectations, their approaches to the acquisition and use of power, the characteristics of their professional networks, the kinds of mentoring relationships they find effective, and their preferred management/ leadership styles. A specific topic of importance to career growth is their attitude towards uncertainty and risk. This is also of interest since Asian cultures differ from American culture along Hofstede's dimension of uncertainty avoidance.

The extensive research done on women in the workplace has identified the persistent and powerful impact of stereotyping, both descriptive and prescriptive. Intriguing research results indicate that stereotypes for Asian women in the workplace could differ significantly from those for other women, as well as those associated with Asian men. However, these stereotypes need in-depth analysis. While there are many stereotypes for Asian women in broader American society, it appears that there is some degree of uniformity of stereotypes in the workplace. It will also be important to determine whether there are generational differences in stereotypes, in particular between immigrant women and second-generation women. Another aspect of this topic that should be researched is related to Asian women who ascend to the highest corporate levels, principally whether they are able to do so by presenting themselves as counter-stereotypical.

Stereotypes reflect the understanding of an individual by others. The counterpart of a stereotype is an individual's identity, which reflects the individual's understanding of herself. Here again, there is a lack of published work regarding Asian women. Given the diversity of Asian cultures, it is likely that the ethnic identities of Asian women vary widely as well. Generational differences are also likely to be significant. Understanding how ethnic, gender, professional, and organizational identities interact and impact Asian women is of critical importance to their career management approaches.

Ethnic identities are in turn impacted by acculturation processes. While there are models describing Asian acculturation in general, they do not identify any gender related differences. An indirect acknowledgement that there are aspects unique to acculturation of Asian women is addressed only in research as related to professional behaviors and parenting styles. It is likely that Asian women different inherently in these processes from Asian men. Since women are generally considered to carry the responsibility of upholding traditions, their acculturation processes likely have much deeper impact on the persistence of Asian values and beliefs in later generations.

Finally, a study of Asian women's career paths in corporate workplaces is likely to reveal similarities and differences within this group. Such a study would provide an understanding of the factors that helped them succeed, such as the active support of extended families, as well as those factors that posed hurdles to their success, such as stereotypes and role expectations. This information would reveal important details about their career preferences and professional orientations.

In addition to providing information about Asian women, research in the aforementioned areas will contribute to the development of broader career models, approaches, and strategies. The experiences of first-generation Asian women in workplaces will aid future generations. A nuanced understanding of organizational workplaces and dynamics, as well as the choices available to them, will help Asian women achieve their professional, career, and personal aspirations.

REFERENCES

Abele, A. E., & Wojciszke, B. (2007). Agency and communion from the perspective of self versus others. *Journal of Personality and Social Psychology*, *93*(5), 751–763. doi:10.1037/0022-3514.93.5.751 PMID:17983298

Adams, R. B., & Funk, P. (2012). Beyond the glass ceiling: Does gender matter? *Management Science*, *58*(2), 219–235. doi:10.1287/mnsc.1110.1452

Adya, M. P. (2008). Women at work: Differences in IT career experiences and perceptions between South Asian and American women. *Human Resource Management*, *47*(3), 601–635. doi:10.1002/hrm.20234

Akutagawa, L. (2013). Breaking stereotypes: An Asian American's view of leadership development. *Asian American Journal of Psychology*, *4*(4), 277–284. doi:10.1037/a0035390

Ashforth, B. E., & Mael, F. A. (1996). Organizational identity and strategy as a context for the individual. *Advances in Strategic Management*, *13*, 19–64.

Ashforth, B. E., & Schinoff, B. S. (2016). Identity under construction: How individuals come to define themselves in organizations. *Annual Review of Organizational Psychology and Organizational Behavior*, *3*(1), 111–137. doi:10.1146/annurev-orgpsych-041015-062322

Bertrand, M., & Hallock, K. F. (2001, October). The gender gap in top corporate jobs. *Industrial & Labor Relations Review*, *55*(1), 3–21. doi:10.1177/001979390105500101

Brass, D. J. (1985). Men's and women's networks: A study of interaction patterns and influence in an organization. *Academy of Management Journal, 28*(2), 327–343.

Burns, J. M. (1978). *Leadership*. Harper & Row.

Census. (2016). Survey of Business Owners and Self-Employed Persons (SBO). *Census.gov*. Retrieved June 24, 2020 from https://www.census.gov/programs-surveys/sbo.html

Chang, T., Tracey, T. J. G., & Moore, T. L. (2005). The dimensional structure of Asian American acculturation: An examination of prototypes. *Self and Identity, 4*(1), 25–43. doi:10.1080/13576500444000155

Conger, J. A., & Kanungo, R. N. (1987). Towards a behavioral theory of charismatic leadership in organizational settings. *Academy of Management Review, 12*(4), 637–647. doi:10.5465/amr.1987.4306715

Cuddy, A. J. C., Fiske, S. T., & Glick, P. (2007). The BIAS map: Behaviors from intergroup affect and stereotypes. *Journal of Personality and Social Psychology, 92*(4), 631–648. doi:10.1037/0022-3514.92.4.631 PMID:17469949

Darley, J. M., & Gross, P. H. (1983). A hypothesis-confirming bias in labeling effects. *Journal of Personality and Social Psychology, 44*(1), 20–33. doi:10.1037/0022-3514.44.1.20

Deloitte. (2018). *Missing pieces report: The 2018 board diversity census of women and minorities on Fortune 500 boards*. https://www2.deloitte.com/us/en/pages/center-for-board-effectiveness/articles/missing-pieces-report-industry-view.html

Dhaliwal, S. (1998). Silent contributors: Asian female entrepreneurs and women in business. *Women's Studies International Forum, 21*(5), 463–474. doi:10.1016/S0277-5395(98)00069-7

Dhingra, P. (2007). *Managing multicultural lives: Asian American professionals and the challenge of multiple identities*. Stanford University Press.

Eagly, A. H., & Carli, L. L. (2003). The female leadership advantage: An evaluation of the evidence. *The Leadership Quarterly, 14*(6), 807–834. doi:10.1016/j.leaqua.2003.09.004

Eagly, A. H., Gartzia, L., & Carli, L. L. (2014). Female advantage: Revisited. In S. Kumra, R. Simpson, & R. J. Burke (Eds.), *The Oxford handbook of gender in organizations* (pp. 153–174). Oxford University Press.

Fong, L. Y. S. (1997). Asian-American women: An understudied minority. *Journal of Sociology and Social Welfare*, *24*(1), 91–111.

Glick, P., Zion, C., & Nelson, C. (1988). What mediates sex discrimination in hiring decisions? *Journal of Personality and Social Psychology*, *55*(2), 178–186. doi:10.1037/0022-3514.55.2.178

Grahame, K. M. (2003). "For the family": Asian immigrant women's triple day. *Journal of Sociology and Social Welfare*, *30*(1), 65–90.

Greenhaus, J. H., & Kossek, E. E. (2014). The contemporary career: A work-home perspective. *Annual Review of Organizational Psychology and Organizational Behavior*, *1*(1), 361–388. doi:10.1146/annurev-orgpsych-031413-091324

Hall, D. T. (2004). The Protean career: A quarter-century journey. *Journal of Vocational Behavior*, *65*(1), 1–13. doi:10.1016/j.jvb.2003.10.006

Harvard Law Forum. (2018). *Missing pieces report 2018: Corporate board.* https://corpgov.law.harvard.edu/2019/02/05/missing-pieces-report-the-2018-board-diversity-census-of-women-and-minorities-on-fortune-500-boards/

Hatch, M. J. (1993). The dynamics of organizational culture. *Academy of Management Review*, *18*(4), 657–693. doi:10.5465/amr.1993.9402210154

Heilman, M. E., Block, C. J., Simon, M. C., & Martell, R. E. (1989). Has anything changed? Current characterizations of men, women, and managers. *The Journal of Applied Psychology*, *74*(6), 935–942. doi:10.1037/0021-9010.74.6.935

Herzberg, F. (2003). One more time: How do you motivate employees? *Harvard Business Review*. Retrieved June 15, 2020 from https://hbr.org/2003/01/one-more-time-how-do-you-motivate-employees

Hirschi, A. (2012, August). The career resources model: An integrative framework for career counsellors. *British Journal of Guidance & Counselling*, *40*(4), 369–383. doi:10.1080/03069885.2012.700506

Hofstede, G., Neuijen, B., Ohayv, D. D., & Sanders, G. (1990, June). Measuring organizational cultures: A qualitative and quantitative study across twenty cases. *Administrative Science Quarterly*, *35*(2), 286–316. doi:10.2307/2393392

Hyun, J. (2005). *Breaking the Bamboo Ceiling*. Harper-Collins.

Ibarra, H., Ely, R., & Kolb, D. (2013, September). Women rising: The unseen barriers. *Harvard Business Review*, 62–66.

Killian, C., & Manohar, N. N. (2016). Highly skilled immigrant women's labor market access: A comparison of Indians in the United States and North Africans in France. *Social Currents*, *3*(2), 138–159. doi:10.1177/2329496515620644

Lim, J. I. (2017). *Perceptions of Asian American and female leadership candidates: The impact of descriptive and prescriptive stereotyping* [Doctoral dissertation, City University of New York]. CUNY Academic Works: Dissertations, Theses and Capstone Projects: Graduate Center.

Little, L. M., Major, V. S., Hinojosa, A. S., & Nelson, D. L. (2015). Professional image maintenance: How women navigate pregnancy in the workplace. *Academy of Management Journal*, *58*(1), 8–37. doi:10.5465/amj.2013.0599

Lyness, K. S., & Thompson, D. E. (1997). Above the glass ceiling? A comparison of matched samples of female and male executives. *The Journal of Applied Psychology*, *82*(3), 359–375. doi:10.1037/0021-9010.82.3.359 PMID:9190144

Mainiero, L. A., & Sullivan, S. E. (2005). Kaleidoscope careers: An alternate explanation for the "opt-out" revolution. *The Academy of Management Executive*, *19*(1), 106–123. doi:10.5465/ame.2005.15841962

Mallon, M., & Cohen, L. (2001). Time for a change? Women's accounts of the move from organizational careers to self-employment. *British Journal of Management*, *12*(3), 217–230. doi:10.1111/1467-8551.00195

Manohar, N. N. (2013). Mothering for class and ethnicity: The case of Indian professional immigrants in the United States. In M. Kohlman, D. Krieg, & B. Dickerson (Eds.), *Notions of family: Intersectional perspectives, advances in gender research* (Vol. 17, pp. 159–185). Emerald Group Publishing Limited. doi:10.1108/S1529-2126(2013)0000017011

McNall, L. A., Nicklin, J. M., & Masuda, A. D. (2010). A meta-analytic review of the consequences associated with work–family enrichment. *Journal of Business and Psychology*, *25*(3), 381–396. doi:10.100710869-009-9141-1

Mukkamala, S., & Suyemoto, K. L. (2018). Racialized sexism/sexualized racism: A multimethod study of intersectional experiences of discrimination for Asian American women. *Asian American Journal of Psychology*, *9*(1), 32–46. doi:10.1037/aap0000104

Na, Y. (2017). *The experiences of Asian immigrant women: Journeys into corporate leadership* [Doctoral Dissertation, Alliant International University]. ProQuest LLC.

Ocampo, A. C. G., Restubog, S. L. D., Liwag, M. E., Wang, L., & Petelczyc, C. (2018). My spouse is my strength: Interactive effects of perceived organizational and spousal support in predicting career adaptability and career outcomes. *Journal of Vocational Behavior*, *108*, 165–177. doi:10.1016/j.jvb.2018.08.001

Oyserman, D., & Sakamoto, I. (1997). Being Asian American: Identity, cultural constructs and stereotype perception. *The Journal of Applied Behavioral Science*, *33*(4), 435–453. doi:10.1177/0021886397334002

Phinney, J. S. (1996). When we talk about American ethnic groups, what do we mean? *The American Psychologist*, *51*(9), 918–927. doi:10.1037/0003-066X.51.9.918

Prendergast, C., & Topel, R. (1993). Discretion and bias in performance evaluation. *European Economic Review*, *37*(2-3), 355–365. doi:10.1016/0014-2921(93)90024-5

Rath, T. S., Mohanty, M., & Pradhan, B. B. (2019). An alternative career progression model for Indian women bank managers: A labyrinth approach. *Women's Studies International Forum*, *73*, 24–34. doi:10.1016/j.wsif.2019.01.005

Remedios, J. D., Chasteen, A. L., & Paek, J. D. (2011). Not all prejudices are experienced equally: Comparing experiences of racism and sexism in female minorities. *Group Processes & Intergroup Relations*, *15*(2), 273–287. doi:10.1177/1368430211411594

Rosenfield, P., Giacalone, R. A., & Riordan, C. A. (1994). Impression management theory and diversity: Lessons for organizational behavior. *The American Behavioral Scientist*, *37*(5), 601–604. doi:10.1177/0002764294037005002

Rudman, L. A., & Glick, P. (2001). Prescriptive gender stereotypes and backlash toward agentic women. *The Journal of Social Issues*, *57*(4), 743–762. doi:10.1111/0022-4537.00239

Smith, M. (2013). *Fact sheet: the state of Asian American women in the United States*. Center for American Progress. https://www.americanprogress.org/issues/race/reports/2013/11/07/79182/fact-sheet-the-state-of-asian-american-women-in-the-united-states/

Sorkin, A. R. (2018, January 15). BlackRock's message: Contribute to society or risk losing our support. *The New York Times*. https://www.nytimes.com/2018/01/15/business/dealbook/blackrock-laurence-fink-letter.html

Srinivasan, S. (2001). "Being Indian," "being American": A balancing act or a creative blend? *Journal of Human Behavior in the Social Environment*, *3*(3/4), 135–158.

Sturges, J. (1999). What it means to succeed: Personal conceptions of career success held by male and female managers at different ages. *British Journal of Management*, *10*(3), 239–252. doi:10.1111/1467-8551.00130

Sullivan, S. E., & Arthur, M. B. (2006). The evolution of the boundaryless career concept: Examining physical and psychological mobility. *Journal of Vocational Behavior*, *69*(1), 19–29. doi:10.1016/j.jvb.2005.09.001

Sullivan, S. E., & Mainiero, L. A. (2007). The changing nature of gender roles, Alpha/Beta careers and work-life issues: Theory-driven implications for human resource management. *Career Development International*, *12*(3), 238–263. doi:10.1108/13620430710745881

Tinkler, J., Zhao, J. J., Li, Y., & Ridgeway, C. L. (2019). Honorary whites? Asian American women and the dominance penalty. *Socius: Sociological Research for a Dynamic World*, *5*, 1–13. doi:10.1177/2378023119836000

Twenge, J. M. (2001). Changes in women's assertiveness in response to status and roles: A cross-temporal meta-analysis, 1931–1993. *Journal of Personality and Social Psychology*, *81*(1), 133–145. doi:10.1037/0022-3514.81.1.133 PMID:11474719

Varghese, A., & Jenkins, S. R. (2009). Parental overprotection, cultural value conflict, and psychological adaptation among Asian Indian women in America. *Sex Roles*, *61*(3-4), 235–251. doi:10.100711199-009-9620-x

Weis, L., & Lay, A. (2019). Gender-specific networking: Mind the gap. In A. Antoniou, C. Cooper, & C. Gatrell (Eds.), *Women, business and leadership: Gender and organisations* (pp. 174–198). Edward Elgar Publishing. doi:10.4337/9781786432711.00018

Wiernik, B. M., & Kostal, J. W. (2019). Protean and boundaryless career orientations: A critical review and meta-analysis. *Journal of Counseling Psychology*, *66*(3), 280–307. doi:10.1037/cou0000324 PMID:30777774

Wojciszke, B., Abele, A. E., & Baryla, W. (2009). Two dimensions of interpersonal attitudes: Liking depends on communion, respect depends on agency. *European Journal of Social Psychology*, *39*(6), 973–990. doi:10.1002/ejsp.595

Related Readings

To continue IGI Global's long-standing tradition of advancing innovation through emerging research, please find below a compiled list of recommended IGI Global book chapters and journal articles in the areas of success of Asian American women in leadership roles in the workplace. These related readings will provide additional information and guidance to further enrich your knowledge and assist you with your own research.

Abdullah, H., & Sahharon, H. (2020). Emerging Digital Social Innovation in Youth Work Practice. In Z. Zaremohzzabieh, S. Ahrari, S. E. Krauss, A. Abu Samah, & S. Z. Omar (Eds.), *Youth Work in a Digital Society* (pp. 62–81). IGI Global. doi:10.4018/978-1-7998-2956-0.ch004

Acharya, B. B. (2019). What Motivates Immigrants for ICT Adoption and Use? In E. C. Idemudia (Ed.), *Handbook of Research on Technology Integration in the Global World* (pp. 436–460). IGI Global. doi:10.4018/978-1-5225-6367-9.ch021

Adewusi, A. O. (2019). Skill Acquisition and Entrepreneurial Intention Among Corp Members in Southwestern Nigeria. In S. Bala & P. Singhal (Eds.), *Gender Issues in Technical and Vocational Education Programs* (pp. 183–199). IGI Global. doi:10.4018/978-1-5225-8443-8.ch009

Adeyinka-Skold, S. (2020). Barriers in Women's Romantic Partner Search in the Digital Age. In R. Kalish (Ed.), *Young Adult Sexuality in the Digital Age* (pp. 113–137). IGI Global. doi:10.4018/978-1-7998-3187-7.ch007

Aguilera, E., Greenstein, I., & Shannon, L. A. (2020). Linguistically-Responsive Literacy Pedagogies Across Primary and Secondary Classrooms. In G. Neokleous, A. Krulatz, & R. Farrelly (Eds.), *Handbook of Research on Cultivating Literacy in Diverse and Multilingual Classrooms* (pp. 496–515). IGI Global. doi:10.4018/978-1-7998-2722-1.ch023

Akhter, S. (2019). Social Workers' Understanding of Bi-Culturalism and Its Cultural Differences in Aotearoa New Zealand. In S. Hameed, S. El-Kafafi, & R. Waretini-Karena (Eds.), *Handbook of Research on Indigenous Knowledge and Bi-Culturalism in a Global Context* (pp. 255–270). IGI Global. doi:10.4018/978-1-5225-6061-6.ch014

Akinpelu, T. O. (2018). The Entrepreneurial Woman in the Nigerian Economy. In D. Chitakunye & A. Takhar (Eds.), *Examining the Role of Women Entrepreneurs in Emerging Economies* (pp. 97–125). IGI Global. doi:10.4018/978-1-5225-5112-6.ch005

Aktepe, S. O. (2020). Gender Inequality in Work Organizations. In B. U. Tan (Ed.), *Macro and Micro-Level Issues Surrounding Women in the Workforce* (pp. 1–36). IGI Global. doi:10.4018/978-1-5225-9163-4.ch001

Allen, J. M., Bracey, P. S., Aguilar, M. G., & Zimmerman, T. D. (2020). Supporting Workforce Wisdom in a Global Economy. In C. Hughes (Ed.), *Strategies for Attracting, Maintaining, and Balancing a Mature Workforce* (pp. 152–178). IGI Global. doi:10.4018/978-1-7998-2277-6.ch007

Andoh, J. S., Ghansah, B., Okogun-Odompley, J. N., & Benuwa, B. (2019). Impact of Workplace Diversity on Employee Performance. *International Journal of R&D Innovation Strategy*, *1*(2), 31–43. doi:10.4018/IJRDIS.2019070103

Andrus-Henry, S. (2018). Imagining Graduate Students. In A. G. Scheg & M. Shaw (Eds.), *Fostering Effective Student Communication in Online Graduate Courses* (pp. 271–297). IGI Global. doi:10.4018/978-1-5225-2682-7.ch015

Anyanwu, C. A. (2020). Politics of Food Distribution. In L. Amadi & F. Allen (Eds.), *Global Food Politics and Approaches to Sustainable Consumption* (pp. 177–200). IGI Global. doi:10.4018/978-1-7998-0125-2.ch009

Aranda, A. S., & Jerrard, M. A. (2019). A Comparison Between Australia and Chile of Factors Facing Women Engineers and ICT Professionals in Their Careers. In I. Williams, O. Millward, & R. Layton (Eds.), *Gender Gaps and the Social Inclusion Movement in ICT* (pp. 1–23). IGI Global. doi:10.4018/978-1-5225-7068-4.ch001

Attah, D. A., Boafo-Arthur, S., & Boafo-Arthur, A. (2018). The Sojourner's Return. In D. M. Velliaris (Ed.), *Study Abroad Contexts for Enhanced Foreign Language Learning* (pp. 218–255). IGI Global. doi:10.4018/978-1-5225-3814-1.ch010

Audley, S., & Ginsburg, J. L. (2019). Caring as an Authoritative Act. In K. Daniels & K. Billingsley (Eds.), *Creating Caring and Supportive Educational Environments for Meaningful Learning* (pp. 154–182). IGI Global. doi:10.4018/978-1-5225-5748-7.ch009

Augustine, T. A., & Redman, D. P. (2019). Using Critical Literacy Skills to Support Civic Discourse. In A. M. Cartwright & E. K. Reeves (Eds.), *Critical Literacy Initiatives for Civic Engagement* (pp. 1–28). IGI Global. doi:10.4018/978-1-5225-8082-9.ch001

Ayari, A. (2018). Women and Careers. In E. Al-A'ali, M. M. Al-Shammari, & H. Masri (Eds.), *Arab Women and Their Evolving Roles in the Global Business Landscape* (pp. 74–86). IGI Global. doi:10.4018/978-1-5225-3710-6.ch004

Baer, J. (2019). Opening the Door to Study Abroad From Community Colleges. In G. F. Malveaux & R. L. Raby (Eds.), *Study Abroad Opportunities for Community College Students and Strategies for Global Learning* (pp. 22–36). IGI Global. doi:10.4018/978-1-5225-6252-8.ch002

Bagasra, A. (2020). Muslim Worldviews. In A. Bagasra & M. Mackinem (Eds.), *Working With Muslim Clients in the Helping Professions* (pp. 1–22). IGI Global. doi:10.4018/978-1-7998-0018-7.ch001

Banerjee, G. (2018). Measuring the Different Facets of Diversity Using Quantitative Methods. In D. K. Bhattacharyya (Ed.), *Statistical Tools and Analysis in Human Resources Management* (pp. 169–196). IGI Global. doi:10.4018/978-1-5225-4947-5.ch008

Banks, S. (2017). Mirrors of Opportunity. In A. Shahriar & G. Syed (Eds.), *Student Culture and Identity in Higher Education* (pp. 18–37). IGI Global. doi:10.4018/978-1-5225-2551-6.ch002

Baporikar, N. (2020). Human Resource Management for Managing Cultural Diversity. *International Journal of Applied Management Sciences and Engineering*, *7*(1), 74–99. doi:10.4018/IJAMSE.2020010104

Baron, A., & McNeal, K. (2019). Strategies for Teaching Online Higher Education Courses With an Eye Towards Retention. In L. Kyei-Blankson, J. Blankson, & E. Ntuli (Eds.), *Care and Culturally Responsive Pedagogy in Online Settings* (pp. 280–298). IGI Global. doi:10.4018/978-1-5225-7802-4.ch014

Barral, L. V., Pinet, F., Tacnet, J., & Jousselme, A. (2020). Combining UML Profiles to Design Serious Games Dedicated to Trace Information in Decision Processes. *International Journal of Information System Modeling and Design*, *11*(2), 1–27. doi:10.4018/IJISMD.2020040101

Battista, L. T., & Wright, L. (2020). Overcoming Implicit Bias in Collaborative Online Learning Communities. In C. N. Stevenson & J. C. Bauer (Eds.), *Enriching Collaboration and Communication in Online Learning Communities* (pp. 19–38). IGI Global. doi:10.4018/978-1-5225-9814-5.ch002

Belay, D. G. (2020). Failure of Governance, State Legitimacy, and Hate Speech in Ethiopia. *International Journal of Political Activism and Engagement*, *7*(1), 64–76. doi:10.4018/IJPAE.2020010104

Belli, S., & Bernal, M. J. (2018). Discursive-Linguistic Devices and Strategies in Spam E-Mail Narratives. *International Journal of Information Communication Technologies and Human Development*, *10*(3), 1–13. doi:10.4018/IJICTHD.2018070101

Bensalloua, C. A., & Hamdadou, D. (2018). Spatial OLAP and Multicriteria Integrated Approach for Decision Support System. *International Journal of Decision Support System Technology*, *10*(3), 1–26. doi:10.4018/IJDSST.2018070101

Bernhardt, S., Braun, P., & Thomason, J. (2019). *Cultural and Social Context*. IGI Global. doi:10.4018/978-1-5225-7975-5.ch005

Bernhardt, S., Braun, P., & Thomason, J. (2019). *Structural Context*. IGI Global. doi:10.4018/978-1-5225-7975-5.ch006

Berthelemy, C. (2018). International College Students' Experience of Racial Prejudice. In B. Blummer, J. M. Kenton, & M. Wiatrowski (Eds.), *Promoting Ethnic Diversity and Multiculturalism in Higher Education* (pp. 148–170). IGI Global. doi:10.4018/978-1-5225-4097-7.ch009

Berti, M., Maranzana, S., & Monzingo, J. (2020). Fostering Cultural Understanding with Virtual Reality. *International Journal of Computer-Assisted Language Learning and Teaching*, *10*(1), 47–59. doi:10.4018/IJCALLT.2020010104

Beyene, Z. (2019). From an Emperor to the Derg and Beyond. In U. T. Onyebadi (Ed.), *Music and Messaging in the African Political Arena* (pp. 1–21). IGI Global. doi:10.4018/978-1-5225-7295-4.ch001

Bilge, N. (2018). Cultural Identity Preservation Through Social Media. In N. Bilge & M. I. Marino (Eds.), *Reconceptualizing New Media and Intercultural Communication in a Networked Society* (pp. 1–17). IGI Global. doi:10.4018/978-1-5225-3784-7.ch001

Black, S. (2019). Diversity and Inclusion. In J. Joe & E. Knight (Eds.), *Social Media for Communication and Instruction in Academic Libraries* (pp. 100–118). IGI Global. doi:10.4018/978-1-5225-8097-3.ch007

Bloom, L., Noltensmeyer, C. J., Hahn, S. A., Rush, C. B., Heidlebaugh-Buskey, P., & Westbrook, T. M. (2020). Pedagogical Considerations in Teaching Implicit Bias. *International Journal of Bias, Identity and Diversities in Education*, *5*(1), 46–63. doi:10.4018/IJBIDE.2020010103

Bogueva, D., & Marinova, D. (2019). Reconciling Not Eating Meat and Masculinity in the Marketing Discourse for New Food Alternatives. In D. Bogueva, D. Marinova, T. Raphaely, & K. Schmidinger (Eds.), *Environmental, Health, and Business Opportunities in the New Meat Alternatives Market* (pp. 260–282). IGI Global. doi:10.4018/978-1-5225-7350-0.ch014

Boltz, L. O. (2017). Like Hearing From Them in the Past. *International Journal of Gaming and Computer-Mediated Simulations*, *9*(4), 1–18. doi:10.4018/IJGCMS.2017100101

Boltz, L. O. (2019). Nervousness and Maybe Even Some Regret. In B. R. Dubbels (Ed.), *Exploring the Cognitive, Social, Cultural, and Psychological Aspects of Gaming and Simulations* (pp. 228–251). IGI Global. doi:10.4018/978-1-5225-7461-3.ch008

Boronat-Navarro, M., & Garcia-Joerger, A. (2020). Family Firm Competitiveness and Organizational Ambidexterity. In C. Camison & T. Gonzalez (Eds.), *Competitiveness, Organizational Management, and Governance in Family Firms* (pp. 67–88). IGI Global. doi:10.4018/978-1-7998-1655-3.ch003

Boston, C. M. (2019). Achievement, Racial Identity, and Connectedness. In K. Daniels & K. Billingsley (Eds.), *Creating Caring and Supportive Educational Environments for Meaningful Learning* (pp. 183–198). IGI Global. doi:10.4018/978-1-5225-5748-7.ch010

Bridges-Bond, S. (2020). A Bilingual Child Diagnosed With Autism Spectrum Disorder (ASD). In D. M. Scott (Ed.), *Cases on Communication Disorders in Culturally Diverse Populations* (pp. 89–112). IGI Global. doi:10.4018/978-1-7998-2261-5.ch005

Brown, C. (2019). CSR and PSR Diversity Engagement Among Ethnic Minority Businesses (EMBs) Within the UK. In C. Brown & U. Nwagbara (Eds.), *Corporate Social Responsibility and Strategic Market Positioning for Organizational Success* (pp. 1–34). IGI Global. doi:10.4018/978-1-5225-5409-7.ch001

Brown, C. (2020). *Findings and Analysis*. IGI Global. doi:10.4018/978-1-7998-1639-3.ch005

Brown, M. H., & West, A. R. (2020). Counseling With a Muslim-American Family. In B. C. King & T. A. Stewart (Eds.), *Cases on Cross-Cultural Counseling Strategies* (pp. 44–65). IGI Global. doi:10.4018/978-1-7998-0022-4.ch003

Brusa, A. P. (2020). The Difficulty of Teaching Historical Landscape. In E. J. Delgado-Algarra & J. M. Cuenca-Lopez (Eds.), *Handbook of Research on Citizenship and Heritage Education* (pp. 378–407). IGI Global. doi:10.4018/978-1-7998-1978-3.ch018

Burleson, S. D., Tyler, W. A., Major, D. A., & Reynoldson, K. R. (2018). Women in STEM Workplaces and Computer-Mediated Communication. *International Journal of Virtual Communities and Social Networking, 10*(3), 1–22. doi:10.4018/IJVCSN.2018070101

Burston, B., & Collier-Stewart, S. (2018). STEM for All. In K. E. Norris & S. Collier (Eds.), *Social Justice and Parent Partnerships in Multicultural Education Contexts* (pp. 274–288). IGI Global. doi:10.4018/978-1-5225-3943-8.ch015

Caceres, Y. D., Gonzalez, S., & Medina, J. R. (2020). Alpaca Meat. In V. Chkoniya, A. O. Madsen, & P. Bukhrashvili (Eds.), *Anthropological Approaches to Understanding Consumption Patterns and Consumer Behavior* (pp. 286–302). IGI Global. doi:10.4018/978-1-7998-3115-0.ch016

Campbell, D. M. (2019). Black Lives Matter vs. All Lives Matter in the Generation of Hashtivism. In O. Ozgen (Ed.), *Handbook of Research on Consumption, Media, and Popular Culture in the Global Age* (pp. 287–310). IGI Global. doi:10.4018/978-1-5225-8491-9.ch017

Carrim, N. M., & Senne, Y. (2019). Life Context Model, Intersectionality, and Black Feminist Epistemology. In E. T. Pereira & P. Paoloni (Eds.), *Handbook of Research on Women in Management and the Global Labor Market* (pp. 136–155). IGI Global. doi:10.4018/978-1-5225-9171-9.ch007

Chapman, C. (2018). Student Acceptance of a Civic Engagement Graduation Requirement in an Urban Community College. In S. Chhabra (Ed.), *Handbook of Research on Civic Engagement and Social Change in Contemporary Society* (pp. 40–62). IGI Global. doi:10.4018/978-1-5225-4197-4.ch003

Chase, J., & Yan, Z. (2017). *Meaningful Individual Differences in Statistics Cognition*. IGI Global. doi:10.4018/978-1-5225-2420-5.ch006

Chennamsetti, P. (2020). Aiding International Students to Thrive in US Higher Education. In D. M. Velliaris (Ed.), *Academic Language and Learning Support Services in Higher Education* (pp. 119–139). IGI Global. doi:10.4018/978-1-7998-2878-5.ch005

Cho, H., Johnson, P., & Somiari, S. S. (2019). Service-Learning as Authentic Practice for Teacher Candidates to Work With English Language Learners. In C. A. Lenkaitis & S. M. Hilliker (Eds.), *Engaging Teacher Candidates and Language Learners With Authentic Practice* (pp. 35–54). IGI Global. doi:10.4018/978-1-5225-8543-5.ch003

Christiansen, B. (2019). Cultural Indoctrination and Management Education Curriculum. *International Journal of Applied Management Theory and Research*, *1*(1), 1–15. doi:10.4018/IJAMTR.2019010101

Chuang, S., & Crowder, C. L. (2019). Gender Characteristics. In J. Keengwe & K. Kungu (Eds.), *Handbook of Research on Cross-Cultural Online Learning in Higher Education* (pp. 253–270). IGI Global. doi:10.4018/978-1-5225-8286-1.ch013

Conway, C. S., Sims, Y., McCrary-Quarles, A., Nicholson, C. S., Ethridge, G., Maultsby, M., Thomas, T. P., & Smith, S. (2018). Strategies to Mentor Female Faculty. In C. S. Conway (Ed.), *Faculty Mentorship at Historically Black Colleges and Universities* (pp. 126–150). IGI Global. doi:10.4018/978-1-5225-4071-7.ch007

Cowart, M. T. (2019). Facilitating Linguistic and Academic Success for Newcomer English Language Learners. In J. Keengwe & G. Onchwari (Eds.), *Handbook of Research on Assessment Practices and Pedagogical Models for Immigrant Students* (pp. 218–234). IGI Global. doi:10.4018/978-1-5225-9348-5.ch011

Cox, M. R. (2020). Creating a Sense of Belonging for Black American Students. In T. Crosby-Cooper (Ed.), *Implementing Culturally Responsive Practices in Education* (pp. 243–263). IGI Global. doi:10.4018/978-1-7998-3331-4.ch014

Cresswell-Yeager, T. J., & Whitaker, R. W. II. (2020). Using Student-Centered Engagement in the Classroom to Develop Cultural Intelligence. In L. O. Tripp & R. M. Collier (Eds.), *Culturally Responsive Teaching and Learning in Higher Education* (pp. 262–279). IGI Global. doi:10.4018/978-1-5225-9989-0.ch012

Delahoussaye, K. (2017). Culture Shock. In K. Jones & J. R. Mixon (Eds.), *Intercultural Responsiveness in the Second Language Learning Classroom* (pp. 62–83). IGI Global. doi:10.4018/978-1-5225-2069-6.ch005

Delello, J. A., & Mokhtari, K. (2020). Student and Faculty Perceptions of Social Media Use and Relationships Inside and Outside the Higher Education Classroom. In M. Sarfraz (Ed.), *Innovative Perspectives on Interactive Communication Systems and Technologies* (pp. 23–44). IGI Global. doi:10.4018/978-1-7998-3355-0.ch002

Demirhan, K. (2019). An Overview of International Students and Discrimination in Higher Education. In S. Wisdom, L. Leavitt, & C. Bice (Eds.), *Handbook of Research on Social Inequality and Education* (pp. 333–347). IGI Global. doi:10.4018/978-1-5225-9108-5.ch018

Desconnets, J., Mougenot, I., & Chahdi, H. (2017). A Methodology for Effective Metadata Design in Earth Observation. In M. C. Malta, A. A. Baptista, & P. Walk (Eds.), *Developing Metadata Application Profiles* (pp. 65–97). IGI Global. doi:10.4018/978-1-5225-2221-8.ch004

Dewan, A. D. (2019). Fulani Herdsmen and Farmers Conflicts in Nigeria. In E. A. Nyam & A. H. Tunde (Eds.), *Impacts of Violent Conflicts on Resource Control and Sustainability* (pp. 1–25). IGI Global. doi:10.4018/978-1-5225-5987-0.ch001

Dickens, K. N. (2020). Just Eat! In B. C. King & T. A. Stewart (Eds.), *Cases on Cross-Cultural Counseling Strategies* (pp. 27–43). IGI Global. doi:10.4018/978-1-7998-0022-4.ch002

Dion, S. K. (2019). Considering Diversity in L2 Teacher Education. In C. A. Lenkaitis & S. M. Hilliker (Eds.), *Engaging Teacher Candidates and Language Learners With Authentic Practice* (pp. 118–138). IGI Global. doi:10.4018/978-1-5225-8543-5.ch008

Dobransky, M. (2020). The Effect of Membership in an Online Cohort Major on Baccalaureate Degree Completion. In L. Kyei-Blankson, E. Ntuli, & J. Blankson (Eds.), *Handbook of Research on Creating Meaningful Experiences in Online Courses* (pp. 119–139). IGI Global. doi:10.4018/978-1-7998-0115-3.ch009

Dolanbay, H. (2019). A Discipline Approach. In M. N. Yildiz, M. Fazal, M. Ahn, R. Feirsen, & S. Ozdemir (Eds.), *Handbook of Research on Media Literacy Research and Applications Across Disciplines* (pp. 50–64). IGI Global. doi:10.4018/978-1-5225-9261-7.ch004

Dorrell, D. (2018). Using International Content in an Introductory Human Geography Course. In S. Dikli, B. Etheridge, & R. Rawls (Eds.), *Curriculum Internationalization and the Future of Education* (pp. 55–80). IGI Global. doi:10.4018/978-1-5225-2791-6.ch004

Dryjanska, L. (2020). Religion and Spirituality Empowering Female Refugee Entrepreneurship. In S. Mosquera & P. Jardim da Palma (Eds.), *Multidisciplinary Approach to Entrepreneurship Education for Migrants* (pp. 41–59). IGI Global. doi:10.4018/978-1-7998-2925-6.ch003

Duru, A. V., & Akinro, N. (2020). Navigating Academia Away From Home. In U. T. Onyebadi (Ed.), *Multidisciplinary Issues Surrounding African Diasporas* (pp. 80–102). IGI Global. doi:10.4018/978-1-5225-5079-2.ch004

Dutot, V., & Lichy, J. (2019). The Role of Social Media in Accelerating the Process of Acculturation to the Global Consumer Culture. *International Journal of Technology and Human Interaction, 15*(1), 65–84. doi:10.4018/IJTHI.2019010105

Eberz, F. (2020). Generational Differences in the Workplace? In B. Christiansen (Ed.), *Global Applications of Multigenerational Management and Leadership in the Transcultural Era* (pp. 163–195). IGI Global. doi:10.4018/978-1-5225-9906-7.ch006

Ekundayo, S., Arasanmi, C. N., & Aliyu, O. A. (2019). International Students' Use of Social Media as Information Sources. In H. C. Lum (Ed.), *Critical Issues Impacting Science, Technology, Society (STS), and Our Future* (pp. 111–123). IGI Global. doi:10.4018/978-1-5225-7949-6.ch005

Endong, F. P. (2018). Female Entrepreneurship in the Nollywood Film Industry. In D. Chitakunye & A. Takhar (Eds.), *Examining the Role of Women Entrepreneurs in Emerging Economies* (pp. 126–144). IGI Global. doi:10.4018/978-1-5225-5112-6.ch006

Endong, F. P. (2019). America in the Camera Obscura of Nigerian â€œVideastesâ. In F. P. Endong (Ed.), *Popular Representations of America in Non-American Media* (pp. 81–105). IGI Global. doi:10.4018/978-1-5225-9312-6.ch004

Endong, F. P. (2019). Exploring U.S. Citizens' Perceptions of Foreign Media's Representations of America. In F. P. Endong (Ed.), *Popular Representations of America in Non-American Media* (pp. 243–260). IGI Global. doi:10.4018/978-1-5225-9312-6.ch010

Endong, F. P. (2020). Body Abjectification as a Tool to Represent Poverty in Black Africa. In F. P. Endong (Ed.), *Deconstructing Images of the Global South Through Media Representations and Communication* (pp. 67–86). IGI Global. doi:10.4018/978-1-5225-9821-3.ch003

Endong, F. P. (2020). Tackling Nigeria's Image Crisis With the Aid of Popular Cinema. In F. P. Endong (Ed.), *Deconstructing Images of the Global South Through Media Representations and Communication* (pp. 187–206). IGI Global. doi:10.4018/978-1-5225-9821-3.ch007

Endong, F. P., & Essoh, G. E. (2020). Ode to Africa's Urban Space. In F. P. Endong (Ed.), *Deconstructing Images of the Global South Through Media Representations and Communication* (pp. 166–186). IGI Global. doi:10.4018/978-1-5225-9821-3.ch006

Essoh, G. E. (2020). Beautifying Controversial African Politicians Through Metaphors. In F. P. Endong (Ed.), *Deconstructing Images of the Global South Through Media Representations and Communication* (pp. 253–272). IGI Global. doi:10.4018/978-1-5225-9821-3.ch011

Falcone, A., & Giroldini, P. (2020). Imagined Archaeologies. In E. Proietti (Ed.), *Developing Effective Communication Skills in Archaeology* (pp. 285–307). IGI Global. doi:10.4018/978-1-7998-1059-9.ch014

Falk, A. F., & Carey, A. J. (2018). Lawrence2College. In O. O. Delano-Oriaran, M. W. Penick-Parks, & S. Fondrie (Eds.), *Culturally Engaging Service-Learning With Diverse Communities* (pp. 169–190). IGI Global. doi:10.4018/978-1-5225-2900-2.ch010

Fallah, S., Reynolds, B., & Murawski, W. (2020). *Themes and Recommendations From One CLD Group*. IGI Global. doi:10.4018/978-1-7998-2069-7.ch008

Farina, D. M., & Coleman, N. (2018). College Student Reception of Next-Generation Learning and Effective Approaches for Instructors. In J. Keengwe (Ed.), *Handbook of Research on Pedagogical Models for Next-Generation Teaching and Learning* (pp. 306–324). IGI Global. doi:10.4018/978-1-5225-3873-8.ch017

Farooqui, J. F., & Kaushik, A. (2020). Situational Analysis of Muslim Children in the Face of Islamophobia. In A. Bagasra & M. Mackinem (Eds.), *Working With Muslim Clients in the Helping Professions* (pp. 96–116). IGI Global. doi:10.4018/978-1-7998-0018-7.ch006

Farr, R. H., Simon, K. A., & Bruun, S. T. (2017). LGBTQ Relationships. In N. R. Silton (Ed.), *Family Dynamics and Romantic Relationships in a Changing Society* (pp. 110–136). IGI Global. doi:10.4018/978-1-5225-2404-5.ch006

Fernandez-Torres, Y., Palomo-Zurdo, R. J., & Gutierrez-Fernandez, M. (2019). Gender Diversity in the Senior Management of Large Technology Companies. In A. Guerra Guerra (Ed.), *Organizational Transformation and Managing Innovation in the Fourth Industrial Revolution* (pp. 48–64). IGI Global. doi:10.4018/978-1-5225-7074-5.ch003

Ferrari, F. (2019). The Daughter's Career in Family Firms. In E. T. Pereira & P. Paoloni (Eds.), *Handbook of Research on Women in Management and the Global Labor Market* (pp. 156–176). IGI Global. doi:10.4018/978-1-5225-9171-9.ch008

Fletcher, E. C. Jr. (2018). Characteristics of Career and Technical Education Faculty across Institutions of Higher Education in the United States. *International Journal of Adult Vocational Education and Technology*, *9*(1), 42–58. doi:10.4018/IJAVET.2018010104

Folostina, R., & Iacob, C. I. (2020). The Inclusion of Children With Special Education Needs. In V. Trif (Ed.), *Analyzing Paradigms Used in Education and Educational Psychology* (pp. 189–209). IGI Global. doi:10.4018/978-1-7998-1427-6.ch009

Fontoura, M. M., & Amaral, M. A. (2020). Femininities and Technologies. In P. Isaias & K. Blashki (Eds.), *Interactivity and the Future of the Human-Computer Interface* (pp. 224–243). IGI Global. doi:10.4018/978-1-7998-2637-8.ch012

Frady, K. K. (2020). A Practical Workforce Development Framework Using Strategies and Initiatives to Strengthen the Mature Workforce. In C. Hughes (Ed.), *Strategies for Attracting, Maintaining, and Balancing a Mature Workforce* (pp. 237–269). IGI Global. doi:10.4018/978-1-7998-2277-6.ch010

Frifita, S., Mathlouthi, I., & Dammak, A. (2020). An Efficient VNS Algorithm to Solve the Multi-Attribute Technician Routing and Scheduling Problem. *International Journal of Applied Metaheuristic Computing*, *11*(1), 23–35. doi:10.4018/IJAMC.2020010102

Fuentes, M. A., Shannon, C. R., Ahluwalia, M. K., & Collier, C. S. (2018). Transgressions on Students and Faculty of Color in Higher Education. In B. Blummer, J. M. Kenton, & M. Wiatrowski (Eds.), *Promoting Ethnic Diversity and Multiculturalism in Higher Education* (pp. 132–147). IGI Global. doi:10.4018/978-1-5225-4097-7.ch008

Gardiner, C. L. (2019). Media Communication Perspectives of African American Males Regarding Criminal Behaviors. In P. H. Hoffman-Miller, M. James, & D. Hermond (Eds.), *African American Suburbanization and the Consequential Loss of Identity* (pp. 28–38). IGI Global. doi:10.4018/978-1-5225-7835-2.ch003

Gasa, V. (2018). Social Justice and Inclusion of Children With Diverse Needs in Mainstream Schools. In I. Tshabangu (Ed.), *Global Ideologies Surrounding Children's Rights and Social Justice* (pp. 171–185). IGI Global. doi:10.4018/978-1-5225-2578-3.ch011

Gbadamosi, A. (2019). A Conceptual Overview of Consumer Behavior in the Contemporary Developing Nations. In A. Gbadamosi (Ed.), *Exploring the Dynamics of Consumerism in Developing Nations* (pp. 1–30). IGI Global. doi:10.4018/978-1-5225-7906-9.ch001

Goette, W., Delello, J. A., & McWhorter, R. R. (2019). Gendered Experiences of Mobile Gaming and Augmented Reality. *International Journal of Virtual and Augmented Reality*, *3*(2), 54–67. doi:10.4018/IJVAR.2019070105

Goksoy, A. (2019). Cultural Integration in Mergers and Acquisitions. In A. C. Moreira & P. Silva (Eds.), *Handbook of Research on Corporate Restructuring and Globalization* (pp. 101–124). IGI Global. doi:10.4018/978-1-5225-8906-8.ch005

Grant, M. C. (2018). Equity, Equality, and Reform in Contemporary Public Education. In M. C. Grant (Ed.), *Equity, Equality, and Reform in Contemporary Public Education* (pp. 1–30). IGI Global. doi:10.4018/978-1-5225-4960-4.ch001

Grant, Y. (2020). Sexism in Medical Communication. In M. I. Bellini & V. E. Papalois (Eds.), *Gender Equity in the Medical Profession* (pp. 75–93). IGI Global. doi:10.4018/978-1-5225-9599-1.ch006

Green, W. M., & De Cruz, V. (2017). Enhancing Intercultural Competency Though Co-Curricular Activities in Higher Education. In A. Shahriar & G. Syed (Eds.), *Student Culture and Identity in Higher Education* (pp. 59–74). IGI Global. doi:10.4018/978-1-5225-2551-6.ch004

Habito, C. D., & Ealdama, S. J. (2019). Identity Construction, Social Media, and Ifugao Rice Terraces Conservation of Indigenous People's Youth Through Appreciative Inquiry. *International Journal of Social Ecology and Sustainable Development*, *10*(4), 47–59. doi:10.4018/IJSESD.2019100104

Hai-Jew, S. (2018). *Exploring Identity-Based Humor in a #Selfies #Humor Image Set From Instagram*. IGI Global. doi:10.4018/978-1-5225-2679-7.ch001

Hai-Jew, S. (2020). Global Evocations of South-Ness Online. In F. P. Endong (Ed.), *Deconstructing Images of the Global South Through Media Representations and Communication* (pp. 383–408). IGI Global. doi:10.4018/978-1-5225-9821-3.ch015

Hammack, R. (2020). A Mile in Their Shoes. In A. M. Ellsworth (Ed.), *Cases on Emotionally Responsive Teaching and Mentoring* (pp. 198–208). IGI Global. doi:10.4018/978-1-7998-2971-3.ch016

Hampton-Garland, P., Sechrest-Ehrhardt, L., & Cooke, B. (2018). *Creating a Stereotype of a Race as Dangerous, Unintelligent, and Lazy*. IGI Global. doi:10.4018/978-1-5225-3843-1.ch001

Hampton-Garland, P., Sechrest-Ehrhardt, L., & Cooke, B. (2018). *Decoding Difference*. IGI Global. doi:10.4018/978-1-5225-3843-1.ch006

Han, P. (2019). Social Constructivism as a Theoretical Foundation of Cross-Cultural Mentoring for Foreign-Born Faculty. In V. X. Wang (Ed.), *Handbook of Research on Transdisciplinary Knowledge Generation* (pp. 201–215). IGI Global. doi:10.4018/978-1-5225-9531-1.ch015

Hardee, S. C., & McFaden, K. L. (2018). Social Foundations of Education and Service-Based Field Experiences. In T. D. Meidl & M. Sulentic Dowell (Eds.), *Handbook of Research on Service-Learning Initiatives in Teacher Education Programs* (pp. 41–57). IGI Global. doi:10.4018/978-1-5225-4041-0.ch003

Harrichand, J. J., Kirk, K., & Mwendwa, J. M. (2020). Deepa's Discovery. In B. C. King & T. A. Stewart (Eds.), *Cases on Cross-Cultural Counseling Strategies* (pp. 192–218). IGI Global. doi:10.4018/978-1-7998-0022-4.ch010

Harushimana, I., & Awokoya, J. (2019). The Threat of Downward Assimilation Among Young African Immigrants in U.S. Schools. In J. Keengwe & G. Onchwari (Eds.), *Handbook of Research on Assessment Practices and Pedagogical Models for Immigrant Students* (pp. 330–354). IGI Global. doi:10.4018/978-1-5225-9348-5.ch018

Heitner, K. L., Sherman, K. C., & Jennings, M. E. (2019). Care and Cultural Responsiveness of Online College Courses. In L. Kyei-Blankson, J. Blankson, & E. Ntuli (Eds.), *Care and Culturally Responsive Pedagogy in Online Settings* (pp. 331–355). IGI Global. doi:10.4018/978-1-5225-7802-4.ch016

Hiatt, M. A., Mc Letchie, A., Bagasra, A. B., Laufersweiler-Dwyer, D. L., & Mackinem, M. (2019). Perceptions of Diversity, Inclusion, and Belongingness at an HBCU. In R. Jeffries (Ed.), *Diversity, Equity, and Inclusivity in Contemporary Higher Education* (pp. 175–193). IGI Global. doi:10.4018/978-1-5225-5724-1.ch011

Hochschild, T. R. Jr, Alvarez-Rivera, L. L., & McIntyre, R. N. Jr. (2019). Go Back to Where You Came From. In G. A. Crews (Ed.), *Handbook of Research on School Violence in American K-12 Education* (pp. 227–243). IGI Global. doi:10.4018/978-1-5225-6246-7.ch010

Horton, R. (2020). Systems-Based Approaches to Speech-Language Pathology Service Delivery for School Age Children. In D. M. Scott (Ed.), *Cases on Communication Disorders in Culturally Diverse Populations* (pp. 113–136). IGI Global. doi:10.4018/978-1-7998-2261-5.ch006

Hoskin, M. N., & Smith, M. D. (2020). Let's Get Real. In L. O. Tripp & R. M. Collier (Eds.), *Culturally Responsive Teaching and Learning in Higher Education* (pp. 122–139). IGI Global. doi:10.4018/978-1-5225-9989-0.ch006

Hu, L. (2019). The Need Towards Bicultural Social Services in Supporting Senior Chinese Migrants Towards Their Pursuit of Mauri Ora in Aotearoa New Zealand. In S. Hameed, S. El-Kafafi, & R. Waretini-Karena (Eds.), *Handbook of Research on Indigenous Knowledge and Bi-Culturalism in a Global Context* (pp. 120–135). IGI Global. doi:10.4018/978-1-5225-6061-6.ch007

Huderson, A., & Huderson, B. (2019). Societal Factors and Workplace Perceptions. In U. Thomas & J. Drake (Eds.), *Women's Influence on Inclusion, Equity, and Diversity in STEM Fields* (pp. 1–21). IGI Global. doi:10.4018/978-1-5225-8870-2.ch001

Hudson, S. A. (2017). Reflective Game Designers. In A. Shahriar & G. Syed (Eds.), *Student Culture and Identity in Higher Education* (pp. 111–125). IGI Global. doi:10.4018/978-1-5225-2551-6.ch007

Hughes, H., Myers, J., & Ward, P. (2019). The Accrual and Use of Social Capital in Workplace Innovation. In B. C. Thomas & L. J. Murphy (Eds.), *Innovation and Social Capital in Organizational Ecosystems* (pp. 98–130). IGI Global. doi:10.4018/978-1-5225-7721-8.ch006

Humiston, J. P., Marshall, S. M., Hacker, N. L., & Cantu, L. M. (2020). Intentionally Creating an Inclusive and Welcoming Climate in the Online Learning Classroom. In L. Kyei-Blankson, E. Ntuli, & J. Blankson (Eds.), *Handbook of Research on Creating Meaningful Experiences in Online Courses* (pp. 173–186). IGI Global. doi:10.4018/978-1-7998-0115-3.ch012

Ibbi, A. A. (2020). Development vs. Underdevelopment. In F. P. Endong (Ed.), *Deconstructing Images of the Global South Through Media Representations and Communication* (pp. 225–237). IGI Global. doi:10.4018/978-1-5225-9821-3.ch009

Ibrahim, N. (2020). Domestic and Family Violence and Associated Correlates Among Muslims in Australia. In A. Bagasra & M. Mackinem (Eds.), *Working With Muslim Clients in the Helping Professions* (pp. 155–185). IGI Global. doi:10.4018/978-1-7998-0018-7.ch009

Idowu, D., & King, G. (2018). Health Literacy and Ethnic Minority Populations. In V. E. Papalois & M. Theodosopoulou (Eds.), *Optimizing Health Literacy for Improved Clinical Practices* (pp. 210–227). IGI Global. doi:10.4018/978-1-5225-4074-8.ch012

Igu, N. C., Ogba, F. N., & Nwinyinya, E. (2020). Managing Diversity in Schools. In T. Crosby-Cooper (Ed.), *Implementing Culturally Responsive Practices in Education* (pp. 195–210). IGI Global. doi:10.4018/978-1-7998-3331-4.ch011

Imai, T. (2020). Benefits and Risks Associated With Use of Social Media by People With Health Issues. In M. F. Wright (Ed.), *Recent Advances in Digital Media Impacts on Identity, Sexuality, and Relationships* (pp. 206–230). IGI Global. doi:10.4018/978-1-7998-1063-6.ch011

Iwasaki, Y. (2020). Centrality of Youth Engagement in Media Involvement. In M. Adria (Ed.), *Using New Media for Citizen Engagement and Participation* (pp. 81–96). IGI Global. doi:10.4018/978-1-7998-1828-1.ch005

Iyengar, K. M. (2020). Identity Construction in Latina Students. In J. Keengwe (Ed.), *Handbook of Research on Diversity and Social Justice in Higher Education* (pp. 238–256). IGI Global. doi:10.4018/978-1-7998-5268-1.ch014

Jackson, B. (2020). The Academic Second Language (L2) Socialization and Acculturation of International Exchange Students. In D. M. Velliaris (Ed.), *Academic Mobility Programs and Engagement* (pp. 80–110). IGI Global. doi:10.4018/978-1-7998-1607-2.ch004

Johnson, L. W. (2020). Healthcare Considerations for the Hispanic Population. In D. M. Scott (Ed.), *Cases on Communication Disorders in Culturally Diverse Populations* (pp. 239–259). IGI Global. doi:10.4018/978-1-7998-2261-5.ch012

Johnson, T., & Lehner, E. (2020). Understanding the Attrition Rates of Diverse Teacher Candidates. In P. D. Keough (Ed.), *Overcoming Current Challenges in the P-12 Teaching Profession* (pp. 268–290). IGI Global. doi:10.4018/978-1-7998-1177-0.ch012

Jones, D. (2017). From Theorizing in the Ivory Tower to Creating Change with the People. *International Journal of Adult Vocational Education and Technology*, *8*(2), 29–41. doi:10.4018/IJAVET.2017040103

Kamasak, R., Ozbilgin, M., & Atay, D. (2020). The Cultural Impact of Hidden Curriculum on Language Learners. In A. Slapac & S. A. Coppersmith (Eds.), *Beyond Language Learning Instruction* (pp. 104–125). IGI Global. doi:10.4018/978-1-7998-1962-2.ch005

Kamberi, S. (2017). A Girls-Only Online Virtual World Environment and its Implications for Game-Based Learning. In A. Stricker, C. Calongne, B. Truman, & F. Arenas (Eds.), *Integrating an Awareness of Selfhood and Society into Virtual Learning* (pp. 74–95). IGI Global. doi:10.4018/978-1-5225-2182-2.ch006

Karataa, K., & Baloglu, M. (2019). Acculturation Stress and Its Reflections in Terms of Social Inequality. In S. Wisdom, L. Leavitt, & C. Bice (Eds.), *Handbook of Research on Social Inequality and Education* (pp. 348–365). IGI Global. doi:10.4018/978-1-5225-9108-5.ch019

Khumalo, K. (2019). Gender Sensitivity in Parliamentary Discourse an Appraisal Approach. In E. Jakaza (Ed.), *Argumentation and Appraisal in Parliamentary Discourse* (pp. 215–244). IGI Global. doi:10.4018/978-1-5225-8094-2.ch009

Kilburn, M., Radu, M. B., & Henckell, M. (2019). Conceptual and Theoretical Frameworks for CRT Pedagogy. In L. Kyei-Blankson, J. Blankson, & E. Ntuli (Eds.), *Care and Culturally Responsive Pedagogy in Online Settings* (pp. 1–21). IGI Global. doi:10.4018/978-1-5225-7802-4.ch001

Kimotho, S. G. (2018). Understanding the Nature of Stigma Communication Associated With Mental Illness in Africa. In B. A. Canfield & H. A. Cunningham (Eds.), *Deconstructing Stigma in Mental Health* (pp. 20–41). IGI Global. doi:10.4018/978-1-5225-3808-0.ch002

King, B. A. (2020). An Approach to Diversity and Cultural Competence Curriculum in Public Administration. In L. O. Tripp & R. M. Collier (Eds.), *Culturally Responsive Teaching and Learning in Higher Education* (pp. 239–261). IGI Global. doi:10.4018/978-1-5225-9989-0.ch011

Kuehn, C. (2020). College-Going and College-Staying Capital. In G. A. Berg & L. Venis (Eds.), *Accessibility and Diversity in the 21st Century University* (pp. 68–98). IGI Global. doi:10.4018/978-1-7998-2783-2.ch004

Kulturel-Konak, S., Konak, A., & D'Allegro, M. L. (2017). Global Awareness Interest of College Students. *International Journal of Bias, Identity and Diversities in Education*, *2*(1), 13–26. doi:10.4018/IJBIDE.2017010102

Kumi-Yeboah, A., Dogbey, J., Yuan, G., & Amponsah, S. (2019). Cultural Diversity in Online Learning. In L. Kyei-Blankson, J. Blankson, & E. Ntuli (Eds.), *Care and Culturally Responsive Pedagogy in Online Settings* (pp. 230–251). IGI Global. doi:10.4018/978-1-5225-7802-4.ch012

Kurebwa, J. (2020). The Evolution of Gender Studies and Its Impact on the African Society in the 21st Century. In J. Kurebwa (Ed.), *Understanding Gender in the African Context* (pp. 1–18). IGI Global. doi:10.4018/978-1-7998-2815-0.ch001

Kurebwa, J., & Ndlovu, S. (2020). The Contribution of Zimbabwean Uniformed Women in Peacekeeping in Africa. In S. Chhabra (Ed.), *Civic Engagement in Social and Political Constructs* (pp. 220–245). IGI Global. doi:10.4018/978-1-7998-2364-3.ch010

Kurylo, A. D. (2018). American People vs. Politicians. In N. Bilge & M. I. Marino (Eds.), *Reconceptualizing New Media and Intercultural Communication in a Networked Society* (pp. 251–279). IGI Global. doi:10.4018/978-1-5225-3784-7.ch010

Kyendo, M. W. (2018). Interethnic Conflicts. In B. L. Cook (Ed.), *Handbook of Research on Examining Global Peacemaking in the Digital Age* (pp. 350–360). IGI Global. doi:10.4018/978-1-5225-3032-9.ch025

Lalas, J. W., & Strikwerda, H. L. (2020). Driving Equity in Action Through a Socially and Culturally Situated Pedagogy. In P. D. Keough (Ed.), *Overcoming Current Challenges in the P-12 Teaching Profession* (pp. 291–315). IGI Global. doi:10.4018/978-1-7998-1177-0.ch013

Lee, L. (2020). Promoting Interpersonal and Intercultural Communication With Flipgrid. In M. Kruk & M. Peterson (Eds.), *New Technological Applications for Foreign and Second Language Learning and Teaching* (pp. 261–281). IGI Global. doi:10.4018/978-1-7998-2591-3.ch013

Leggett-Robinson, P. M., & Villa, B. C. (2019). Navigating the Landscape of the STEM Professoriate. In U. Thomas & J. Drake (Eds.), *Women's Influence on Inclusion, Equity, and Diversity in STEM Fields* (pp. 22–65). IGI Global. doi:10.4018/978-1-5225-8870-2.ch002

Lehner, E., & Ziegler, J. R. (2019). Re-Conceptualizing Race in New York City's High School Social Studies Classrooms. In S. Wisdom, L. Leavitt, & C. Bice (Eds.), *Handbook of Research on Social Inequality and Education* (pp. 24–45). IGI Global. doi:10.4018/978-1-5225-9108-5.ch002

Leung, L. Y. (2020). Representation of Gender Equality From the Perspective of the Medical Trainee and its Ripple Effect. In M. I. Bellini & V. E. Papalois (Eds.), *Gender Equity in the Medical Profession* (pp. 29–50). IGI Global. doi:10.4018/978-1-5225-9599-1.ch003

Lewis, A. S. (2019). What's Respect Got to Do With It? In U. Thomas (Ed.), *Navigating Micro-Aggressions Toward Women in Higher Education* (pp. 181–201). IGI Global. doi:10.4018/978-1-5225-5942-9.ch009

Ligocki, D., & Wilkins, M. A. (2020). The Truth We Can't Afford to Ignore. In J. S. Mitchell & E. N. Vaughn (Eds.), *Participatory Literacy Practices for P-12 Classrooms in the Digital Age* (pp. 57–72). IGI Global. doi:10.4018/978-1-7998-0000-2.ch004

Lima, B., & Dart, H. (2019). The Hemispheres Connection. In P. Romanowski & E. Bandura (Eds.), *Intercultural Foreign Language Teaching and Learning in Higher Education Contexts* (pp. 162–176). IGI Global. doi:10.4018/978-1-5225-8128-4.ch008

Little, J. M., Gaier, S., & Spoutz, D. (2018). The Role of Values, Beliefs, and Culture in Student Retention and Success. In R. C. Black (Ed.), *Critical Assessment and Strategies for Increased Student Retention* (pp. 54–72). IGI Global. doi:10.4018/978-1-5225-2998-9.ch004

Liu, X., & Wachira, P. (2020). Perceptions of Gender Stereotypes About Computer Game-Based Learning Among Pre-Service Teachers. In J. Keengwe & P. Wachira (Eds.), *Handbook of Research on Integrating Computer Science and Computational Thinking in K-12 Education* (pp. 107–123). IGI Global. doi:10.4018/978-1-7998-1479-5.ch007

Loew, D. J. (2019). Exploring Peace Perspectives Through the Lens of Gender Inequality. In M. W. Lutfy & C. Toffolo (Eds.), *Handbook of Research on Promoting Peace Through Practice, Academia, and the Arts* (pp. 405–426). IGI Global. doi:10.4018/978-1-5225-3001-5.ch020

Logan, S. R., & Dudley, H. S. (2019). The â€œDouble-Whammyâ€ of Being Black and a Woman in Higher Education Leadership. In H. L. Schnackenberg & D. A. Simard (Eds.), *Challenges and Opportunities for Women in Higher Education Leadership* (pp. 84–104). IGI Global. doi:10.4018/978-1-5225-7056-1.ch006

Louber, I. (2017). Racial Discrimination and TESOL. *International Journal of Bias, Identity and Diversities in Education*, *2*(2), 29–41. doi:10.4018/IJBIDE.2017070103

Loza, J., & Garino, A. (2020). Gender and Ethnic Identities Against Neoliberalism in Bolivia. In P. A. Baisotti & P. Pozzi (Eds.), *Historical and Future Global Impacts of Armed Groups and Social Movements* (pp. 161–192). IGI Global. doi:10.4018/978-1-7998-5205-6.ch007

Mackinem, M. B., & Sporl, C. (2020). A Primer on Substance Use and Islam. In A. Bagasra & M. Mackinem (Eds.), *Working With Muslim Clients in the Helping Professions* (pp. 23–39). IGI Global. doi:10.4018/978-1-7998-0018-7.ch002

Madichie, N. O., & Opute, P. A. (2019). Regulatory Challenges in Sub-Saharan Africa and Marketing Malpractices of â€œBigâ€ Tobacco. In A. Gbadamosi (Ed.), *Exploring the Dynamics of Consumerism in Developing Nations* (pp. 101–123). IGI Global. doi:10.4018/978-1-5225-7906-9.ch005

Maheshkar, C., & Sharma, V. (2018). Cross-Cultural Business Education. In C. Maheshkar & V. Sharma (Eds.), *Handbook of Research on Cross-Cultural Business Education* (pp. 1–35). IGI Global. doi:10.4018/978-1-5225-3776-2.ch001

Malizia, P. (2017). Watercolour. In P. Malizia, C. Cannavale, & F. Maimone (Eds.), *Evolution of the Post-Bureaucratic Organization* (pp. 1–18). IGI Global. doi:10.4018/978-1-5225-1983-6.ch001

Martinovic, D. (2017). Internationally Educated Mathematics Teacher Candidates. *International Journal of Semiotics and Visual Rhetoric*, *1*(1), 36–46. doi:10.4018/IJSVR.2017010105

Mathiyalakan, S., Ho, K. K., Heilman, G. E., & Law, W. K. (2017). An Investigation into the Impact of Ethnicity and Culture on the Motivation for using Facebook for Academics and Socialization in Guam. *International Journal of Systems and Service-Oriented Engineering*, *7*(4), 1–21. doi:10.4018/IJSSOE.2017100101

Maulana, I. (2019). Mobile Devices and the Prevention of Human Rights Violations. In S. Umair & M. Y. Shah (Eds.), *Mobile Devices and Smart Gadgets in Human Rights* (pp. 1–26). IGI Global. doi:10.4018/978-1-5225-6939-8.ch001

Mayakis, C. G., & Robinson, J. (2018). Girls in STEM K-12 Subjects. In M. C. Grant (Ed.), *Equity, Equality, and Reform in Contemporary Public Education* (pp. 110–125). IGI Global. doi:10.4018/978-1-5225-4960-4.ch006

Mazur, E. (2020). The Trouble With Tinder. In M. F. Wright (Ed.), *Recent Advances in Digital Media Impacts on Identity, Sexuality, and Relationships* (pp. 99–118). IGI Global. doi:10.4018/978-1-7998-1063-6.ch006

McDonald, C. P. (2020). When Worlds Collide. In T. Crosby-Cooper (Ed.), *Implementing Culturally Responsive Practices in Education* (pp. 211–229). IGI Global. doi:10.4018/978-1-7998-3331-4.ch012

McKoy, H. C. Jr, & Johnson, J. H. Jr. (2018). Do Business Ecosystems See Color? *International Journal of Social Ecology and Sustainable Development*, *9*(3), 80–91. doi:10.4018/IJSESD.2018070106

McLaughlin, A. C., Pryor, M., & Feng, J. (2019). Design the Technological Society for an Aging Population. In H. C. Lum (Ed.), *Critical Issues Impacting Science, Technology, Society (STS), and Our Future* (pp. 218–250). IGI Global. doi:10.4018/978-1-5225-7949-6.ch010

Mensch, S. E., & Wilkie, L. (2018). Cell Phone Security. *International Journal of Strategic Information Technology and Applications*, *9*(3), 15–31. doi:10.4018/IJSITA.2018070102

Midkiff, B. (2017). Higher Education for Whom? Higher Education for What? In H. C. Alphin Jr, J. Lavine, & R. Y. Chan (Eds.), *Disability and Equity in Higher Education Accessibility* (pp. 104–134). IGI Global. doi:10.4018/978-1-5225-2665-0.ch005

Miller, C. H., Dunbar, N. E., Jensen, M. L., Massey, Z. B., Lee, Y., Nicholls, S. B., Anderson, C., Adams, A. S., Cecena, J. E., Thompson, W. M., & Wilson, S. N. (2019). Training Law Enforcement Officers to Identify Reliable Deception Cues With a Serious Digital Game. *International Journal of Game-Based Learning*, *9*(3), 1–22. doi:10.4018/IJGBL.2019070101

Miller, O. P., & Banks-Hall, R. L. (2019). Parental Involvement in Education. In P. H. Hoffman-Miller, M. James, & D. Hermond (Eds.), *African American Suburbanization and the Consequential Loss of Identity* (pp. 116–140). IGI Global. doi:10.4018/978-1-5225-7835-2.ch007

Mir, S. H., & Baddar, A. (2020). Association between Urinary Bisphenol A Concentration and Obesity Prevalence in Children and Adolescents. In K. A. Wani, L. Ariana, & S. Zuber (Eds.), *Handbook of Research on Environmental and Human Health Impacts of Plastic Pollution* (pp. 214–245). IGI Global. doi:10.4018/978-1-5225-9452-9.ch012

Moore, A., & Brand, S. T. (2018). A Grand Challenge. In T. D. Meidl & M. Sulentic Dowell (Eds.), *Handbook of Research on Service-Learning Initiatives in Teacher Education Programs* (pp. 429–444). IGI Global. doi:10.4018/978-1-5225-4041-0.ch023

Moore, M. N., & Smith, M. D. (2019). Multicultural Critical Consciousness. In K. Daniels & K. Billingsley (Eds.), *Creating Caring and Supportive Educational Environments for Meaningful Learning* (pp. 36–49). IGI Global. doi:10.4018/978-1-5225-5748-7.ch003

Moridpour, S., Toran Pour, A., & Saghapour, T. (2019). *Neighbourhood Influences on Vehicle-Pedestrian Crash Severity*. IGI Global. doi:10.4018/978-1-5225-7943-4.ch005

Mugweni, R. (2018). Managing Bias in Teacher Preparation in Higher Education. In U. Thomas (Ed.), *Advocacy in Academia and the Role of Teacher Preparation Programs* (pp. 182–189). IGI Global. doi:10.4018/978-1-5225-2906-4.ch010

Mupepi, K., Mupepi, T., & Mupepi, C. (2019). Workforce Diversity. In M. Mupepi & R. Costello (Eds.), *Strategic Collaborative Innovations in Organizational Systems* (pp. 119–139). IGI Global. doi:10.4018/978-1-5225-7390-6.ch006

Nakayama, M. (2017). Exploratory Study on the Stability of Consumer Rationality in Judging Online Reviews. *Journal of Electronic Commerce in Organizations*, *15*(1), 1–22. doi:10.4018/JECO.2017010101

Nava, M. R. (2017). The Development of Intercultural Competences in Post-Bureaucratic Organizations. In P. Malizia, C. Cannavale, & F. Maimone (Eds.), *Evolution of the Post-Bureaucratic Organization* (pp. 401–421). IGI Global. doi:10.4018/978-1-5225-1983-6.ch019

Nave, L., & Khalid, A. H. (2019). The Boone-Kabul Project. In M. W. Lutfy & C. Toffolo (Eds.), *Handbook of Research on Promoting Peace Through Practice, Academia, and the Arts* (pp. 229–249). IGI Global. doi:10.4018/978-1-5225-3001-5.ch012

Ndlovu, R. (2020). Gender Mainstream. In J. Kurebwa (Ed.), *Understanding Gender in the African Context* (pp. 41–62). IGI Global. doi:10.4018/978-1-7998-2815-0.ch003

Niu, Y. (2020). Improving the Employability of Mature Workers. In C. Hughes (Ed.), *Strategies for Attracting, Maintaining, and Balancing a Mature Workforce* (pp. 28–60). IGI Global. doi:10.4018/978-1-7998-2277-6.ch002

Norris, K. E. (2018). Effective Parent Partnerships Between Schools and Diverse Families. In K. E. Norris & S. Collier (Eds.), *Social Justice and Parent Partnerships in Multicultural Education Contexts* (pp. 1–17). IGI Global. doi:10.4018/978-1-5225-3943-8.ch001

Nyemba, F. (2019). An Examination of How Legal Status Affects Enrollment and Graduation Rates. In S. Wisdom, L. Leavitt, & C. Bice (Eds.), *Handbook of Research on Social Inequality and Education* (pp. 130–148). IGI Global. doi:10.4018/978-1-5225-9108-5.ch007

Ohme, R., Matukin, M., & Wicher, P. (2020). Merging Explicit Declarations With Implicit Response Time to Better Predict Behavior. In V. Chkoniya, A. O. Madsen, & P. Bukhrashvili (Eds.), *Anthropological Approaches to Understanding Consumption Patterns and Consumer Behavior* (pp. 427–448). IGI Global. doi:10.4018/978-1-7998-3115-0.ch023

Ojo, S. (2019). *Being and Belonging*. IGI Global. doi:10.4018/978-1-5225-7631-0.ch007

Okoya, J. (2017). Interfacing with Diaspora/Ethnic Entrepreneurship. In S. Ojo (Ed.), *Diasporas and Transnational Entrepreneurship in Global Contexts* (pp. 173–187). IGI Global. doi:10.4018/978-1-5225-1991-1.ch010

Olszewski, C. A., & Hansman, C. A. (2020). Faculty Socialization and Gaining Tenure. In V. Wang (Ed.), *Handbook of Research on Ethical Challenges in Higher Education Leadership and Administration* (pp. 51–71). IGI Global. doi:10.4018/978-1-7998-4141-8.ch004

Onyebadi, U. T., Bland, D., Howard, H., & Walcott, C. (2020). Issues in Academic Leadership. In U. T. Onyebadi (Ed.), *Multidisciplinary Issues Surrounding African Diasporas* (pp. 220–244). IGI Global. doi:10.4018/978-1-5225-5079-2.ch010

Onyebadi, U. T., Satti, M. A., & Mbunyuza-Memani, L. (2020). Diversity and the Media. In U. T. Onyebadi (Ed.), *Multidisciplinary Issues Surrounding African Diasporas* (pp. 54–79). IGI Global. doi:10.4018/978-1-5225-5079-2.ch003

Oppong, N. Y. (2017). Mastering Talent Management. In M. Mupepi (Ed.), *Effective Talent Management Strategies for Organizational Success* (pp. 31–46). IGI Global. doi:10.4018/978-1-5225-1961-4.ch003

Oralkan, A. (2019). The Interaction of Memes and Digital Rhetoric With Stereotypes. In R. Yilmaz (Ed.), *Handbook of Research on Narrative Advertising* (pp. 227–237). IGI Global. doi:10.4018/978-1-5225-9790-2.ch020

Palomares, A., Hearld, K. R., & Budhwani, H. (2020). Research Findings From the American Muslim Women's Health Project (MWHP). In A. Bagasra & M. Mackinem (Eds.), *Working With Muslim Clients in the Helping Professions* (pp. 117–135). IGI Global. doi:10.4018/978-1-7998-0018-7.ch007

Papakitsos, E. C., Kiousi, E., Florakos, G., Patsiada, E., & Makrygiannis, P. S. (2020). Gender Equality and Relevant European Policies Regarding Vocational Education and Labour Market. In U. C. Okolie (Ed.), *Socio-Economic Perspectives on Vocational Skill Development* (pp. 1–30). IGI Global. doi:10.4018/978-1-5225-4145-5.ch001

Parnell, T. A. (2018). Weaving Health Literacy Strategies Throughout the Fabric of Healthcare Organizations. In V. E. Papalois & M. Theodosopoulou (Eds.), *Optimizing Health Literacy for Improved Clinical Practices* (pp. 17–31). IGI Global. doi:10.4018/978-1-5225-4074-8.ch002

Perelli, L. (2020). Evaluating Barriers to and Opportunities for Higher Education in the Hispanic Community. In S. L. Johnson (Ed.), *Examining Social Change and Social Responsibility in Higher Education* (pp. 107–115). IGI Global. doi:10.4018/978-1-7998-2177-9.ch008

Perrotta, K. A., & Mattson, M. F. (2018). Using Counterstories and Reflective Writing Assignments to Promote Critical Race Consciousness in an Undergraduate Teacher Preparation Course. In U. Thomas (Ed.), *Advocacy in Academia and the Role of Teacher Preparation Programs* (pp. 42–64). IGI Global. doi:10.4018/978-1-5225-2906-4.ch003

Petersen, A. J. (2017). Intersectionality and the Construction of Inclusive Schools. In C. M. Curran & A. J. Petersen (Eds.), *Handbook of Research on Classroom Diversity and Inclusive Education Practice* (pp. 1–26). IGI Global. doi:10.4018/978-1-5225-2520-2.ch001

Piscitelli, M. (2019). Promotion of Heritage Tourism Through Branding and Graphic Communication. In S. Srivastava (Ed.), *Conservation and Promotion of Heritage Tourism* (pp. 87–107). IGI Global. doi:10.4018/978-1-5225-6283-2.ch004

Plazas, J. E., Bimonte, S., De Sousa, G., & Corrales, J. C. (2019). Data-Centric UML Profile for Wireless Sensors. *International Journal of Agricultural and Environmental Information Systems, 10*(2), 21–48. doi:10.4018/IJAEIS.2019040102

Porter, P. D. (2018). Using Culturally Responsive Teaching and Data-Driven Instruction in Mathematics to Create Equity and Equality. In M. C. Grant (Ed.), *Equity, Equality, and Reform in Contemporary Public Education* (pp. 197–222). IGI Global. doi:10.4018/978-1-5225-4960-4.ch010

Powell, A. M. (2017). Cultural Bias, Self-Identity, and Self-Efficacy. In K. Jones & J. R. Mixon (Eds.), *Intercultural Responsiveness in the Second Language Learning Classroom* (pp. 51–61). IGI Global. doi:10.4018/978-1-5225-2069-6.ch004

Raby, R. L. (2019). Changing the Conversation. In G. F. Malveaux & R. L. Raby (Eds.), *Study Abroad Opportunities for Community College Students and Strategies for Global Learning* (pp. 1–21). IGI Global. doi:10.4018/978-1-5225-6252-8.ch001

Raghunandan-Jack, N. (2018). Revolutionizing Education. In M. C. Grant (Ed.), *Equity, Equality, and Reform in Contemporary Public Education* (pp. 31–52). IGI Global. doi:10.4018/978-1-5225-4960-4.ch002

Rajesh, S. (2019). Mood Pattern for Savory and Confectionary Food Item Among Gen-Y Women From Social Identity Standpoint. In S. Dasgupta & P. Grover (Eds.), *Optimizing Millennial Consumer Engagement With Mood Analysis* (pp. 118–156). IGI Global. doi:10.4018/978-1-5225-5690-9.ch006

Raposo, D., Oliveira, F., & Farinha, L. (2020). From Identity Into Brand Visual Identity. In L. Farinha & D. Raposo (Eds.), *Handbook of Research on Driving Industrial Competitiveness With Innovative Design Principles* (pp. 66–85). IGI Global. doi:10.4018/978-1-7998-3628-5.ch005

Ravazzani, S. (2017). Communication in Post-Bureaucratic Organizations. In P. Malizia, C. Cannavale, & F. Maimone (Eds.), *Evolution of the Post-Bureaucratic Organization* (pp. 297–320). IGI Global. doi:10.4018/978-1-5225-1983-6.ch014

Reid-Griffin, A. (2020). Communication as Social Influence on Academic and Developmental Growth of Today's Adolescent. In Z. Zaremohzzabieh, S. Ahrari, S. E. Krauss, A. Abu Samah, & S. Z. Omar (Eds.), *Youth Work in a Digital Society* (pp. 82–99). IGI Global. doi:10.4018/978-1-7998-2956-0.ch005

Reynolds, H. M., & Wagle, A. T. (2018). Utilizing Program Specific Data to Develop Case Studies for Use With Preservice Teachers. In D. Polly, M. Putman, T. M. Petty, & A. J. Good (Eds.), *Innovative Practices in Teacher Preparation and Graduate-Level Teacher Education Programs* (pp. 1–20). IGI Global. doi:10.4018/978-1-5225-3068-8.ch001

Rhodes, C. M., & Lohr, K. D. (2019). Culturally Inclusive Teaching of Adult English Language Learners. In D. P. Peltz & A. C. Clemons (Eds.), *Multicultural Andragogy for Transformative Learning* (pp. 115–132). IGI Global. doi:10.4018/978-1-5225-3474-7.ch007

Richards, K. A., Ivy, V. N., Lawson, M. A., & Alameda-Lawson, T. (2018). Teaching Personal and Social Responsibility in Physical Education Teacher Education. In T. D. Meidl & M. Sulentic Dowell (Eds.), *Handbook of Research on Service-Learning Initiatives in Teacher Education Programs* (pp. 143–162). IGI Global. doi:10.4018/978-1-5225-4041-0.ch008

Rockinson-Szapkiw, A. J., & Caldwell, L. R. (2019). Improving STEM Career Aspirations in Underrepresented Populations. In J. L. Wendt & D. L. Apugo (Eds.), *K-12 STEM Education in Urban Learning Environments* (pp. 208–237). IGI Global. doi:10.4018/978-1-5225-7814-7.ch008

Rockinson-Szapkiw, A. J., & Wade-Jaimes, K. (2019). Gendered and Racial Microaggressions in STEM. In J. L. Wendt & D. L. Apugo (Eds.), *K-12 STEM Education in Urban Learning Environments* (pp. 162–182). IGI Global. doi:10.4018/978-1-5225-7814-7.ch006

Rodriguez, S. (2019). Latina Efficacy. In P. D. Keough (Ed.), *Ethical Problem-Solving and Decision-Making for Positive and Conclusive Outcomes* (pp. 162–180). IGI Global. doi:10.4018/978-1-5225-7582-5.ch009

Rogers, R., & Sun, Y. (2019). *A Three-Pillar Approach to Preparing Tomorrow's STEM Professionals*. IGI Global. doi:10.4018/978-1-5225-6341-9.ch004

Rogers, R., & Sun, Y. (2019). *Opening the Doors to STEM Employment Opportunities for Rural Youth*. IGI Global. doi:10.4018/978-1-5225-6341-9.ch005

Roy, S. (2019). Challenges for Asian American and Immigrant Asian Women in the U.S. Higher Education Administration. In H. L. Schnackenberg & D. A. Simard (Eds.), *Challenges and Opportunities for Women in Higher Education Leadership* (pp. 105–124). IGI Global. doi:10.4018/978-1-5225-7056-1.ch007

Sapeg, R. (2020). Underrepresentation of Latina Faculty in Academia. In G. A. Berg & L. Venis (Eds.), *Accessibility and Diversity in the 21st Century University* (pp. 115–139). IGI Global. doi:10.4018/978-1-7998-2783-2.ch006

Saripalle, R. K. (2018). A Software Modeling Perspective of UMLS Semantic Network. In J. Tan (Ed.), *Handbook of Research on Emerging Perspectives on Healthcare Information Systems and Informatics* (pp. 305–322). IGI Global. doi:10.4018/978-1-5225-5460-8.ch013

Sarma, S. (2018). Cultural Nuances in Changing Consumer Behavior. In S. Sarma (Ed.), *Global Observations of the Influence of Culture on Consumer Buying Behavior* (pp. 279–293). IGI Global. doi:10.4018/978-1-5225-2727-5.ch016

Shah, T. M. (2020). Victimization, Cultural Imperatives, and Empowerment of People of Color in the United States. In J. O. Ayodele (Ed.), *Global Perspectives on Victimization Analysis and Prevention* (pp. 96–113). IGI Global. doi:10.4018/978-1-7998-1112-1.ch006

Sharma, M. (2020). Racial/Ethnic Diversity and Economy - A Broad Overview of U.S. Counties, 2000-2014. *International Journal of Applied Geospatial Research, 11*(2), 18–41. doi:10.4018/IJAGR.2020040102

Shiau, H., & Xiang, C. H. (2018). Learning English With Texting on Social Media. In C. H. Xiang (Ed.), *Cases on Audio-Visual Media in Language Education* (pp. 240–260). IGI Global. doi:10.4018/978-1-5225-2724-4.ch010

Simon, R. (2019). Constructing Happiness. In N. R. Silton (Ed.), *Scientific Concepts Behind Happiness, Kindness, and Empathy in Contemporary Society* (pp. 156–177). IGI Global. doi:10.4018/978-1-5225-5918-4.ch008

Slapac, A., Kim, S., & Coppersmith, S. A. (2020). Preparing and Enriching Linguistically and Culturally Responsive Educators Through Professional Development. In A. Slapac & S. A. Coppersmith (Eds.), *Beyond Language Learning Instruction* (pp. 282–304). IGI Global. doi:10.4018/978-1-7998-1962-2.ch012

Smith, T. T., & Johnson, N. N. (2019). Creating Support Systems for Black Women in Nontraditional STEM Career Paths. In U. Thomas & J. Drake (Eds.), *Women's Influence on Inclusion, Equity, and Diversity in STEM Fields* (pp. 108–142). IGI Global. doi:10.4018/978-1-5225-8870-2.ch005

Sonesson, G. (2017). Ego Meets Alter and Alius on the Marketplace. *International Journal of Semiotics and Visual Rhetoric, 1*(2), 55–78. doi:10.4018/IJSVR.2017070104

Song, G. (2018). Cultural Evolution and Cultural Translation. In O. I. Seel (Ed.), *Redefining Translation and Interpretation in Cultural Evolution* (pp. 121–140). IGI Global. doi:10.4018/978-1-5225-2832-6.ch007

Sowad, A. S. (2019). Is Gender a More Important Axis of Representation Than Race, Ethnicity or Class in Politics? *International Journal of Social Ecology and Sustainable Development, 10*(2), 29–36. doi:10.4018/IJSESD.2019040103

Stacey, E. (2019). *Gender Diaspora and International Women's Movements*. IGI Global. doi:10.4018/978-1-5225-7757-7.ch004

Swiderska, A., Krumhuber, E. G., & Kappas, A. (2019). Behavioral and Physiological Responses to Computers in the Ultimatum Game. *International Journal of Technology and Human Interaction, 15*(1), 33–45. doi:10.4018/IJTHI.2019010103

Szymanski, M., & Kalra, K. (2019). Foreign Language Acquisition, Bilingualism, and Biculturalism. In B. Christiansen & E. Turkina (Eds.), *Applied Psycholinguistics and Multilingual Cognition in Human Creativity* (pp. 31–54). IGI Global. doi:10.4018/978-1-5225-6992-3.ch002

Tadlaoui, M., Khaldi, M., & Carvalho, R. (2019). *A Comparative Study of the Functionalities and Characteristics of a Learner Model in Adaptive Hypermedia Educational Systems*. IGI Global. doi:10.4018/978-1-5225-7413-2.ch001

Tadlaoui, M., Khaldi, M., & Carvalho, R. (2019). *A Comparative Study of the Modeling Techniques and Models of a Learner Model in Adaptive Hypermedia Educational Systems*. IGI Global. doi:10.4018/978-1-5225-7413-2.ch002

Tadlaoui, M., Khaldi, M., & Carvalho, R. (2019). *The Combination of Bayesian Networks and Stereotypes to Initialize the Learner Model in Adaptive Educational Hypermedia Systems*. IGI Global. doi:10.4018/978-1-5225-7413-2.ch006

Tadlaoui, M. A., El Moudden, F., & Khaldi, M. (2020). Implementing a Probabilistic Learner Model Into a Course Creation Application. In M. A. Tadlaoui & M. Khaldi (Eds.), *Personalization and Collaboration in Adaptive E-Learning* (pp. 244–258). IGI Global. doi:10.4018/978-1-7998-1492-4.ch012

Tagne, J. S., & Evou, J. P. (2020). Cultural Diversity and Performance of Cameroonian Companies. In B. Christiansen, J. D. Branch, & J. Karmowska (Eds.), *Cultural Factors and Performance in 21st Century Businesses* (pp. 144–163). IGI Global. doi:10.4018/978-1-7998-3744-2.ch007

Tan, B. U. (2020). The Effects of Values and Gender Role Perceptions on Attitudes Towards Women Managers. In B. U. Tan (Ed.), *Macro and Micro-Level Issues Surrounding Women in the Workforce* (pp. 37–57). IGI Global. doi:10.4018/978-1-5225-9163-4.ch002

Tan, C. K., Wijaya, O. I., & Tubal, E. (2019). Self-Esteem and Associated Factors of International Tertiary Students in New Zealand and the Implications on Acculturation and Well-Being. In S. Hameed, S. El-Kafafi, & R. Waretini-Karena (Eds.), *Handbook of Research on Indigenous Knowledge and Bi-Culturalism in a Global Context* (pp. 271–288). IGI Global. doi:10.4018/978-1-5225-6061-6.ch015

Tarboush, E. A. (2019). Bridging Cultures. In J. Keengwe & G. Onchwari (Eds.), *Handbook of Research on Assessment Practices and Pedagogical Models for Immigrant Students* (pp. 235–248). IGI Global. doi:10.4018/978-1-5225-9348-5.ch012

Tello, A. M. (2020). Lucia's Journey of Bridging Two Worlds. In B. C. King & T. A. Stewart (Eds.), *Cases on Cross-Cultural Counseling Strategies* (pp. 107–123). IGI Global. doi:10.4018/978-1-7998-0022-4.ch006

Thiagarajan, P., & Garcia, M. (2020). Cultural Influence on Employee Behavior Impacting Organizational Sustainability. In G. Jain, H. Singh, S. Akter, A. Munjal, & H. S. Grewal (Eds.), *Technological Innovations for Sustainability and Business Growth* (pp. 253–269). IGI Global. doi:10.4018/978-1-5225-9940-1.ch014

Thomas, T. P., & Maultsby, M. L. (2018). Mentoring African American Women at Historically Black Colleges/Universities. In C. S. Conway (Ed.), *Faculty Mentorship at Historically Black Colleges and Universities* (pp. 97–125). IGI Global. doi:10.4018/978-1-5225-4071-7.ch006

Thorsos, N. J. (2019). Language Loss. In P. D. Keough (Ed.), *Ethical Problem-Solving and Decision-Making for Positive and Conclusive Outcomes* (pp. 181–195). IGI Global. doi:10.4018/978-1-5225-7582-5.ch010

Tigert, J. M., & Armstrong, A. A. (2019). Teaching for Diversity Online. In G. Onchwari & J. Keengwe (Eds.), *Handbook of Research on Engaging Immigrant Families and Promoting Academic Success for English Language Learners* (pp. 1–19). IGI Global. doi:10.4018/978-1-5225-8283-0.ch001

Tomasiak, M. A., & Chamakiotis, P. (2017). Understanding Diversity in Virtual Work Environments. In B. Christiansen & H. C. Chandan (Eds.), *Handbook of Research on Human Factors in Contemporary Workforce Development* (pp. 283–307). IGI Global. doi:10.4018/978-1-5225-2568-4.ch013

Tran, B. (2018). Understanding and Addressing the Stigma in Mental Health Within the Asian and Asian-American Culture. In B. A. Canfield & H. A. Cunningham (Eds.), *Deconstructing Stigma in Mental Health* (pp. 70–107). IGI Global. doi:10.4018/978-1-5225-3808-0.ch004

Travers, C. S. (2019). Mapping Mindset and Academic Success Among Black Men at a Predominantly White Institution. In J. T. Butcher, J. R. O'Connor Jr, & F. Titus (Eds.), *Overcoming Challenges and Creating Opportunity for African American Male Students* (pp. 151–171). IGI Global. doi:10.4018/978-1-5225-5990-0.ch009

Tsai, C. (2019). The Role of Self-Confidence in the Criteria of Aesthetic Labour Recruitment. *International Journal of Tourism and Hospitality Management in the Digital Age*, *3*(1), 1–22. doi:10.4018/IJTHMDA.2019010101

Tsang, K. T., & Ip, C. F. (2018). SSLD and Senior Service. In B. Fong, A. Ng, & P. Yuen (Eds.), *Sustainable Health and Long-Term Care Solutions for an Aging Population* (pp. 238–258). IGI Global. doi:10.4018/978-1-5225-2633-9.ch013

Turner, S. (2020). Service Learning as a Scholarly Pursuit. In R. F. Kronick (Ed.), *Emerging Perspectives on Community Schools and the Engaged University* (pp. 190–204). IGI Global. doi:10.4018/978-1-7998-0280-8.ch012

Urick, M. J. (2020). The Millennial Label. In B. Christiansen (Ed.), *Global Applications of Multigenerational Management and Leadership in the Transcultural Era* (pp. 263–283). IGI Global. doi:10.4018/978-1-5225-9906-7.ch009

Uzun, F. V. (2018). Natural Resources Management. In A. N. Eneanya (Ed.), *Handbook of Research on Environmental Policies for Emergency Management and Public Safety* (pp. 1–21). IGI Global. doi:10.4018/978-1-5225-3194-4.ch001

Vakaloudi, A. D. (2020). Concepts of Propaganda. In R. Z. Zheng (Ed.), *Examining Multiple Intelligences and Digital Technologies for Enhanced Learning Opportunities* (pp. 184–214). IGI Global. doi:10.4018/978-1-7998-0249-5.ch010

Vallera, F. L., Thorpe, L., & Kleintop, L. (2019). Developing Diversity Awareness and Multicultural Competence Across Liberal Arts Campuses. In J. Keengwe & R. Byamukama (Eds.), *Handbook of Research on Promoting Higher-Order Skills and Global Competencies in Life and Work* (pp. 37–55). IGI Global. doi:10.4018/978-1-5225-6331-0.ch003

Venkatesan, S. (2018). Changing Socio-Cultural Models and Policy Programs in Rehabilitation of Persons With Communication Disorders. In S. K. Gupta & S. Venkatesan (Eds.), *Handbook of Research on Psychosocial Perspectives of Human Communication Disorders* (pp. 284–304). IGI Global. doi:10.4018/978-1-5225-4955-0.ch015

Vij, R. (2018). Do Women Perceive Organizational Culture Differently From Men? In S. Chhabra (Ed.), *Handbook of Research on Civic Engagement and Social Change in Contemporary Society* (pp. 253–271). IGI Global. doi:10.4018/978-1-5225-4197-4.ch015

Vogt, K. (2020). Towards a Culturally Reflective Practitioner. In D. M. Velliaris (Ed.), *Academic Mobility Programs and Engagement* (pp. 143–197). IGI Global. doi:10.4018/978-1-7998-1607-2.ch006

Vommaro, P. (2020). Social Movements and Territorial Dynamics in Argentina and Latin America (1980-2018). In P. A. Baisotti & P. Pozzi (Eds.), *Historical and Future Global Impacts of Armed Groups and Social Movements* (pp. 129–160). IGI Global. doi:10.4018/978-1-7998-5205-6.ch006

von Rosing, M., Arzumanyan, M., & Zachman, J. A. Sr. (2017). The Relationship Between Ontology and Modelling Concepts. *International Journal of Conceptual Structures and Smart Applications*, *5*(1), 25–47. doi:10.4018/IJCSSA.2017010102

von Rosing, M., & Zachman, J. A. Sr. (2017). The Need for a Role Ontology. *International Journal of Conceptual Structures and Smart Applications*, *5*(1), 1–24. doi:10.4018/IJCSSA.2017010101

Wambu, G. W., & Nkabinde, Z. P. (2019). Supporting Immigrant Children in College and Career Readiness. In G. Onchwari & J. Keengwe (Eds.), *Handbook of Research on Engaging Immigrant Families and Promoting Academic Success for English Language Learners* (pp. 246–268). IGI Global. doi:10.4018/978-1-5225-8283-0.ch013

Wang, K. Y. (2018). Online Ethnic Media Consumption, Acculturation, and Enculturation Among Asian Americans. In N. Bilge & M. I. Marino (Eds.), *Reconceptualizing New Media and Intercultural Communication in a Networked Society* (pp. 18–46). IGI Global. doi:10.4018/978-1-5225-3784-7.ch002

Wang, V. L., Wu, Y., & Lou, H. (2020). Hispanic Humor Styles on Facebook. *International Journal of E-Business Research, 16*(1), 60–73. doi:10.4018/IJEBR.2020010104

Warner-Ault, A. (2020). Promoting Intercultural Learning through Synchronous Video Exchange. *International Journal of Computer-Assisted Language Learning and Teaching, 10*(1), 1–14. doi:10.4018/IJCALLT.2020010101

Wheaton, M. M., & Kezar, A. (2019). Interlocking Systems of Oppression. In H. L. Schnackenberg & D. A. Simard (Eds.), *Challenges and Opportunities for Women in Higher Education Leadership* (pp. 61–83). IGI Global. doi:10.4018/978-1-5225-7056-1.ch005

Whitaker, M. C., & Hines, D. E. (2018). Teaching What We Don't Know. In T. D. Meidl & M. Sulentic Dowell (Eds.), *Handbook of Research on Service-Learning Initiatives in Teacher Education Programs* (pp. 315–332). IGI Global. doi:10.4018/978-1-5225-4041-0.ch017

Whitney, J., Hultgren, M., Jennex, M. E., Elkins, A., & Frost, E. (2020). Using Knowledge Management and Machine Learning to Identify Victims of Human Sex Trafficking. In M. E. Jennex (Ed.), *Knowledge Management, Innovation, and Entrepreneurship in a Changing World* (pp. 360–389). IGI Global. doi:10.4018/978-1-7998-2355-1.ch014

Williams, L. S., & McGivern, M. H. (2017). Women in the Military Who Have Shattered the Glass Ceiling. *International Journal of Strategic Information Technology and Applications, 8*(1), 1–20. doi:10.4018/IJSITA.2017010101

Williams, Y. (2020). An Analysis of Organizational Behavior Diversity Management and Positive Psychology. In E. Baykal (Ed.), *Handbook of Research on Positive Organizational Behavior for Improved Workplace Performance* (pp. 21–33). IGI Global. doi:10.4018/978-1-7998-0058-3.ch002

Wudie, A. A. (2020). Society and State in Ethiopia for Quality Education. In M. Sony, K. T. Karingada, & N. Baporikar (Eds.), *Quality Management Implementation in Higher Education* (pp. 240–255). IGI Global. doi:10.4018/978-1-5225-9829-9.ch012

Yeung, H. Y. (2017). What the Future America Will Look Like. In N. R. Silton (Ed.), *Family Dynamics and Romantic Relationships in a Changing Society* (pp. 226–244). IGI Global. doi:10.4018/978-1-5225-2404-5.ch012

Zakria, M., Nova dos Santos, P. M., Moreira, A. C., & Mota, J. (2019). Exploring Female Entrepreneurship. In E. T. Pereira & P. Paoloni (Eds.), *Handbook of Research on Women in Management and the Global Labor Market* (pp. 239–258). IGI Global. doi:10.4018/978-1-5225-9171-9.ch012

Zamani, B., & Rasoulzadeh, S. (2018). A Domain Specific Modeling Language for Enterprise Application Development. *International Journal of Information Technologies and Systems Approach, 11*(2), 51–70. doi:10.4018/IJITSA.2018070104

Zhang, H., & Dunn, R. A. (2020). The Facebook Me. In R. Kalish (Ed.), *Young Adult Sexuality in the Digital Age* (pp. 176–193). IGI Global. doi:10.4018/978-1-7998-3187-7.ch010

Zucchero, R. A. (2018). Engaging Vital Older Adults in Intergenerational Service-Learning. In O. O. Delano-Oriaran, M. W. Penick-Parks, & S. Fondrie (Eds.), *Culturally Engaging Service-Learning With Diverse Communities* (pp. 266–287). IGI Global. doi:10.4018/978-1-5225-2900-2.ch016

About the Author

Sambhavi Lakshminarayanan has a PhD in Management from the University of Texas at Dallas and Master of Statistics from the Indian Statistical Institute. Dr. Lakshminarayanan has been in academia for more than 25 years and has extensive experience teaching courses at both undergraduate and graduate levels. Her publications include papers, books, and cases in the fields of management and business. Over the last decade, Dr. Lakshminarayanan has been an informal consultant and career coach to several (Asian) women professionals and executives. These interactions provided the direct impetus for this book.

Index

F

I

L

M

N

O

P

R

S

T

W

www.ingramcontent.com/pod-product-compliance
Lightning Source LLC
LaVergne TN
LVHW081327300926
849161LV00008B/1895
* 9 7 8 1 7 9 9 8 4 3 8 4 9 *